The
Fast Forward MBA
Pocket Reference

SECOND EDITION

THE FAST FORWARD MBA SERIES

The Fast Forward MBA Series provides time-pressed business professionals and students with concise, one-stop information to help them solve business problems and make smart, informed business decisions. All of the volumes, written by industry leaders, contain "tough ideas made easy." The published books in this series are:

The Fast Forward MBA Pocket Reference, Second Edition
(0-471-22282-8)
by Paul A. Argenti

The Fast Forward MBA in Selling
(0-471-34854-6)
by Joy J.D. Baldridge

The Fast Forward MBA in Financial Planning
(0-471-23829-5)
by Ed McCarthy

The Fast Forward MBA in Negotiating and Dealmaking
(0-471-25698-6)
by Roy J. Lewicki and Alexander Hiam

The Fast Forward MBA in Project Management
(0-471-32546-5)
by Eric Verzuh

The Fast Forward MBA in Business Planning for Growth
(0-471-34548-2)
by Philip Walcoff

The Fast Forward MBA in Business Communication
(0-471-32731-X)
by Lauren Vicker and Ron Hein

The Fast Forward MBA in Investing
(0-471-24661-1)
by John Waggoner

The Fast Forward MBA in Hiring
(0-471-24212-8)
by Max Messmer

The Fast Forward MBA in Technology Management
(0-471-23980-1)
by Daniel J. Petrozzo

The Fast Forward MBA in Marketing
(0-471-16616-2)
by Dallas Murphy

The Fast Forward MBA in Business
(0-471-14660-9)
by Virginia O'Brien

The
Fast Forward MBA
Pocket Reference

SECOND EDITION

PAUL A. ARGENTI

The Tuck School of Business
Dartmouth College

John Wiley & Sons, Inc.

This publication is designed to provide accurate and authoritative information in regard to the subject matter covered. It is sold with the understanding that the publisher is not engaged in rendering professional services. If
professional advice or other expert assistance is required, the services of a
competent professional person should be sought.

Wiley also publishes its books in a variety of electronic formats. Some content that appears in print may not be available in electronic books.

ISBN: 0-471-22282-8

Printed in the United States of America.

10 9 8 7 6 5 4 3 2 1

For my parents, Nick and Elenora

Professor Paul A. Argenti has taught management and corporate communication starting in 1977 at the Harvard Business School, from 1979 to 1981 at the Columbia Business School, and since 1981 as a faculty member at Dartmouth's Tuck School of Business. He has also taught as a visiting professor at the International University of Japan, the Helsinki School of Economics, and Erasmus University. He currently serves as faculty director for the Tuck Leadership Forum and as chair of Tuck's Curriculum Committee. He has previously served as faculty director for the Tuck Executive Program (TEP), Update 2000, and for Tuck's senior executive program at the Hanoi School of Business in Vietnam.

Professor Argenti has provided management and corporate communication consulting and training for over 50 corporations and nonprofit organizations in both the United States and abroad over the past 23 years. His clients cover a broad range that includes Goldman Sachs, Sony, Kmart, and Martha Stewart.

This second edition of Professor Argenti's *The Fast Forward MBA Pocket Reference* is a revision of the work published in April 1998 by John Wiley & Sons. He has also authored two editions of his McGraw-Hill/Irwin textbook *Corporate Communication;* the textbook will appear in a third edition in 2003. His new book *The Power of Corporate Communication* (coauthored with UCLA's Janis Forman) will be published in 2002. Professor Argenti is the editor of *The Portable MBA Desk Reference,* a best-seller, which was published in 1994 by John Wiley & Sons. He has written over 75 case studies, and is the author of articles for both academic and managerial journals. Professor Argenti also currently serves on the editorial board of *Journal of Business Communication* and is associate editor of *Corporate Reputation Review.* He sits on the board of advisors for the Institute for Brand Leadership.

Both *The Wall Street Journal* (2001) and *U.S. News & World Report* (1994) have rated Professor Argenti's department number one in the nation. He received a Fulbright Fellowship in 1987 to study in England. He also earned an undergraduate degree from Columbia College (in 1975), and graduate degrees from Brandeis (in 1979) and Columbia (in 1981) Universities.

ACKNOWLEDGMENTS

Writing a book that takes an author beyond his own area of expertise leads inevitably to help from others. Professor James Seward from Tuck provided the raw material for the chapters on accounting and finance; Cathy Sirett shaped the chapter on organizational behavior; Mary Munter's ideas shaped much of the chapter on communication; Steve Lubrano, assistant dean at Tuck, provided the material for the chapter on the job search; Maura Harford, a writer and consultant from New York, and Mary Tatmau a former research assistant here at Tuck were instrumental in creating the other chapters in the book; and Laura Turner, an undergraduate research assistant from Dartmouth, helped immeasurably with the development of key terms. But this book would have taken much longer to produce without the incessant cajoling of my most trusted research assistant here at Tuck, Abbey Nova. She made the book come together and deserves credit for what you hold in your hands. I would also like to thank Lorri Hamilton, Kimberley Tait, and Jamie Neidig for their assistance with this edition. Finally, I would like to thank Larry Alexander and Paula Sinnott at Wiley for their patience and interest in this second edition.

CONTENTS

INTRODUCTION   XV

CHAPTER 1—STRATEGY   1

Case Example: Redd's Fun Park, Hatsville, Texas   2

Understanding the Customer   6

The BCG Matrix   7

Competitor Analysis   9

Implementing a Strategy   12

Strategic Intent   14

Summary   17

Internet Resources   18

Strategic Management Critical Reference Materials   18

CHAPTER 2—COMMUNICATION   23

Management Communication   24

Communication Strategy   24

Managerial Writing   30

Cross-Cultural Communication   36

Corporate Communication   38

Functions within the Discipline of Corporate
      Communication   45

Summary   48

Internet Resources   49

Communication Critical Reference Materials   49

CHAPTER 3—MARKETING   53

    The Customer   54
    The Buying Process   55
    Customer Retention   58
    Customer Satisfaction   58
    Customer Relationship Management   61
    Market Segmentation   61
    The Product   62
    Summary   76
    Internet Resources   77
    Marketing Critical Reference Materials   77

CHAPTER 4—ORGANIZATIONAL BEHAVIOR   81

    Individual Level of Analysis—Managing Individuals 82
    Group Level of Analysis   96
    Organizational Level of Analysis   103
    Summary   108
    Internet Resources   108
    Organizational Behavior Critical Reference
        Materials   109

CHAPTER 5—ECONOMICS   113

    Macroeconomics   113
    Leading Economic Indicators   114
    The Federal Reserve Bank System   118
    Microeconomics   122
    Summary   128
    Internet Resources   129
    Economics Critical Reference Materials   129

CHAPTER 6—ACCOUNTING   133

    Types of Accounting   133
    Managerial Accounting   134
    Financial Accounting   139
    Financial Statement Analysis   155
    Uses and Limitations of Ratio Analysis   168
    Summary   170
    Internet Resources   170
    Accounting Critical Reference Materials   171

CHAPTER 7—FINANCE 175

Financial Goals of the Modern Corporation 177
What Is Financial Management? 178
The Role of the Modern Financial Manager 184
Management Decisions and Shareholder Value 187
A Basic Methodology for Measuring Value 192
Recent Innovations in Applied Value Measurement 195
Summary 200
Internet Resources 201
Finance Critical Reference Materials 201

CHAPTER 8—ENTREPRENEURSHIP 205

The Entrepreneurial Profile 206
Entrepreneurial Opportunities 207
Business Plans 210
Sources of Financing 212
Business Forms 215
Summary 216
Internet Resources 217
Entrepreneurship Critical Reference Materials 217

CHAPTER 9—INTERNATIONAL BUSINESS 219

The Global Marketplace 220
The Competitive Advantages Needed for Global
    Competition 220
The Determinants of National Advantage Model 222
Opportunities Associated with a Global Approach—
    Joint Ventures 223
The Backlash Against Globalization 228
Summary 229
Internet Resources 230
International Business Critical Reference Materials 230

CHAPTER 10—THE JOB SEARCH 233

First, a Coherent Career Plan 235
Establishing a Career Plan 235
The Online Search 237
Resume Writing for Success 237
Basic Resume Organization 238

Resume Types   240
Resume Red Flags   242
Now That It's Done . . . Posting a Resume
     on the Internet   245
Networking   246
Interview   247
What If You Don't Get the Job—What Next?   253
Summary   254
Internet Resources   255
Job Search Critical Reference Materials   256

KEY CONCEPTS   259

NOTES   341

INDEX   345

You know that the skills taught in MBA programs are essential to success in business today, but you can't afford either the tuition or the time away from your job. Or maybe you received an MBA several years ago and feel that some of the ideas and references you have in your notebooks are outdated.

This book is geared to those of you who want to learn more about the kinds of material covered in the top business schools without actually having to spend the time and money involved in attending an MBA program. Each chapter introduces you to the most important ideas from some of the most critical business school disciplines: strategy, communication, marketing, organizational behavior, economics, accounting, finance, entrepreneurship, and international business.

In addition, we have included a chapter on conducting the job search. Most top business school programs put a heavy emphasis on helping students to get jobs, and this chapter reflects that emphasis.

Each chapter follows a similar format. Chapters start with the basics of each discipline. We have tried to provide you with the most current thinking culled from top experts in each field. The overview is not meant to be comprehensive, but rather to give readers the essence of a topic.

Lists of *Internet Resources* and *Critical References* follow the basics for each chapter. These are the most critical and up-to-date resources to mine the ideas that have shaped and continue to shape the thinking behind each discipline. Those of you who want more detailed information will benefit from this extensive list of the best sites, books, articles, and journals in each field.

The *Key Concepts* section is found at the end of the book—these are terms that you really need to know to understand each field, alphabetized for easy reference. Here you will find all of the most important terms and ideas that people who work in these fields use and understand.

This second edition has been thoroughly updated and revised to reflect the dramatic changes that have taken place in the world of business since the first edition was published in 1997. In addition, we have moved the Key Concepts section to the back of the book to provide you with a handy reference for terms you need defined both as you read and in your daily work.

In all, the second edition of the *Fast Forward MBA Pocket Reference* should become an invaluable companion for you whether you just want to know a little bit about a topic or are seeking a more comprehensive look into a discipline. We hope that you will find the information easy to use, and that you use it to great success.

Paul A. Argenti
Hanover, New Hampshire
June 2002

Strategy

Strategy, in simplest terms, is one's plan to reach predetermined goals. A corporation frequently sets goals to increase profitability, to reach new revenue levels, and to be the leading producer of its products. This company's strategy then becomes a roadmap to reach these goals through a series of actions and analyses.

However, a company's strategy is rarely crystal clear. Many managers find it extremely difficult to state their corporate strategies, let alone describe how these may differ from those of their competitors and business partners. Deciphering—and in many cases redefining—one's strategy can be a time-consuming yet effective process to help propel a business forward into a more efficient or profitable enterprise and a more cohesive culture.

Countless theories and frameworks have been developed to assist business leaders in evaluating their corporate strategies. As opposed to going through dry and lengthy discussions of each strategic tool, this chapter offers a case example to illustrate how to analyze a business situation strategically. We will follow this case example to explore a few of the strategic frameworks a manager might use. And, finally, we will briefly discuss some additional strategic frameworks you may want to keep in mind. Note that different businesses at various stages in their life cycles may require different strategic tools, and a specific business problem or competitive environment may require a completely unique strategic response. These tools are only meant to be frameworks from which a manager can create an applicable and effective strategy.

CASE EXAMPLE: REDD'S FUN PARK, HATSVILLE, TEXAS

Redd's is an outdoor fun park situated on 15 acres of land in Hatsville, Texas, 30 miles outside of San Antonio. Redd's is owned and operated by Bill and Joan Redd and their extended family, and has been known in the area as a good family fun place for the past 12 years. For the first 10 years, the fun park had two main attractions: a nine-hole mini golf course, and a speedway race track with mini race cars similar to those found at Disneyland. Two years ago, Redd's expanded and built a new high-speed roadster racetrack and a building that houses a snack-bar-type restaurant, full-service bar, pool tables, and the latest in high-tech video games (3D, etc.). See park layout in Figure 1.1.

One day, sitting at his desk in the new building, Bill started thinking about some changes he was noticing in his clientele, and then he began wondering which parts of his park were

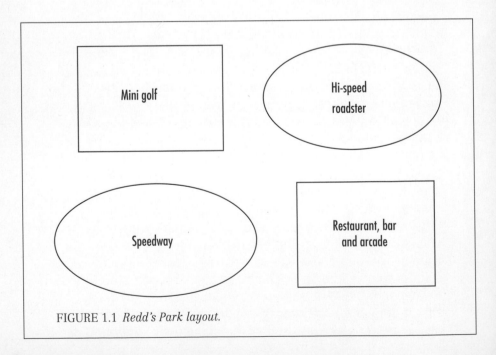

FIGURE 1.1 *Redd's Park layout.*

most profitable. He and Joan had expanded to deal with new competition cropping up in San Antonio, but he had the uneasy feeling that the family business was taking a turn that he couldn't control. Bill had several questions and really no idea how to start answering them.

Background on Redd's

Bill and Joan started Redd's Fun Park 12 years ago when their four kids kept complaining that there was nothing to do. To get the youngsters away from the television set, Joan came up with the idea for a mini golf course, and then their eldest son Baxter pleaded for a racetrack that he and his friends could ride on. Bill and Joan set about building these attractions on their private land, and the park soon became a Hatsville weekend tradition for families seeking outdoor fun.

Times changed, and Bill started seeing bigger attractions build up in nearby San Antonio, such as other speedways and new, shiny indoor entertainment centers that boasted the latest in arcade games. His teenage sons were driving out to the big city on the weekends with their friends. Bill and Joan talked with some friends and were persuaded to add the two new features they hoped would win back clients and maybe even draw in some new ones.

Case Analysis

Sitting at his desk that day, Bill realized he needed to reassess his decisions and think about what was driving his business. Joan had successfully run her own shoe store for 15 years and had read several business books that she said helped her succeed. Bill had always chuckled at this, but now he threw on his Stetson and headed home to check out her books.

Once home, Bill started pulling out anything that wasn't too thick and had the word "strategy" in the title. He poured himself some iced tea and soon was deep into reading and trying to understand what was making his business tick.

Starting to Analyze

Bill's first read was *Competitive Strategy,* a book by Michael Porter. Admittedly, he skimmed through some sections, but he liked when Porter was discussing how internal and external forces affect a corporation. Porter stipulated that for an organization to succeed, its managers have to have:

- A good command of its internal workings
- A comprehensive understanding of the industry in which it functions
- A working knowledge of what the competition is doing

Bill felt he knew his fun park pretty well. His 10 employees all made $7 an hour and all shifted through the various activities, with the exception of the bartender. His hours were from 3:00 to 7:00 P.M. Monday through Thursday, and from 11:00 A.M. to 7:00 P.M. on Friday through Sunday. He wrote his weekly revenues in a table (see Table 1.1).

In addition to this, the restaurant brought in $500 per week and the bar brought in about $1,800. So the fun park's total weekly revenue was $7,650.

Thinking about his internal costs was a bit trickier:

- His total labor cost was $2,800/week (he didn't pay himself or Joan).
- His snack shop was making slim margins, with 75 percent cost ($375), and the bar was doing well with a 60 percent margin (cost = $1,080).
- Then there was upkeep of his facilities . . . Bill worked this out in Table 1.2.

When Bill summed everything up, he had costs at $6,555. A little more quick math produced a smile as he confirmed that he was operating profitably at a 14 percent margin, making $1,095 each week. Not bad he thought. But could he do better?

TABLE 1.1 REDD'S FUN PARK WEEKLY REVENUES

Attraction	Price	Volume/Week	Revenue/ Week
Mini golf	$3/round	150	$ 450
Speedway	$2/ride or 3 for $5	50; 200	$1,100
Hi-speed roadster	$4/ride	400 (2 ride average)	$3,200
Video games and pool	$1 each	200 (3 games each)	$ 600

TABLE 1.2 REDD'S FUN PARK WEEKLY EXPENSES

Attraction	Cost	Volume/ Week	Cost/ Week
Mini golf	0 (just dry land and rusty putters)	150	$ 0
Speedway	$.50/ride (gas, maintenance, insurance)	650 rides	$ 325
Hi-speed roadster	$2/ride (hi-quality gas, maintenance, higher insurance)	800 rides	$1,600
Video games and pool	Flat rental and service fee of $1,500/month	N/A	$ 375

Continuing with the internal analysis, Bill started looking at the profitability of each activity (see Table 1.3). He realized that he needed to allocate his labor costs, and once he did this, he was shocked by what he saw.

Bill had previously had no idea that he was losing money on the speedway, and he had thought that his indoor activity center would be more profitable. Bill remembered now that he never saw lines forming by the speedway, but that the hi-speed roadster was frequently jam-packed with people waiting to

TABLE 1.3 REDD'S FUN PARK WEEKLY PROFIT

Attraction	Revenue/ Week	Total Cost/Week	Profit/ Week
Mini golf	$ 450	$280 (1 worker)	$170
Speedway	$1,100	$1,165 ($325 + 3 workers)	−$ 65
Hi-speed roadster	$3,200	$2,440 ($1,600 + 3 workers)	$760
Video games and pool	$ 600	$515 ($375 + 1/2 worker)	$ 85
Restaurant and bar	$2,300	$2,155 (base + 2.5 workers)	$145

ride. Bill began to realize that he either needed to reallocate his labor costs or give more consideration to which track was now the true focus of his business. He'd noted that his customer base seemed to change of late, but was this the cause for the imbalance in activity profitability? To answer this, Bill decided to continue along with Porter's analysis, and look at his customers.

UNDERSTANDING THE CUSTOMER

After reading more, Bill stepped outside to think. Three years ago, Bill and Joan had noticed their customer base declining, looked at what some of the places downtown were building, and decided to copy them to keep their current customers from going all the way to San Antonio for family fun. It seemed logical at the time, but now as Bill walked toward the park, he realized that some of those actions might have conflicted dramatically with his original business strategy.

Porter had discussed the importance of understanding customers, and watching for changes in market trends and external forces. As Bill walked around the park, he finally understood what one of his business problems was: He had two conflicting customer bases.

The two original attractions had targeted families like Bill and Joan's, where parents could take their kids to participate in outdoor activities. The speedway added the excitement that kept the older children interested even when their parents became "embarrassing." But these families were not the ones, as it turns out, who were impressed with the new attractions. Looking at the lines for the hi-speed roadster, Bill saw men in their twenties and thirties out with their buddies for some thrill rides. Knowing well enough that these were the same patrons that made his bar a success, it hit Bill that these new customers were actually discouraging his old clientele from visiting Redd's Fun Park.

Bill walked back inside and made a new list based on some of Porter's discussion points and his own realizations. He knew that to think about his customers strategically, he needed to incorporate the following (see the Marketing chapter for more information):

1. Define your current customers.

2. Understand what these customers value.

3. When considering any change in your business, think about what value it adds to your customers' experiences.

4. If you're looking to add new customers, think about who they are and how they will affect existing customers.

Bill smiled. At least he was learning from some of his mistakes, but how could he fix what he had done? And did he need to? How could he frame his current understanding of his business in terms of which parts might need some changes? Bill knew he needed to frame the numbers he'd just run and his knowledge of his business into a more standard and structured analytical format so that any action he took would be grounded in rational analysis, as opposed to "gut feelings."

THE BCG MATRIX

Bill continued leafing through some of his wife's strategy books and came across a section describing a process for analyzing strategy developed by the Boston Consulting Group. BCG proposes that the best way to understand how a business is functioning is to break the business down into its smaller operating parts, commonly known as *standard business units,* or SBUs. SBU management became a very popular trend in the 1980s, and drove managers away from considering their companies as integrated entities. Rather, managers began to view companies as a portfolio of SBUs.

Bill read on to understand that the BCG Matrix is a framework to assist companies by using the same approach in classifying the performance of any given specific product in relation to the overall performance of the firm. Matrix identifies products or business units across two dimensions: market share and market growth. *Market share* refers to the percent of sales one product earns in relation to the total market sales for all products in that category. For example, Tide may have a 30 percent market share of the domestic laundry detergent market. *Market growth* refers to the potential for a product category to attract more consumer spending.

Figure 1.2 illustrates how these two forces work together to create four SBU categories. If a product or SBU is in a high-growth market with high market share, it is called a *star.* Products or businesses in this category usually require a good deal of capital investment from the company to capitalize on market growth opportunities. Products that have a

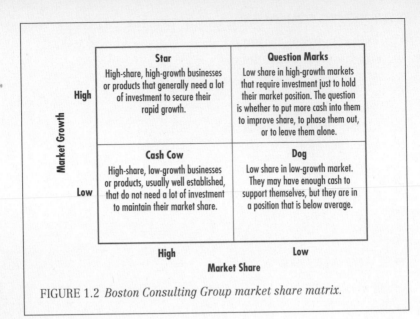

FIGURE 1.2 *Boston Consulting Group market share matrix.*

high market share in a low market growth business are called *cash cows*. Typically, companies can enjoy high revenues on these products without much additional investment or attention to maintain market share.

A product or business with a low market share in a low growth industry is referred to as a *dog*. Products or SBUs in this category usually generate enough revenue to be self-supporting, but they are probably poor performers in relation to the other products or SBUs in the firm. Lastly, products or SBUs that have a low market share in a high growth industry are called *question marks*, because they beg the most questions of management. Usually these products require investment to maintain their market share in an industry, so management must decide if the investment is worth it.

Bill defined his business units as: Mini Golf, Speedway, Hi-Speed Roadster, Video Games and Pool, and Restaurant. The cost and profit analyses he did earlier gave him some sense of how to place his units on the BCG Matrix, but Bill realized from what Michael Porter had said that he also needed a better understanding of his competitors before he should begin thinking about making any changes.

COMPETITOR ANALYSIS

The components of a competitor analysis provide managers with a framework to complete a successful and informative assessment of their industry competitors. Central to the model, and to the analysis, are four questions that comprise what Porter deems a "Competitor's Response Profile." The questions, located in the center box of Figure 1.3, emphasize the need for managers to consider what moves a competitor might make on his or her own, as well as what moves a competitor might make in response to the manager's own moves.

To begin such an analysis, a manager should start by considering what a competitor's performance goals and objectives might be. For example, a product manager for Coca-Cola should wonder if Pepsi's performance goals for the year are to

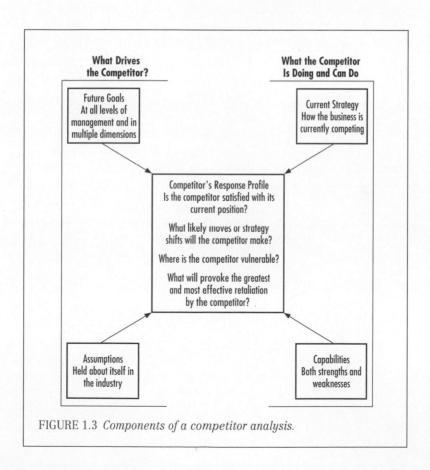

FIGURE 1.3 *Components of a competitor analysis.*

beat their prior year's earnings, or are they to outsell Coke at any cost? Clearly, these goals need not be identical.

Next, the manager should assess how close the competitor is to actually achieving these goals and what moves the competitor might make to get there. (If Pepsi's goal is to outsell Coke, is Pepsi willing to engage in head-to-head combat to do so, as in the case of the nationally televised "Pepsi Challenge"?) Further, a manager should contemplate the competitor's weaknesses—both those the competitor may be aware of as well as those the competitor may be oblivious to. (Perhaps the brand manager at Pepsi does not know that you, the Coke brand manager, negotiated as part of your multibillion-dollar advertising contract with the networks that Pepsi commercials which engage in head-to-head tactics can only be aired between the hours of 2:00 and 4:00 A.M.) Lastly, the manager must evaluate, given the information ascertained through making the previous considerations, how the competitor might react to a specific strategic move made by the manager's firm. (You must realize that the brand manager at Pepsi may be none too pleased when she discovers what you have done, and may resort to strategic tactics of her own.)

Armed with this central information gleaned from the Competitor Response Profile, a manager can work towards gaining a deeper understanding of the competitor's capabilities and motivations. To return to our study of Figure 1.3, focus your attention on the arrows emanating from the Competitor Response Profile in the center box. Porter, again, defines four forces broken up into two subcategories. On the left side of Figure 1.3 are the two forces stemming from considerations of "What Drives the Competitor?" Under this heading, Porter identifies the "Future Goals" of the competitor. These are a firm's goals as they have been communicated to all persons within the company. Porter also identifies "Assumptions" the firm may have about itself and its position within the industry. These two forces, taken together, provide a skeletal archetype of the firm's industry motivation, its process for internal motivation and its self-perception. These are all important factors in shaping the Competitor's Response Profile.

The right side of Figure 1.3 is dedicated to forces that stem from an assessment of the behavior of the competitor, as captured in the subheading "What the Competitor Is Doing and Can Do." Specifically, the forces identified are the competitor's

"Current Strategy," or a status report of the basis on which the business is competing and how it is doing in the industry. In conjunction with current strategy is the consideration of the firm's "Capabilities," both in terms of its core competencies and in terms of its weak points.

Lastly, Porter emphasizes the interactive nature of the concerns driven by the right and left sides of the model on the center of the model. More specifically, any change in any of the four forces will affect the Competitor's Response Profile directly. Moreover, a change in the competitor's response profile could prompt changes in any or all of the other forces.

Returning to our case example, Bill knew that he had no competitors with the exact profile of Redd's Fun Park, but rather that all of the high-tech video arcades and the larger speedways in San Antonio, as well as local bars and restaurants, were his competition. Since every one of these is different, how could Bill possibly compare his business with them? This is a question that managers often struggle with when defining strategy, but, as is true for Bill, every competitor needs to be considered as strategy is developed and refined.

Bill's Response

Bill now understood that there could be multiple answers to the complex issues he faced. Indeed, several possible solutions immediately came to Bill's mind:

1. Cut back on open hours for attractions like the mini golf and extend hours on the hi-speed roadster and bar. Bill had a hunch this could push his revenues up while maintaining the status of his mini golf as the company "dog." However, he also knew this would mean a significant shift toward one of his customer bases over the other.

2. Offer "family day" packages for the video games, restaurant, and mini golf, and then "party fast" nights for the hi-speed roadster and bar. Bill knew this might mean additional labor costs at night and two different strategies, one for the day customer and the other for the night customer.

Indeed, several solutions occurred to Bill, and he realized that he might want to spend some additional time researching his customers (see the Marketing chapter) and his investment alternatives (see the Finance chapter) before he'd make any decisions. The frameworks showed that there could be a variety of "good" strategies, and he knew that he wanted to discuss any ideas with Joan before making significant changes. What he wanted to know now was once he and Joan figured out what they wanted to do, what did they need to do as managers to ensure success?

IMPLEMENTING A STRATEGY

Bill continued looking through books and came across a very interesting section about the "McKinsey Seven S Framework"—the product of a marriage between theory and practice.[1] It said that McKinsey's primary objective in developing the 7S framework was to put a new spin on management style and suggest that "soft issues" could and should be managed. Further, the use of the "Wheel," a format borrowed from Porter, also emphasizes the idea that a firm is the comprehensive, inextricable sum of its parts.

After conducting the equivalent of a Ph.D.-level research project on how America's best-run companies were managed, the best minds at McKinsey arrived at two key findings. First, the consultants learned that both the strategy and the structure of the organization determined a manager's effectiveness. Their second discovery was that no linear relationship governs these three components, although they are interdependent.

In reality, the management, structure, and strategy of an organization are interrelated through a complex network of seven characteristic factors in the organization. Managers who try to run their firm as if it were a collection of several independent units soon learn about the spoke-and-hub concept of the wheel. A wheel is nothing more than a collection of spokes when there is no hub, and vice versa. Neither part alone can replicate the functions of a wheel. Similarly, an organization without common goals and strategy cannot function in the way it was intended. Sure, each unit can perform independent functions, but without a unifying force to bring the units together, they are merely spokes. Hence, McKinsey developed its Wheel to illustrate this very point. Figure 1.4 provides you with all of the categories in a typical organization that must operate under a common goal.

The McKinsey study produced another interesting finding.

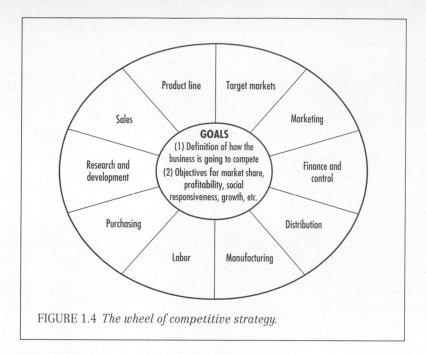

FIGURE 1.4 *The wheel of competitive strategy.*

The McKinsey people discovered that most successful organizations, regardless of their line of business, had several practices in common. The McKinsey model incorporates these practices into eight characteristics:

1. *Maintain a bias for action.* Successful companies are not afraid to make changes, even if it means making a mistake along the way.

2. *Learn from the customers by staying close to them.* Successful firms maintain close relationships with their customer base. In this way, the firm can anticipate and plan for changes in customers' needs before the customer is aware of the change.

3. *Encourage autonomy and entrepreneurship in staff and management.* Management encourages others to find new and creative solutions to problems by allowing managers/employees to challenge old rules and methods and by providing the latitude to try new approaches.

4. *Respect contributions of all employees, especially those traditionally undervalued.* If a manager wants his or her staff to buy into the goals of the firm, those who report to

him or her must feel that the firm respects and values their individual contributions.

5. *Use a hands-on, highly visible management approach.* When management is present and involved in every part of the businesses, employees have more respect and include managers more in the everyday workings of the firm.

6. *Stick to the knitting—know your core competency and stay with it.* Do not abandon your core competencies and core products in search of products or services that are glamorous today. Stick to whatever it is that you are good at.

7. *Keep the organizational structure simple and staff only as much management as is required for bare-minimum operations.* Creating many levels of middle and upper management only serves to create division within the ranks of a company.

8. *Allow core values to govern.* Manage with loose and tight properties when appropriate. Trust that your staff knows and shares the core values of the company. Allow enough managerial latitude so that employees can try new ideas and methods. Provide enough managerial guidance so that everyone remains committed to the same goals.

The McKinsey Wheel is an especially valuable tool for two reasons. Not only does the Wheel (1) reemphasize that all parts of an organization must work together to achieve common goals, it also (2) provides specific areas and business activities to examine when diagnosing the health of a firm.

Bill knew that he and Joan had some work ahead of them with their employees to get everyone's buy-in to whatever strategic path they decided to undertake. As it stood now, Bill had some employees who loved hanging out with the partying young men, and others who would prefer to see Redd's "return to its roots" as the local family-oriented fun center. He had a good sense now of how to frame his and Joan's discussion about Redd's future and what they'd need to do once they decided, but he wanted one more thing: what was best to include in his newly-developed strategy.

STRATEGIC INTENT

Bill wasn't sure yet what path he and Joan would select for Redd's, but he knew that after he spent additional time analyzing the profits/costs of his business units, researching his competitors, and learning more about his customers, he'd need to be certain that his strategy was the one that best positioned Redd's for success. Michael Porter's works had given him a good starting point, but Bill wanted more. Looking for this final nugget of information, Bill came across a more recent article by Gary Hamel and C.K. Prahalad, entitled "Strategic Intent," in the *Harvard Business Review*.[2]

In this article, Prahalad and Hamel argue that companies need more than a formal model to define strategy. Companies need, as one of their self-defining goals, a desired leadership position within an industry. The authors insist that a company must develop "a competitive obsession with winning at all levels of the organization and then sustain that obsession over a 10- to 20-year quest for global leadership." They must develop a strategic intent.

A famous example of a strategic intent was President John F. Kennedy's initiative for the United States to be the first country to send a man to the moon. Although many people believed this to be an impossible feat, Kennedy maintained that it was imperative that we, as a nation, succeed to preserve our national identity. Americans, from the scientists at NASA to the American public in general, internalized this statement. Taxpayers did not complain about the allocation of money to NASA, while scientists worked around the clock to achieve "the impossible." When the goal was reached, it inspired unity and pride throughout the country.

Strategic intent is a long-term goal, and one that the business will stick to, even as the tides of business change. Equally as important, this strategy concept also includes an accompanying management process. Prahalad and Hamel suggest the following practices:

- Focus the organization's attention on the essence of winning.
- Motivate people by communicating the value of the target.
- Leave room for individual and team contributions.
- Sustain enthusiasm by providing new operational definitions as circumstances change.
- Use this intent to consistently guide resource allocations.

While strategic intent requires commitment in terms of a long-term focus, it also enables a company to be flexible because it only requires the firm to commit to plans for short-term action, leaving many opportunities to reevaluate and take advantage of new opportunities as they emerge.

Strategic intent must be communicated in such a way that all members of a company buy into the idea and are committed to it personally. It must be inescapable. When Honda issued the strategic intent to beat GM's sales in the American markets in the late 1960s, it seemed like an impossible goal. Yet within 20 years, it was a reality, and it became a reality because every member of the Honda company force was committed to making it happen.

This kind of internalization, coupled with operational flexibility, allows for entrepreneurial management styles within the company. Styles that can help a company overcome resource constraints by inspiring innovation and creativity towards achieving the same goal. Means are flexible, since the end has been determined and bought into by all. This style of management also requires flexibility to take advantage of short-term competitive advantages. The firm does not have to be married to one competitive advantage, but should be flexible enough to be benefited by all.

The firm cannot be wed to typical evaluation schemes, either. Instead of considering projects in terms of whether they yield benefits of either quality *or* cost, firms should be thinking in terms of quality *and* cost advantages. Firms should also engage in a collaborative style of management, where the company encourages its staff to find creative solutions and to challenge all rules and realities that prohibit the company from achieving its goals.

The last critical part of a successful strategic intent initiative is that it must be perceived as a personal challenge made to every member of the company. This, in turn, will inspire a response of drive and determination to achieve the goal across all organizational levels. For a strategic intent to work, managers must:

1. Create a sense of urgency. Perpetuating a bias for action avoids crisis from inaction.

2. Develop a competitor focus at every level through widespread use of competitive intelligence.

3. Encourage employees to set personal benchmarks based on beating the best-in-class procedures of the firm's competitors.

4. Provide employees with the skills they need to work effectively. Do not ever skimp on providing employees with as much training as they need or seek out.

5. Avoid competing initiatives by launching one challenge at a time. Allowing enough time for a challenge to be absorbed and personalized by the staff before launching another will alleviate a sense of confusion and foster a more competitive environment.

6. Establish clear milestones and review mechanisms. Managers need to set specific goals and to review processes in a timely fashion. Managers must also establish a clear and consistent rewards system.

7. Reciprocate responsibility. If the organization is to remain responsible and competitive, managers must share credit for every victory as well as share responsibility for every setback.

8. Innovate rather than imitate. Focus on developing and playing your own game well instead of trying to imitate someone else's game. Better to be a first-rate original than a second-rate imitation.

9. Manage creatively. Rewrite the rules and use every tactic that will advance you towards your goal. Dump rules of strategy that confine instead of advance the company toward the goal.

Bill realized that in a number of ways the concepts described in the strategic intent article resemble those described in Porter and in the McKinsey Wheel frameworks. In sum, the article was pushing for a style of management that focuses on harnessing the creative energy and entrepreneurial spirit of every employee within the firm towards attaining a difficult but highly rewarding goal.

SUMMARY

By now, you're beginning to see what Bill was learning: there are multiple strategic frameworks for understanding where and how to take your business into the future. Which will prove to be most useful or will guarantee the most success is really dependent on your ability as a manager to match the issues of your firm with a particular tool and your desired outcomes.

However, even after you've developed a comprehensive strategic plan, grounded in knowledge about your customer, research about your competitor, and your firm's current performance, it is perhaps most important to remember that successful strategy requires careful and consistent implementation. It is not enough for you as a manager to develop the strategy; you must follow through with actions that imbue that strategy throughout the culture of your firm. A good strategy may be a perfectly realistic roadmap, but it will be your actions that determine whether you ever reach those goals.

INTERNET RESOURCES

E-Business Forum (www.ebusinessforum.com). This web site from the Economist Intelligence Unit (EIU) is designed to help senior executives build successful strategies for the global digital economy. Features daily e-business news, best practices, and a search of the latest research reports.

Ideas@Work on the Air (www.hbsp.harvard.edu/products/radio/index.html). This site contains an archive of radio programs offering insights from the leading management thinkers and practitioners every business day. Based on articles in *Harvard Business Review,* the *Harvard Management Update,* and *Harvard Management Communication Letter* newsletters.

McKinsey Quarterly (www.mckinseyquarterly.com). McKinsey's on-line journal offers great research summaries on current management and industry issues, from strategizing in uncertain environments to winning Asian strategies. Offers a monthly e-mail newsletter for easy access to all new articles.

Quick MBA (www.quickmba.com). Keeps all elementary business information right at your fingertips. Offers great section on strategic management, outlining everything from the fundamentals of game theory to Porter's Diamond of National Advantage.

Social Science of Research Network (www.ssrn.com). Offers an array of strategy and finance-focused articles.

STRATEGIC MANAGEMENT CRITICAL REFERENCE MATERIALS

Baye, Michael. *Managerial Economics and Business Strategy,* 3rd edition. New York: McGraw-Hill College Division, 1999.

This managerial economics textbook is one of the most successful in the market. This is due in no small part to the fact that it combines tools from intermediate microeconomics, game theory, and industrial organization. Its balanced coverage of traditional and modern topics makes this third edition a flexible and up-to-date text that will be useful to a wide audience.

Collins, James, and Jerry Porras. *Built to Last.* New York: Harperbusiness, 1997.

In *Built to Last,* Collins and Porras identify 18 "visionary" companies and then set out to determine what makes each one "special," what sets that company above the hundreds of thousands of others in the global economy. To earn the designation "visionary," each company had to be world famous, have a strong brand image, and be at least 50 years old.

McGrath, Michael. *Product Strategy for High Technology Companies,* 2nd edition. New York: McGraw-Hill Professional Publishing, 2000.

Product strategy is one of the key components of success for high-technology companies, and this guide is one of the few written specifically for the twenty-first-century high-tech industry. This book provides an in-depth examination of the entire area of product strategy, from changing strategies to Web technologies, providing market-tested strategies and techniques. McGrath uses more than 250 examples from technological leaders including IBM, Compaq, and Apple to illustrate his book—and in this second edition he includes new sections on growth strategies and on Internet-based businesses. This book helps define how high-tech companies can use product strategy to be more competitive, increase profitability, and continue to grow.

Peters, Thomas J., and Robert H. Waterman, Jr. *In Search of Excellence: Lessons from America's Best-Run Companies.* New York: Warner Books, 1982.

The number-one bestseller in 1983, *In Search of Excellence* describes eight basic strategic principles that the best-run companies utilize to foster continued success. The principles are: (1) a bias for action; (2) staying close to the customer; (3) autonomy and entrepreneurship; (4) productivity through people; (5) insisting executives stay in touch with the firm's essential business; (6) remaining with the business that the firm knows best; (7) few administrative layers and few people at the upper levels; (8) simultaneous loose-tight properties. The book develops each of the principles in depth with theoretical support and extensive examples of successful companies.

Porter, Michael E. *Competitive Advantage: Creating and Sustaining Superior Performance.* New York: The Free Press, 1985.

Competitive Strategy introduced techniques for industry and competitor analyses. *Competitive Advantage* further develops these concepts for exploration of additional complexities and then presents definitive guidelines for developing sound competitive strategies and instituting them within a firm. Porter describes how companies can create and then maintain a competitive advantage within a given industry by establishing an appropriate competitive range of focus. Value-chain analysis, which enables the manager to differentiate integral activities of a company in different functional business components for its product or service is introduced. These business components, which include design, marketing, production and distribution, are all linked through value-chain analysis demonstrating the importance of considering all company activities in an integrated manner.

Porter, Michael E. *Competitive Strategy: Techniques for Analyzing Industries and Companies.* New York: The Free Press, 1980.

This is a comprehensive book about competitive strategy in business. Written for managers and other business professionals, the book assumes a conceptual approach extending industrial organizational theory with case examples as support. The underlying premise is that significant benefits can be gained though an explicit process of strategy formulation as a coordinated effort amongst different functional business units. The book is divided into three sections. Part I develops the criteria for analyzing the structure of an industry and competitors. Part II applies the framework from Part I to formulate competitive strategy for different types of business environments. Part III evaluates an array of business strategic decisions that challenge companies competing in a single industry.

Porter, Michael E. "How Competitive Forces Shape Strategy," *Harvard Business Review,* vol. 57, no. 2, March-April 1979.

A Harvard Business School faculty specialist in business strategy and industrial economics, Michael E. Porter develops a discussion concerning the identification and degree of business competition in industry. The level and source of competition is dependent upon five forces: threat of new entrants, bargaining power of customers, bargaining power of suppliers, threat of substitute products or services and jockeying for position among current rivals. The collaborative power of these forces determines the profit potential for an industry. Within an industry the bottom-line purpose of forming competitive strategy is to cope with and ideally outmaneuver competition. This is an excellent, concise source for understanding the forces that govern competition in an industry as well as development of strategy formulation to specifically address identified competitive forces.

Communication

This chapter describes effective communication techniques for both internal and external audiences using oral, written, and electronic communications. Communication, more than any other subject in business, has implications for everyone in the organization, from the newest mailroom clerk to the CEO. We all have to communicate no matter what our role, and as a result the subject is often taken for granted.

Given the broad nature of the topic, we will narrow our focus to two areas:

1. The management communication discipline, which is communication related to individuals

2. The corporate communication function, which is communication at the organizational level

What makes communication in business different from other kinds of communication is its focus on audience or constituencies. *The American Heritage Dictionary* defines a constituency as "a group served by an organization or institution; a clientele." The concept of communicating with constituencies is important for companies to understand because messages can quickly move from intended audiences to other, secondary constituencies with an interest in the company.

Although in the past most management communication could easily be contained within the organization, changes in communication technology, such as e-mail and the Internet, have made it difficult to communicate internally without information leaking to the outside world. The fields of management and corporate communication are thus converging, making it essential that managers and companies alike communicate precisely and effectively.

MANAGEMENT COMMUNICATION

The field of management communication is one of the more recent additions to the business school curriculum. Most graduate business schools added such courses to their rosters about 20 years ago in response to requests from the business and academic communities for better written and oral skills from graduates.

Although all college and even high school graduates in the United States receive some formal instruction in writing, this training tends to focus on minutia (grammar, spelling, usage, etc.) rather than on communication strategy or issues of organization, which are critical in business writing. And few graduates receive any training prior to graduate school in the art of oral presentation.

Thus, the first management communication courses developed in the early part of this century (Harvard Business School and Dartmouth's Tuck School of Business were pioneers in this effort) tended to focus on developing writing and speaking skills to help students prepare themselves for managerial careers. Today, virtually all graduate schools teach a combination of management communication, which includes: communication strategy, managerial writing, oral presentation, cross-cultural communication, as well as corporate communication.

COMMUNICATION STRATEGY

Communication skills become more, not less, important as you progress up the corporate ladder. In fact, several studies have shown that CEOs spend as much as 85 percent of their time communicating. Most managers have learned to think strategically about their business overall, but few think strategically about what they spend most of their time doing—communicating. Management communication expert Mary Munter writes in her *Guide to Managerial Communication* that managerial communication is only successful if you get the desired response from your audience.[1] To get that response, you have to think strategically about your communication before you start to write or speak.

In addition, a more strategic focus on communication allows managers to determine their communicator strategy, to analyze their audiences, to determine whether their messages should be direct or indirect, and to choose the appropriate communication channel.

Communicator Strategy

Managers who set objectives before communicating are more efficient and more effective. Setting objectives in this context means putting yourself in the shoes of your audience and determining their response ("As a result of this communication, my audience will . . .").

For example, instead of saying that you want to write a memo requesting funding for a business trip to meet with the sales force, you would set your communication objective as follows: "As a result of reading this memo, my boss will agree that I need to travel to meet with the sales force." This subtle shift makes all the difference in how you organize your message, what tone you use, and what information to include.

In addition, the communicator must think about what communication style to use. Tannenbaum and Schmidt wrote about communication style in a landmark *Harvard Business Review* article. Their approach (as translated for management communication by Munter) breaks down style into four categories: tell, sell, consult, and join. If you want simply to instruct or explain something (e.g., "use this exit in an emergency"), use a "tell" style. If, instead, you want to persuade your audience to do something (as in the previously noted request for funding), use a "sell" style. If you need to confer with your audience and require more information from them (as in a question and answer session after a presentation), use a "consult" style. If you need collaboration (as in preparation for a meeting), use a "join" style of communication.

Finally, the communicator must also think about what kind of credibility he or she has with the audience. This can be based on rank, goodwill, expertise, image, or even shared values. Communicating strategically means thinking about what kind of credibility you have going into the communication and what you might do to acquire such credibility over time.

To get back to our earlier example, if the communicator has asked for travel funding several times over the last year and accomplished little as a result, chances are that the boss will not grant the request because the communicator has lost goodwill credibility.

Audience Analysis

In addition to thinking about the objectives for a given communication, you need to determine who the audience is, what they know about you and the topic, how they feel about it, and what sorts of appeals might work best.

When you communicate with someone, you are in essence communicating with all of the people that person communicates with as well. Many managers do not think about this beforehand. Thus, the secondary or hidden audience is as important to think about as the primary audience when communicating in business. If, for example, you are sending a message about employee benefits to the person who works for you, you must also think about the needs of that person's family who will be a part of the audience for that communication.

One of the great difficulties in management communication is that the same message may appeal to some members of your audience but not to others. This requires you to tailor your message for different audience members depending upon their needs. For example, something that is in the company's best interest may not be as good for its employees and their families.

As important as analyzing the audience is analyzing their knowledge base. How much do they know about the topic you are discussing? If they know very little, you have to include more background information; if they know a lot, you need to come up with a new approach to the topic.

Similarly, what do they know about *you?* If they do not know you very well, your credibility will be low, making it hard for you to achieve your objective. This means you will need to build credibility with the audience as you are covering the main topic. Their feelings about the topic are also an important part of the analysis. If the audience is positively disposed toward your topic, they will be more inclined to agree with you; if their feelings are negative, you have to work harder to reach your objective.

In addition to tailoring your message to your intended audience, you must also consider others who may view the communication, as well as others with whom your intended audience will communicate. This is your secondary audience. Advances in communications technologies have made tailoring messages to secondary audiences important, as information can be quickly passed to many people. For example, it is not uncommon to see "internal" information posted on web sites. One such site, thevault.com, allows employees of a company to anonymously post their grievances online, where they can be read by investors, analysts, and potential employees. Be sure when crafting a message that it is tailored to both the primary and secondary audiences.

Message Strategy

Once you have determined your objectives as a communicator and analyzed your audience, you must also think about how you want to organize your message for the communication. As writing expert Barbara Minto[2] has pointed out, the two most important ways to structure a message are: (1) the direct approach and (2) the indirect approach.

The *direct approach* follows the old dictum, "tell them what you are going to tell them, tell them, and then tell them what you told them again." Most communications experts agree that the direct approach is preferable in business because of the emphasis on efficiency and the bottom-line orientation of managers. Moreover, the audience prefers a more direct approach in business. Thus you should use the direct approach whenever possible.

The *indirect approach,* which requires you to build your argument or get to the main point last, however, may be appropriate when communicating bad news, when dealing with an analytical or academic audience, or when trying to create interest within your audience. Remember that this approach is harder to understand and takes longer for the audience to process.

Despite agreement among experts that the direct approach is best, most people in business still tend to communicate in an indirect manner. This is the legacy of years of training by

English teachers who tend to focus on narrative derived from literature and from a lack of strategic thinking. Several studies have shown that millions of dollars a year are wasted in trying to decipher indirect messages in business.

Channel Choice

Managers today have a much greater range of choices than ever before when it comes to distribution channels. Aside from the obvious choice of whether to write or speak, for example, we must also consider new technologies that have dramatically changed the *way* we write and speak.

Speaking is still the dominant form of communication in business because it allows for two-way interaction. Even in a speech to a large group, the speaker can sense the audience's reaction by observing their nonverbal responses. The choices for managers include speaking to groups, conducting meetings, engaging in conversations with one person at a time, making telephone calls, leaving voice mail messages, and holding videoconferences.

Writing in the past has been a one-way communication activity because of the considerable time involved waiting for a response. Electronic mail (e-mail) and chat rooms have changed that somewhat, but the nonverbal portion is still missing from the picture. The choices for managers include traditional memos, letters, and reports, as well as e-mail. Writing is preferable when the message must be formal or include a written signature.

E-mail has become the ubiquitous communications channel. Although once scorned in favor of written documents when a record of the communications were necessary, e-mail has become the communication channel of choice for many companies. The passage of electronic signature laws and the development of secure transfer technologies have led to the creation of virtual legal documents and binding contracts. These documents, however, are more difficult to contain than written documents, as copies may exist on a foreign server long after a company has deleted the e-mail.

E-mail may seem the best way to communicate because it is convenient and fast. E-mail can be overused, however. According to Munter, you should use e-mail when you want to:

- *Reach many people simultaneously,* in multiple locations or time zones
- *Offer your readers flexibility,* since they can respond at their convenience
- *Save your readers' time,* since reading is faster than listening
- *Impart good or neutral news,* such as confirming, clarifying, updating, and announcing
- *Write the equivalent* of a handwritten note or postcard
- *Record the conversation and leave a conversation trail,* since oral communication leaves no record
- *Distribute documents,* especially for team editing faster and cheaper than overnight mailing

Conversely, you should *not* use e-mail if you:

- *Are angry or in radical disagreement.* Wait until you have time to cool off before you send your reply. With e-mail, you may tend to answer rapidly in the heat of the moment, often before you have time to think through the repercussions of your answer. Avoid "flaming"—that is, responding to an e-mail in an inappropriately uninhibited, irresponsible, or destructive way.
- *Need to convey sensitive performance-related, or negative information* about the recipient.
- *Need to interact, see, or hear your audience.* E-mail lacks nonverbal interaction, immediate "give and take," and is ineffective for confrontation or consensus building.
- *Need an immediate reply.* Do not send a highly time-constrained message by e-mail—unless, of course, your reader stays connected and alerted all day.
- *Need confidentiality or privacy.* Nothing on e-mail is completely confidential or private. Your message might be printed, distributed, forwarded, or saved by the recipient; monitored (even if you delete it from your files) by systems operators or management; or subpoenaed for use in a legal suit.[3]

The key strategic choice is often not between electronic, oral, and written communications. Frequently the key strategic choice is deciding whether to communicate at all. Thinking about this can prevent you from communicating something you may later regret. This is particularly true in e-mail and writing.

MANAGERIAL WRITING

Managerial writing differs from other types of writing in terms of its focus on brevity, its emphasis on the direct approach, and the severe time pressure associated with its production. While style is part of managerial writing, it is much less important than in other kinds of writing, such as fiction or journalism. Given the emphasis on efficiency in business, managerial writers need to produce the material quickly for an audience that is interested in getting to the core idea as soon as possible. Perhaps the easiest way to understand managerial writing is to think of it in terms of the process as well as the final product.

The Managerial Writing Process

This section will explain the process used to compose a managerial communication. Most people have experienced what is known as "writer's block" when trying to produce important documents. Most of the time this results from writers trying to do too many things at once. Many students, for example, under pressure to produce reports in college, will try to develop ideas, organize material, draft, and edit all at the same time. Each part of the process is equally important and takes a different set of skills to succeed. An attempt to do all of these things simultaneously is likely to produce frustration.

Step 1: Develop Ideas

Developing ideas, for example, takes research skills. To come up with ideas that will help you reach your objective, you might need to go to the library, search for information on the Internet, brainstorm, or interview people. Most of us would not consider this "writing," but it is an important part of the process nonetheless.

Step 2: Organize Ideas

Once you have the ideas, you then need to organize them in coherent form. As mentioned earlier, the best approach in business is to use the direct approach, but organization involves more than just choosing between using the direct or indirect approach in managerial writing.

Managerial writers also need to decide how to categorize or "batch" the information developed earlier. This is simple for ideas that are easy to put into categories. Usually, however, this is one of the most difficult steps for writers. Impressed by all of the research he or she has done, the writer will fight valiantly to fit all of the material into some category.

Once the information has been placed in the appropriate categories, you then need to decide which order is best for the categories themselves. For example, you might decide to organize the material chronologically or by some logical method. Chronological organization is easy because one idea flows obviously into the next, but logic is much more difficult to achieve and demands that writers think of ways to link material through transitions.

Step 3: Draft the Document

This part of the process is sometimes referred to as *drafting* by writing experts. It means actually putting the words onto the page or computer screen.

Drafting is the most creative part of the writing process as you struggle to put your stamp on the material. As a result it should not be mixed with editing, which is a much more logical process that can easily stifle creativity. You should feel free to write sections in any order without thinking about whether words are spelled correctly or if the punctuation is just right.

Step 4: Edit the Document

Once you have produced a draft, you are ready to go back and edit the material in several different ways. First, you should see if it fits in with your overall communication strategy and whether you should be writing at all. Next, you should be sure that the material is organized logically with transitions that help bridge ideas. Third, you should edit to see if the document is easy to skim for busy readers. And, finally, you should edit for micro issues such as spelling and grammar. Most writers spend an inordinate amount of time on the last step—at the expense of the more important issues of strategy and organization.

Although the process might proceed easily from step 1 to step 4 as just outlined, it is more likely to involve movement from one step to the next and back again. For example, you might find when editing (step 4) your draft (step 3) that you need more material (step 1). This leads you back to the drafting and organizing (step 2) steps before editing all over again. Writing is recursive and thus involves going over the material repeatedly in a quest for the best way to reach your communication objective.

The Written Product

The product is the end result of the writing process. Managerial communications expert Mary Munter has broken the product into two separate categories: (1) macrowriting and (2) microwriting.

Macrowriting refers to the document as a whole—including its organization, logic, flow, and design. The biggest difference between managerial writing and other kinds of writing (like fiction or academic writing) is the importance of design, or visual appearance.

Good document design enables the reader to grasp the organizational structure of a document more readily through the use of such devices as headings, subheadings, white space, paragraphs, typography, lists, indentations, bullet points, and enumeration.

In addition to design, macrowriting refers to the use of effective introductions and conclusions in your documents. An effective introduction tells the reader why you wrote the document and how it is organized; the introduction should also give the reader a context for the information. For example, to put a document in perspective, you might refer the reader back to a conversation that led to its creation.

The conclusion should either summarize what you wrote in a longer document or refer the reader to the next step in the communication process. Both of these devices used to end the document, as well as the logical flow of information within the body of the document, go into the development of effective macrowriting.

Microwriting refers to issues at the sentence and word level. Most writers have had extensive training in dealing with microlevel issues through composition courses in school and thus feel more comfortable with their microwriting.

As taught at the top business schools in the United States,

however, microwriting strives to make business writers easier to understand and more conversational by stressing use of the active rather than the passive voice; by stressing the importance of writing short sentences with varied structure; by stressing the importance of brevity in style; and by teaching the importance of avoiding jargon in managerial settings.

Managerial writing comes in many different forms—from memos and reports to letters and e-mail messages. These different forms are often called *genres* by writing experts. While they certainly differ in terms of the way they look or the style you might use to produce one versus another, all share the need for good macro- and microwriting as well as a clear communication strategy.

Oral Presentation

Let's turn our attention away from writing and focus on speaking through a detailed approach to mastering the art of oral presentation.

Oral presentations in business are both prevalent and varied. Included in this area are speeches to large audiences, group presentations, meetings, and brainstorming sessions. Each of these activities, while different in form, relies upon three basic components for success: *structure, visual aids,* and *nonverbal delivery.*

Structure

Presentation structure should include four parts: the opening (or grabber), the preview (or agenda), the main points (or body), and the conclusion (or next steps).

Part 1: The Grabber. Speakers need to "connect" with their audience at the beginning of the presentation. Traditionally, this has led many to make the mistake of telling inappropriate jokes. Instead, speakers should establish rapport by arousing the audience's interest in the topic. Using statistics that present the topic in a new light can often help focus the audience's attention on your topic.

For example, if you were making a presentation to a group of potential customers about an investment opportunity, you might begin by citing relevant numbers: "While even the most optimistic investors only count on a return of 10 percent a year from their investments, our mutual fund has produced returns over 25 percent for each of the last three years . . ."

Part 2: The Agenda.   Since an audience cannot skim your presentation in the same way one can skim a document, the speaker must provide an introduction or "table of contents" that will help guide the listener through the main points of the presentation. This preview should be explicit and presented both visually and orally for the greatest impact.

For example, to continue with the presentation on the mutual fund just described, the speaker might continue as follows: "Today I would like to share with you how this fund has been able to achieve such success by first looking at our investment philosophy, by looking at how we determine which stocks to include in our portfolio, and by describing how we have been able to build the portfolio to its current size through investors like you . . ."

Part 3: The Main Points.   As in writing, the body of a presentation should be coherently organized based on some principle such as chronology, importance, or just the logic of the material itself.

To ensure that they have enough to say, speakers often make the mistake of including too much information in their presentations. In general, instructors in management communication courses suggest limiting the number of main points to between five and seven items. In addition to limiting the number of main points, speakers need to provide clear transitions between sections to connect ideas for listeners. Transitions can be as simple as enumeration (e.g., the second reason) or as complex as repeating ideas in a couple of sentences for longer sections in a complicated presentation.

Part 4: The Conclusion.   Speakers often fail to take advantage of one of the most critical parts of any presentation—the ending. Most communications experts agree that audiences are most likely to pay close attention and remember what you say at the beginning and end of your presentation. This means you have an obligation to provide a coherent closing.

You can achieve such a conclusion by referring back to the grabber ("So, if you are interested in taking part in this investment opportunity with greater than average returns . . ."); by referring to next steps ("Now that we have seen how this company is able to provide such staggering returns, let's set up a meeting for you to meet with our investment advisors . . ."); or by summarizing the main ideas ("So let me repeat the ideas that we have covered today . . .").

Visual Aids

Speakers have a variety of choices in how to present ideas visually. Options include PowerPoint presentations, Internet-based simulations, overhead transparencies, and 35mm slides. The medium you pick should be based on the audience's needs and the level of formality you are looking for in the presentation. Whatever medium you choose, however, the visuals themselves will fall into one of two categories: text and graphics.

Text visuals are used to show the structure of the presentation. Many speakers tend to use text visuals for every idea they present rather than reserving them for just the most important ideas. In general, the best way to use text visuals is for the agenda, which tells the reader what the presentation is all about, and for major sections within a longer presentation.

These text visuals should be well-designed and easy to read. They should also include message titles that indicate the main idea of the visual to the viewer. Good design means lettering that is large enough for the situation and a font that is pleasing to the eye.

Graphic visuals include pictures (such as photographs, drawings, or videos) as well as charts and graphs (including pie charts, bar charts, flow charts, and other diagrams).

Visual communication expert Edward Tufte suggests that speakers should avoid graphics that are too complicated and that include what he refers to as "chartjunk" (e.g., shading, 3-D effects, legends, and hash marks).[4] Researchers have shown repeatedly that simple charts and graphs with message titles that act as topic sentences are best to use in almost all situations. Unfortunately, technology has made it easier for us to create overly complex visual aids.

Nonverbal Delivery

While communication strategy, presentation structure, visual aids, and the content itself are all critical to the success of a presentation, what really keeps many speakers awake at night in a cold sweat are the nonverbal components of a presentation. Most communications studies have shown that speaking in front of a group is one of the greatest fears that people have. Practice can help speakers lose their fear over time, so repeated rehearsals are the best antidote for anyone preparing a presentation.

But speakers also need to be aware of the specific physical and vocal characteristics that determine successful nonverbal delivery. These include: posture, body movement, eye contact, hand gestures, facial expressions, inflection, speaking rate, filler words, and enunciation.

Most oral communications experts suggest that the best way to improve nonverbal delivery and avoid nervousness is to relax both the body and the mind. Exercising specific parts of the body and warming up the voice before a presentation help the speaker to gain confidence during the performance. Likewise, trying to build your self-confidence by avoiding self-criticism, and observing yourself in a videotaped practice session can do wonders for timid speakers. You might also try to use some of Dale Carnegie's proven methods of positive thinking to relax yourself mentally before a presentation.

CROSS-CULTURAL COMMUNICATION

In addition to providing training in skills such as written and oral presentation, management communication courses in business schools also cover the cultural context for managers who wish to succeed in an increasingly diverse and global environment.

Managers can become more sensitive to cultural differences by studying about or experiencing different cultures firsthand. But this is not always possible, given the pressures of contemporary business life. Instead, they should try to apply frameworks like the following three examples culled from a variety of disciplines that are used to teach business students how to succeed in diverse cultures.

Cultural Values Systems

Anthropologists Kluckhohn and Strodtbeck's "Cultural Values Systems" framework looks at how attitudes differ about nature, time, social relations, activity, and humanity across cultures.[5] For example, in the United States we tend to believe that we can control and challenge nature, while in Middle Eastern cultures such as Saudi Arabia, they tend to believe that life is determined by God or fate. This can have many implications for you in terms of the success or failure of your communication objective if you are trying to communicate with someone in Saudi Arabia.

Other cultures have beliefs about humanity that differ widely; from a feeling that people are basically evil and hard to change to a feeling that people are basically good and should be trusted. Understanding these cultural distinctions makes a difference in how you motivate your audience.

Work-Related Values

Hofstede's "Differences in Work-Related Values" shows how to analyze a culture's attitude toward authority.[6] Hofstede studied managers in 40 countries to look at how they accept unequal distribution of power, their attitudes toward individualism versus a group orientation, their tolerance for ambiguity, and their materialism versus concern for others.

Hofstede refers to power distribution in a culture in terms of "power distance," the extent to which power is autocratic. Cultures such as Sweden and Israel tend to be more democratic—which would imply that communication is more participative. France, on the other hand, exemplifies a high-power distance, which means they tend to have less concern for participative management and greater concern with who has the power.

In terms of the individual versus the group, the United States was one of the most individualistic out of the 40 countries that Hofstede studied, while Venezuela and Peru tended to be much more collectivist in orientation. These attitudes have implications for what communication style might work best in a particular culture.

High- and Low-Context Cultures

Another framework that is useful to study in terms of management communication across cultures is Hall's analysis of high- and low-context cultures. Hall finds that cultures range from "high-context," which implies the need for a prior relationship or "context," to "low-context" cultures that like to get right to the business at hand.[7]

Several Asian countries such as China, Japan, and Vietnam were "high-context" in their orientation in Hall's study. This means that they tend to establish social trust first, value personal relationships and goodwill, agree by general trust, and negotiate slowly and ritualistically.

Low-context cultures, on the other hand, such as Germany, Switzerland, and North America tend to get down to business first; value expertise and performance; agree by specific, legalistic contracts; and negotiate as efficiently as possible.

This framework has implications for communicators in terms of how you establish credibility in different cultures, how you socialize with people in those cultures, and how you approach business situations such as a simple negotiation.

For example, if a stereotypical American were to begin negotiating a contract with a Chinese bureaucrat without trying to understand the high-context nature of that individual, he or she might try to do business before socializing (such as sharing a meal), which could easily prevent the American from reaching the ultimate communication objective (to get the bureaucrat to sign the contract).

Thus, effective cross-cultural communication in business relies on the sensitivity of the communicator in dealing with diverse cultures, specific knowledge about a particular culture, and the ability of the communicator to use analytical frameworks such as those already described in dealing with a more complex and diverse environment.

CORPORATE COMMUNICATION

In the first part of this chapter we looked at the field of management communication, which tends to focus on specific skills and frameworks that managers can use individually to succeed in any organization. The term *corporate communication,* however, refers to how the organization itself communicates.

In most companies today, corporate communication is a distinct functional area similar to the marketing, finance, production, accounting, and human resource functions. In this section, we will look at the changing environment for business and its influence on the development of a corporate communication function, the rise of public relations firms, as well as the specific subfunctions that make up the core of a modern communication department in a corporation.

The Changing Environment for Business

Although corporations had no specific strategy earlier in this century for dealing with communication as a functional area, they often had to respond to external and internal constituencies whether they wanted to or not. As the environment for business became more hostile, laws also began to change, forcing companies to communicate in new and much more public ways.

According to three different polls, while close to 75 percent of the populace agreed in the late 1960s that business balanced profit and the public interest, only 15 percent would agree with the same statement by the mid 1970s. This radical shift in attitudes created a dramatic need for corporate communication to develop as a functional area in business.

The Development of the Function

Because of the changing environment, the responses to constituencies became frequent enough that someone who was not responsible for another function, such as marketing or administration, had to take control of certain aspects of communication. This function was almost always called either *public relations* (also known as PR) or *public affairs.* Typically, it included a component that would attempt to allow the organization to interact with the press. More often than not, however, the function in its emerging days really existed to keep the press away from the inner workings of the corporation. Thus, the pejorative term *flak* came into existence as a way to describe what PR people were actually doing: shielding top managers from "bullets" thrown at them from outside the boundaries of the organization.

Since the press was used to this sort of relationship, and the general public was less interested in the inner workings of business than they are today, the flak era of public relations lasted for many years. As companies needed to add other communications activities to the list, public relations personnel were the obvious choice. For example, in the 1960s it was not unusual to find public relations officials handling speech-writing, annual reports, and the ubiquitous "house organ" (or company newspaper).

Given that the majority of work in this area involved dealing with the press (television was not a factor until the early 1970s), former journalists were typically hired to handle this job. They could, after all, write quickly and coherently, which were the most important skills necessary for a discipline revolving around the writing of press releases and speeches.

These journalists-turned-flaks brought the first real expertise in the area of communication to the corporation. Most other managers in large companies, until recently, came from very traditional business-oriented backgrounds such as engineering, accounting, finance, production, or at best (in terms of sensitivity to communication issues) sales or marketing. Their understanding of how to communicate depended on abilities that they might have gained by chance or through excellent undergraduate or secondary school training rather than years of experience in the workplace. Given their more quantitative orientations, these old-style managers welcomed a professional communicator who could take the heat for them and offer guidance based on something other than seat-of-the-pants reasoning.

The Rise of Public Relations Firms

At the same time these developments were taking place within corporations, other communications professionals were working independently to handle the growing need for communications advice. The legends of the public relations field like Edward Bernays, David Finn, Harold Burson, and more recently, Linda Robinson, helped the profession develop away from its journalism roots into a more refined and respected field. These were the founders and leaders of the PR firms that were often hired by corporations to deal with the inadequacies in their own public relations or public affairs departments.

As a result, schools of communication sprang up to train the consultants who would work in these firms. Shandwick, Hill and Knowlton, and Burson Marsteller, just to name a few, still exist today to service the needs of organizations in the area of public relations. And schools of communication still provide resources for entrants into these firms.

For many years, those PR firms dominated the communications field. They essentially operated as outsourced communications departments for many organizations who could not afford their own or who needed extra help for special situations, such as crises or promotional activities. Even today, these firms provide some of the best advice available on a number of issues related to corporate communication. But, for the most part, they are unable to handle the day-to-day activities required for a smooth flow of communications from an organization to its constituents.

Thus, as problems in the 1970s developed outside of companies requiring more than the simple internal PR function supplemented by the outside consultant from a PR firm, the roots of the new corporate communication function started to take hold within companies. Accordingly, this new functional area started to look more like other functional areas within the corporation. These changes created the need for business-school-trained professionals who could understand and converse with other managers in their own language. It also created a much more complex functional area with many different subfunctions besides just media relations. The corporate communication strategy framework (see Figure 2.1) shows that corporate communication is a cyclical process.[8] Organizations use corporate communications to get a group of people to do something; buy a product, work for the company, or simply have a favorable opinion of the company. Organizations establish the objective and match that objective with the organization's current situation and resources. Those resources are then used to communicate a carefully structured message to constituencies, who then respond or react to the communication. The organization, in turn, assesses the reaction and decides what it wants the constituency to do. Thus the cycle continues.

Organization

As with managerial communications, you must first establish an objective if you are to communicate effectively. You must also select a communication channel. For example, suppose you were heading the Korean car company, Kia, as it entered the U.S. market. Your objective would be to create demand among American consumers for a car made by a company they previously knew nothing about. You might decide to use

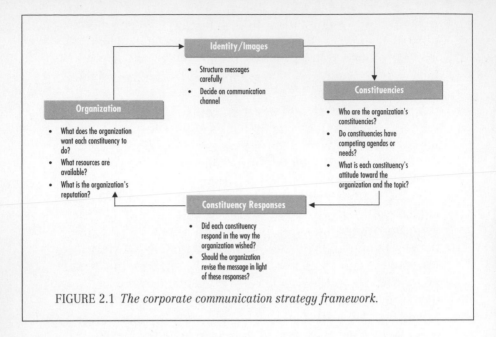

FIGURE 2.1 *The corporate communication strategy framework.*

television advertising as your channel. Achieving your objective is constrained by two factors: available resources and reputation. Resources include money, human resources, and time. For example, airing an advertisement during the Superbowl would certainly raise awareness of Kia. It might, however, be too expensive, or there might not be enough time to create the advertisement to meet the production deadline.

Reputation is based on the constituency's perception of the company, rather than on the company itself. As will be described in more detail later, a company's reputation is a valuable asset. You must have a realistic assessment of your company from the constituency's point of view. Many company's internal views of their strengths and weaknesses are different from actual consumer perception of those elements. Marketing consulting firms can assist you in obtaining an accurate assessment of your company's current reputation.

Image, Reality, Identity, and Reputation[9]
Communication can be used to enhance a company's reputation through image and identity. Messages must be structured carefully and communicated through the correct channels. For example, Philip Morris used advertising about its corporate

philanthropy feeding the hungry in the United States and abroad to enhance its reputation with television viewers, especially those viewing family-friendly programs, who may have had a more negative perception of the company than younger, single consumers.

Image is a reflection of the organization's reality. It is the corporation as seen through the eyes of constituents. Thus, an organization can have different images with different constituencies. For example, forest products companies may have a very negative image among environmental activists, but a very positive image among employees of firms engaged in this endeavor. Corporate communications departments conduct research (similar to marketing research for products and services) to understand different constituents' needs and attitudes. They then try to work on better communications with those constituents to enhance their image.

Reality, on the other hand, is the visual manifestation of a company's image as seen in the corporate logo, stationery, uniforms, buildings, brochures, and advertising that form the company's *identity.* Identity consulting firms work with organizations to create logos and other manifestations of identity. These firms increasingly rely on business schools to provide personnel for this growing field.

Reality combines with image to create *reputation,* which is a product of how all constituencies view a company (see Figure 2.2). A company's reputation may be its most valuable asset. Companies with strong reputations generally command premium prices for their products, have more stable revenues, and are given more latitude in a crisis. For example, Johnson & Johnson was able to regain its Tylenol market share after the poison scandal of the mid-1980s due to fast remedial action, the public's long-standing faith in the corporation, and its excellent reputation.

Constituencies, as described earlier, are groups with an interest in your organization. *Primary constituencies* include employees, customers, shareholders, and communities. Although communications are most commonly targeted to primary constituencies, *secondary constituencies* are also important to organizations. Some examples of secondary constituencies are media, suppliers, government, and creditors. Remember that communications intended for one constituency often reach others. Moreover, constituencies can

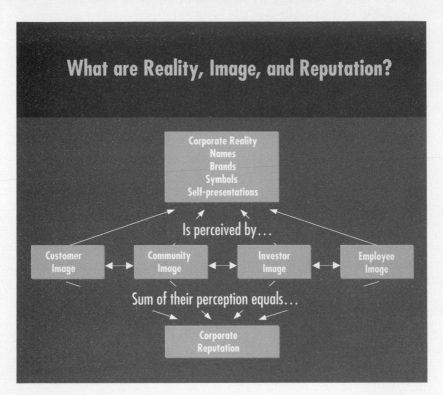

FIGURE 2.2 *Reality, image, and reputation.*

have competing interests and different perceptions of a company. For example, although cutting employee benefits may be viewed positively by a company's stockholders, its employees will most likely have a negative view.

Constituency Responses

After communicating with a constituency, you must assess the results of your communication and determine whether the communication had the desired result. For example, did sales rise in response to an advertising campaign? After determining the results, you must determine how you will react. Has your reputation changed? Do you need to change your communications channel? Thus the cycle continues.

FUNCTIONS WITHIN THE DISCIPLINE OF CORPORATE COMMUNICATION

Once an organization has a coherent corporate communication strategy, it must then think about the function of communication. Perhaps the best way to discuss the function of corporate communication is to look at the different parts of a modern corporate communication function. The areas under consideration are corporate advertising and advocacy, media relations, financial communications, employee relations, community relations and corporate philanthropy, government relations, and crisis communications. Although this is not an all-encompassing list of activities, it represents the most important subfunctions within a large corporation.

Corporate Advertising and Advocacy

Image and identity are often reflected in a company's *corporate advertising.* Corporate advertising differs from product advertising or marketing communication. Instead of trying to sell a company's product or service, corporate advertising tries to sell the company itself—usually to a completely different constituency than customers. For example, companies with a diverse product range might try to run "umbrella" ads that show potential shareholders what the company is all about; oil companies might try to influence public opinion about their environmental friendliness; and chemical companies might try to show themselves as good places to work for young people entering the job market.

Advocacy programs are a subset of corporate advertising and represent the organization's attempt to influence public opinion on an important issue related to the firm's business. The most famous examples are ExxonMobil's ads, which run as op-ed pages and cover a broad range of topics important to the corporation, and Philip Morris's advertising to defend itself against those who would attack the tobacco industry.

Professionals in a corporate communication department typically develop the strategy and shape the messages for these advertisements. They then act as liaisons with advertising agencies.

Media Relations

Unlike the paid advertising just described, the *media relations* subfunction allows an organization to shape its image through third parties. This is the last vestige of the old PR department and a mainstay of any corporate communication function. Most of the personnel for corporate communications will typically be found within this subfunction, and the person in charge of the department as a whole must also be capable of dealing with the media as a spokesperson (in addition to other top managers) for the firm.

Media relations specialists today go far beyond their predecessors in managing this subfunction. They must be more adept at conducting background material on writers and producers, at training managers for interviews based on their best guess of what the story is all about, and at handling the actual relationships with reporters and editors themselves. Given the typically adversarial relationship between business and the media, this is often one of the most critical subfunctions to senior managers hoping to present a positive image to shareholders and other critical constituents.

Financial Communications

Also called *investor* or *shareholder relations,* this subfunction has emerged as one of the fastest growing subsets of the corporate communication function and an area of intense interest at all companies. Traditionally, this area has been handled by the finance or treasury department, but the focus today has moved away from just the numbers to the way the numbers are actually communicated to various constituencies.

Investor relations (IR) also deals with securities analysts on both the buy and sell sides who are often a direct source for the financial media, which this subfunction cultivates in conjunction with experts from the media relations area. Financial communication also involves direct contact with investors, both large and small. In addition, every public firm must produce financial statements and annual reports, which are produced by financial communications professionals.

Financial communicators must have a broad understanding of business in general and finance and accounting in particular. Training in these subjects is most often found today within business schools.

Employee Communications

As companies become more focused on retaining a happy workforce with changing values and different demographics, they have to think more seriously about how they communicate with employees. This process of communicating with employees is referred to as *internal communications*. Companies today must explain complicated health and benefit packages, changes in laws that affect employees, and changes in the marketplace that might affect the company in the future. And increasingly, they must boost the morale of employees after "downsizing" and "restructuring."

While many of these activities can be handled through human resources departments, the communication itself and the strategy for communicating these ideas should come from communications experts in the corporate communication function. Most of the *Fortune 500* corporations now use corporate communication departments (rather than human resource departments) to deal with these issues. Corporate Intranets, web sites that can be accessed only by company employees, have brought information online not only at large, global companies like 3Com and Accenture, but also at small companies. Like financial communications, this area is growing at a rapid rate in most organizations and requires a deeper understanding of the business as a whole than it did in the past.

Community Relations and Corporate Philanthropy

Many companies have a separate subfunction outside of the corporate communications function to deal with each of these areas. For historical reasons, community relations is often housed in the human resource department, while in larger companies corporate philanthropy is often set up as a separate foundation from the organization itself. But the need for a more strategic focus and the difficulties in dealing with growing concerns in communities about the role of the corporation create the need for corporate communication departments to handle both of these subfunctions. In addition, given the limited resources available today in communities and not-for-profit organizations, most companies are much more strategic in their focus on philanthropy. Many try to balance the need to help people in need within the communities in which they do business with the demands of shareholders.

Government Relations

This subfunction, often called by the more global name of *public affairs,* is more important in some industries than others, but virtually every company can benefit by having ties to legislators on both a local and national level. Many U.S. companies have established offices in Washington, DC, to keep tabs on what is going on in government that might affect the company. Because of its importance in heavily regulated industries such as utilities, government relations are often dealt with at an industry level (as in the electric utilities and tobacco industries) in addition to the individual company effort. In these industries, companies and lobbying groups spend far more time trying to influence legislation that might have an effect on the industry or firm than one would find in less heavily regulated industries.

Crisis Communication

While not specifically a separate function, responses to potential crises need to be planned for and coordinated by the corporate communication function. Usually, a broad group of managers from throughout the organization are included in all planning for crises, but the actual execution of a crisis communication plan is the purview of the corporate communication department. Responsibilities for planning include risk assessment, setting communication objectives for potential crises, assigning teams to each crisis, planning for centralization, and deciding what to include in a formal plan. In terms of actual execution of a crisis communication plan, communicators are responsible for taking control, gathering information, creating a centralized crisis management center, doing the actual communication, and making plans to avoid other crises.

SUMMARY

The field of communication in business—which includes both management communication and corporate communication— is one of the most critical areas of concern to managers in a rapidly changing and increasingly hostile environment. The Key Concepts section in the back of the book offers readers an opportunity to learn more about specific terms you may want to refer back to later. Finally, the reference section following this chapter includes web sites with valuable information about the field of communication.

INTERNET RESOURCES

Dow Jones Interactive (djinteractive.com). Extensively tracks PR coverage through company profiles. Track the success of a specific company's press releases and communication initiatives through Dow Jones' publications library.

Facilitation Factory (www.facilitationfactory.com). While Calian Technology Ltd's facilitation web site targets professional facilitators, the site offers features of interest to all managers hoping to improve their facilitation skills. A "FacilitateThis!" feature asks visitors how they would facilitate various meeting scenarios and are able to compare their answers with those of other respondents.

MediaNet Presentation Skills (www.medianet-ny.com). MediaNet's site brims with advice on how to give effective presentations, including topics on scripting messages, designing supportive visuals, and translating group skills into one-on-one settings. The "Presentation Tip of the Week" gives advice on messaging, methods, mechanics, and logistics.

PR Week (www.prweekus.com/index.htm). PR Week's online component offers nationwide coverage of the public relations business—carrying the latest news, in-depth analysis, top columnists and reviews of campaigns. Also lists an extensive list of job opportunities for PR professionals nationwide.

COMMUNICATION CRITICAL REFERENCE MATERIALS

Articles

Argenti, Paul A. "Corporate Communication as a Discipline: Toward a Definition," *Management Communication Quarterly,* August 1996.

    This article traces the academic development of corporate communication as a discipline.

Munter, Mary M. "Cross-Cultural Communication for Managers," *Business Horizons,* May–June 1993.

    This article synthesizes multiple insights about cross-cultural communications—from fields as diverse as anthropology, psychology, communication, linguistics, and organizational behavior—and applies them specifically to managerial communication.

Tannenbaum, R., and W. Schmidt. "How to Choose a Leadership Pattern," *Harvard Business Review,* March–April 1958, pp. 95–101.

> Describes how managers need to use different communication styles to reach various communication objectives.

Books

Argenti, Paul A., and Janis Forman. *The Power of Corporate Communication.* New York: McGraw-Hill, 2002.

> Argenti and Forman discuss the roots of corporate communication as well as various subfunctions within the function of communication—reputation, corporate advertising, internal communication, investor relations, government relations, media relations, and crisis communication. A thorough treatment of the subject of communications, this book should be read by anyone who works in and with the field of communications.

Argenti, Paul A. *Corporate Communication,* 3rd edition. Burr Ridge, IL: McGraw-Hill, 2003.

> Presents the new concept of corporate communication as a functional area of business management. The goal, in theory, is to facilitate unified internal and external communication strategies to create a totally integrated communication function. Evolution of corporate communication is explained in an historical context with specific emphasis on current business demands for a more strategic approach to communications. Case studies on General Electric, Dow Corning, and Adolph Coors and others are included to demonstrate application of theory to companies as well as the importance of communication as a tool for resolving corporate crises.

Aristotle. *The "Art" of Rhetoric.* Vol. 22, Translator John Henry Freese. Cambridge: Harvard University Press, 1982.

> Aristotle was head of the Lyceum of Athens in 336 B.C., and this collection of his works encompasses his teachings on the art of communication. Aristotle defines the tripartite system in terms of speech that includes a speaker, the subject of discussion, and the person to whom it is addressed. This concept forms the basis for communication strategy at both the individual and organiztional level.

Barton, Laurence. *Crisis in Organizations: Managing and Communicating in the Heat of Chaos.* Cincinnati: South-Western Publishing Co., 1993.

Explains strategic challenges facing hundreds of organizations such as Chrysler, Coca-Cola, Dow Corning, Walt Disney, and Tylenol. The book examines potential crises such as strikes, hostile takeovers, product recalls, and accidents through case studies supplemented with interviews of CEOs, managers, and attorneys. The gamut of potential business problems is covered as well as the development and implementation of crisis management plans to resolve these actual corporate disasters.

Cutlip, Scott M. *Public Relations History: From the 17th to the 20th Century.* Hillsdale, NJ: Lawrence Erlbaum Associates, 1995.

Traces dynamics of public relations in its practices and manifestations of events from the seventeenth through the twentieth centuries. Analyzes public relations in the foundation of America and throughout its history. Demonstrates that public relations continues to play an important role in a modern context for businesses, colleges, and non-profit agencies.

Lanham, Richard A. *Revising Business Prose.* New York: Charles Scribner's Sons, 1981.

Promotes the more effective use of language. Postulates that modern communication has assumed a bureaucratic writing format in the business world. Lanham proposes the Paramedic Method as a means of solving the "plague" of bureaucratic writing by offering a quick, self-teaching method for translation of verbose language into comprehensible English.

Munter, Mary. *Guide to Managerial Communication,* 6th edition. Englewood Cliffs, NJ: Prentice Hall, 2002.

Offers practical communication strategies and skills for speaking and writing. Organized and easy-to-read format provides general guidelines of managerial communication as well as answers to specific questions.

Schultz, Majken, Mary Jo Hatch, and Mogens Holten Larsen. *The Expressive Organization: Linking Identity, Reputation, and the Corporate Brand.* London: Oxford University Press, 2000

Suitable for both academics and practitioners, this book discusses ideas and problems related to identity, reputation, brand management, and communication. While slightly academic in tone, the book is an important contribution to the field. The editors argue that organizations are increasingly competing based on their ability to express who they are and what they stand for—hence the title of the book. The chapters are written by a number of different authors with backgrounds in communication, marketing, and strategy, as well as organizational behavior and accounting.

University of Chicago Press, *The Chicago Manual of Style*. 13th edition. Chicago: The University of Chicago Press, 1982.

Comprehensive reference tool for authors, editors, copywriters, and proofreaders, with guidelines on written communication.

Zelazny, Gene. *Say It With Charts: The Executive's Guide to Visual Communication*. 3rd edition. Homewood, IL: Irwin Professional Publishing, 1996.

Explores the selection and use of charts in the 1990s. Advice on how to take advantage of new technology to create impressive graphics and visual aids for business presentations.

Marketing

According to the American Marketing Association, marketing is "the process of planning and executing the conception, pricing, promotion and distribution of ideas, goods and services to create changes that satisfy individual and organizational objectives."[1] Simply put, marketing is a way of doing business that focuses on identifying the customer's needs and preferences. By focusing on satisfying the customer, a company can shape the goods and services it provides, as well as the strategy it uses to bring these goods and services to the public.

Marketing is not just a functional area, it is now a pervasive concern at companies trying to make headway in an increasingly competitive global market. High-level positions once limited to finance gurus and operations experts now include marketing executives, and, in fact, many companies have combined the role of the chief marketing officer with that of the chief strategy officer. From law firms to dot.coms to the United States Postal Service, the creation of a chief marketing officer has led to strategic successes and a trimmer bottom line.

This chapter introduces marketing terms, equations, and models, and explains how they fit together. It focuses on providing a clear understanding of how companies operate within a market-oriented framework. The chapter also explains how companies identify customer's needs and preferences, create products, set prices, and then promote these products so that they will be consumed.

In many of the important phases of this marketing process (e.g., identifying consumer needs, promoting new products to customers) marketers rely on statistical analyses as a source of information. Specifically, marketers use a statistical analysis tool called *regression* to gather information about the strength of customer preferences and the power of marketing efforts in relation to the impact on sales. In addition, marketing managers use statistical analysis to draw conclusions about customer preferences. Lastly, marketing managers use statistical sampling techniques to draw conclusions about an entire population of customers based on information obtained from a small sample of those customers. Thus the customer is the central focus of the marketer.

THE CUSTOMER

Any detailed account of the marketing process must begin with a discussion of the *customer* or *consumer.* For the purpose of this chapter, these words will be used interchangeably. A consumer refers to any individual or household that purchases or acquires goods or services for personal use. Similarly, the population of all consumers is referred to as the *consumer market* or *mass market.* A consumer market has four key characteristics:

1. A large number of buyers and sellers
2. A wide geographic distribution
3. Small individual purchases (as opposed to business to business at a volume discount, for example)
4. A wide variety of products to choose from.

An example of a consumer market is the market for laundry detergent. Most people buy some sort of laundry detergent, and thus they comprise a large number of buyers. Since there are many different manufacturers of laundry detergent, ranging from major companies like Procter & Gamble to generic brands, there are also a large number of sellers. People all over the world buy laundry detergent, thus it has wide geographic distribution. Consumers buy the detergent in individual containers, not by the truckload, so that criterion is also met. Finally, a wide variety of products exist, ranging from Tide to Woolite to white-labeled brands. Thus, marketers vie to influence consumer markets' purchases. Marketers view the purchase not as a single-step decision, but as a process, known as the *buying process.*

THE BUYING PROCESS

The consumer buying process consists of five stages:

1. Need Recognition
2. Alternative Search
3. Alternative Evaluation
4. Purchase Decision
5. Postpurchase Feelings[2]

Need Recognition

The customer begins the purchase cycle by recognizing an unmet need. This simply means that the customer becomes aware that he or she wants a good or a service and makes a decision to acquire it.

A. H. Maslow, in his book *Motivation and Personality,* postulated that people experience a hierarchy of needs, where higher needs do not engage until all earlier needs in the hierarchy have been met. Maslow outlines the hierarchy as follows:

Physiological Needs. This category refers to the needs of the human body, like food, water, and sex.

Safety Needs. This category refers to the need of humans to be protected from physical harm and unknown and potentially detrimental influences. These needs engage once a person's physiological needs have been met.

Social Needs. This category refers to the need for humans to interact socially in groups and to feel a sense of connection with others in a given group.

Esteem Needs. This category refers to the need for humans to be recognized as important in other people's lives. These feelings are the basis for self-confidence and prestige.

Self-Actualization Needs. This category refers to the need people have to recognize all of their potential and to become everything they have the potential to become.[3]

Within the population of the mass market, all needs influence the purchase decision. Hence, marketing efforts attempt to communicate how a given product can address these needs and to specify why the product is attractive to the target consumer. For example, home security systems can be marketed to appeal to one individual's safety needs (I need protection from criminals), while appealing to another's esteem needs (I am important enough to my spouse that he or she would invest in a home security system).

Alternative Search and Alternative Evaluation

Returning to the discussion of the five stages, after a need has been identified and realized, the alternative search and alternative evaluation stages begin. These stages can be considered together because the process is somewhat cyclical. The consumer acquires information on available products that fulfill the identified need. The consumer then compares available products against each other. This process repeats until the consumer is satisfied that enough alternatives have been considered and evaluated. As an example, a first-year college student with dirty clothes might identify the need for laundry detergent for the first time in his or her life. Upon arriving in the detergent aisle at the local grocery store, the student is confronted with his or her different purchase options (Tide, Era, Gain, Cheer, etc.) and begins to compare them (Do I care if it is fragrance-free? Do I need detergent with bleach? How much did that one cost compared to this one? What is the real difference between these two? What did we use at home?) until he or she reaches a decision.

The alternative search and alternative evaluation stages tie directly into Michael Porter's concept of threat of new entrants and threat of substitutes explained in his Competitive Forces within an Industry Model (see Strategy chapter for more on Porter). Thus the same model that managers use to develop corporate strategy also has a direct application in marketing a product. In this context, a company with an existing product out in the market is constantly establishing or maintaining its position for the product in the consumer market. In the case of the laundry detergent example, the student is in the grocery store trying to decide, and to a degree, will go through this process each time she or he enters the store. The concept of threat of new entrants appears if some new product on the market, WonderClean, promises to clean clothes so well that the clothes develop a resistance to getting dirty again. If this feature especially appeals to the student, he or she will purchase this product instead of the widely known products (Tide or Era).

The threat of substitutes concept can come into play as well. Say, for example, that while the student evaluates laundry choices, he or she notices a different kind of product on the shelf. This product is not laundry detergent at all, but a bag of small organic rocks. The rocks themselves allegedly contain deionizing properties when submerged in water that repel dirt and other toxins from clothing. In fact, according to the package, these rocks clean clothes better than any laundry detergent can, and they never wear out. If the college student purchases these rocks, then he or she has chosen a substitute product that may keep him or her from ever buying laundry detergent again.

The ideas captured in the Porter framework integrate the buying process with concerns about the market in which the company is doing business, as well as the external forces affecting that market. Using these frameworks in tandem allows marketing managers to consider a more complete picture when making marketing decisions about a product.

Purchase Decision

After recognizing needs, identifying products that meet those needs, and evaluating each product's ability to meet those needs, the consumer makes a purchase decision. Remember that the purchase decision also includes the possibility of not purchasing any product, thereby leaving the needs unmet. For example, if the price of laundry detergent is too high, the student may decide to drive home and use a friend's detergent to wash his or her clothes.

Postpurchase Feelings

The last stage of the buying process, postpurchase feelings, is important to marketing professionals because of the connection between a customer's feelings after a purchase and the long-term retention of that customer.

CUSTOMER RETENTION

The overall success of a product hinges not on the initial sale to a customer, but on repeated sales to that same customer. Simply put, a company makes the most profit when its customer base has a long-term commitment to a product. The reason long-term, loyal customers make the most profit for a company is that the cost of acquiring new customers (through advertising campaigns or promotions) is high. Therefore, if a company can acquire a customer and then turn that customer into a long-term, loyal customer, the company's initial investment in acquiring that customer pays off. Further, companies are aware that not only are loyal customers the most profitable ones, but they are also the most credible source of advertising: for some products and services, more than half of all new business is the result of word-of-mouth customer referrals. Hence, a company should want to enter into a long-term relationship with every customer.

An important measure related to customer retention is *lifetime value of a customer* (LVC). Marketers use LVC to determine how changing the length of a relationship with a customer affects the company's bottom line. For example, assume an Internet service provider is considering giving one month of free service to each customer who renews his service for a year. In evaluating whether the plan increases profits, marketers consider not only the likelihood of customers signing up for the additional year, but also the likelihood of customers retaining service for years beyond. If customers display no loyalty from year to year, the promotion may be a bad idea. On the other hand, if customers are much less likely to change service if they have been satisfied with their service for more than two years, the promotion is probably worthwhile. Customer satisfaction, then, is a vital component of LVC.

CUSTOMER SATISFACTION

Customer satisfaction is an overarching concern for marketing professionals. Simply put, *customer satisfaction* is how happy a customer is with a product or service, both in the product's performance as well as the company's delivery of the product to the market. One commonly used measure of customer satisfaction is the *gap model.* The gap model is defined by the following equation:

Customer satisfaction = delivery − expectations

Delivery refers to the customer's perception of the actual delivery of the product or service. *Expectations* refer to the customer's expectations about that product or service. Thus customer satisfaction is the difference, or "gap," between what the consumer expected and what he or she received. For example, if a consumer purchases a product that he expects to last three months and it lasts six (the delivery of the product was six months of use), he will be very satisfied with the product. Conversely, if the product only lasts one month (the delivery then is one month of use), the consumer is likely to be highly dissatisfied. Thus, expectations serve as the base point for the customer's assessment of delivery and satisfaction.

Therefore, beyond the operational functions involved in bringing a product or service to the market, marketing executives work to manage the customer's perceptions of delivery, or the quality of the product or service the customer has received. And, they both track and attempt to manipulate the customer's perceptions. Similarly, marketing can help customers to set more realistic expectations. Fully integrating the gap model reduces the proclivity of marketing professionals to overpromise or to create unrealistic expectations. Additionally, the gap model, depicted in Figure 3.1, identifies the major components operating within the customer/provider relationship and serves as a good tool for the provider's marketing agent to identify current weaknesses in the company's programs or strategies.

The gap model says that a customer has two sources from which he or she builds expectations about a product or service.

1. Internally, a customer's expectations are based on personal needs; past experience with the product, service, or company; and word-of-mouth communications from other customers.

2. Externally, the customer also receives information from the company about its products or services.

The gap model identifies five possible gaps between delivery and customer expectations.

Gap 1.   The difference between management's perception of customer expectations and the actual customer expectations.

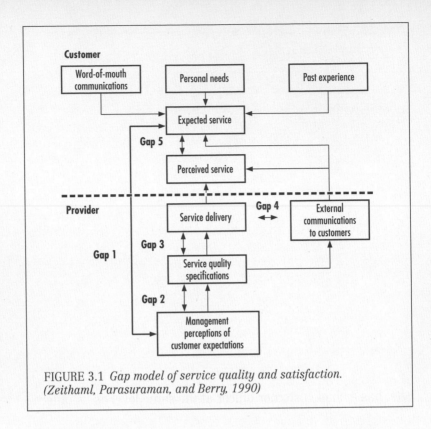

FIGURE 3.1 *Gap model of service quality and satisfaction.*
(Zeithaml, Parasuraman, and Berry, 1990)

Gap 2.   The difference between management's perception of customer expectations and the quality specifications the company communicates to the customer.

Gap 3.   The difference between the quality specifications and actual service delivery.

Gap 4.   The difference between the actual service delivery and what was promised to the customer through external communications, such as advertising.

Gap 5.   The difference between the expected service and the perceived service from the point of view of the customer.

Marketers use the model to monitor the production process at all its critical points, enabling managers to improve service empirically. Moreover, the model accommodates customer perceptions, enabling a manager to identify customer perceptions and correct unfavorable ones occurring at any point in the process. Marketers use many tools ranging from conducting focus groups and surveys to purchasing information from research firms to help identify gaps. Once a specific gap type is identified, management can close that gap and improve customer satisfaction.

CUSTOMER RELATIONSHIP MANAGEMENT

A newly evolved, holistic approach to managing customer retention and customer satisfaction is customer relationship management (CRM). Companies use CRM to organize interactions with customers using methodologies, software, call centers, and Internet applications. For example, many companies use software applications like Oracle to build and maintain a detailed database of their customers and any interactions with them, including sales, customer support, credit history, and so forth. Marketing professionals can then identify and target the best customers, as well as analyze the data to create effective sales campaigns. CRM seeks to anticipate customers' needs and integrate them into the company's products and processes. Increased focus on organized customer interaction has led to the creation of many high-level positions in customer relationship management. For example, Monster.com, a popular career site, has a chief customer officer at the same level as its other "C-Level" (chief financial officer, chief technology officer, etc.) executives. Furthermore, large consulting firms have created specialized consultant groups to assist clients with CRM.

MARKET SEGMENTATION

Marketers understand that not all customers buy the same product to address the same need. And, customer satisfaction levels may vary depending on identifiable attributes within groups of customers such as age, sex, race, religion, geographical location, income, sexual preference, profession, and educational background, just to name a few. Therefore, marketers break customer populations down into smaller markets using these shared personal attributes and other statistics; this is called *market segmentation*. Customers within these smaller populations share needs that are more closely aligned and singularly identifiable. This makes it easier to develop new products and to design specific marketing efforts. For example, a cigar manufacturer may choose to run an advertisement for its product in *Golf* magazine, because research shows that those who golf and read golf magazines often also smoke cigars, and can afford to smoke expensive cigars. Alternatively, cigar manufacturers would not run an ad in *Prevention* magazine, or *Health and Fitness,* because data suggests people who read these magazines typically do not smoke.

A more specific and individualized practice of market segmentation is *database marketing.* Database marketing uses population statistics to identify and target individuals within a group to determine who is most likely to buy a product. For example, suppose Sears kept a database of all its customers who use a Discover card to buy baby clothes sized zero to six months. Sears could hypothesize that these consumers are either expecting a child or know someone who is. Sears could then use the database to send these customers specialized baby catalogs or coupons to motivate them to buy more baby products at Sears.

Use of, and specifically the selling of databases containing an individual's purchase history has sparked debate among privacy advocates. Any company that sells customer's information must also give consumers the option to "opt-out" of having their information sold. A law passed in 2001 granted financial services corporations the legal right to sell individual's transactional information if the individual did not "opt-out." Thus the responsibility is usually placed on the individual to "opt-out," rather than on a company to ask him or her to "opt-in." Nonetheless, great care should be taken before selling information. If you are considering selling your customer database, you should inform customers first, to avoid the risk of negatively affecting customer satisfaction.

Potential privacy issues aside, market segmentation is an important tool for marketing professionals in determining who their customers are and what those customers want. With this basic understanding of who their customers are and how those customers make decisions, marketing professionals then develop products and services and entice customers to buy them. The marketing model that describes this process is known as the *five Ps.*

THE PRODUCT

Marketers combine information from the buying process, customer segmentation, and other customer-centric tools to sell a product. In fact, the popular marketing model, the five Ps, begins with the product.

The five Ps[4] are:

- Product
- Positioning
- Price
- Promotion
- Packaging

The Product Life Cycle

The product life cycle and the perceptual map are two frequently used models for analyzing a product. Figure 3.2 represents the product life cycle. The product life cycle relates sales volumes for a given product to the amount of time the product is available on the market and thereby identifies the stages of a product across these measures. Keep in mind that the efforts of marketing professionals can have a significant effect on shaping any given product's sales. Further, any market segment, as identified using market segmentation, can have its own independent life cycle for a given category of products. Still, the product life cycle model serves as an excellent basis to chart the development of a product within its market.

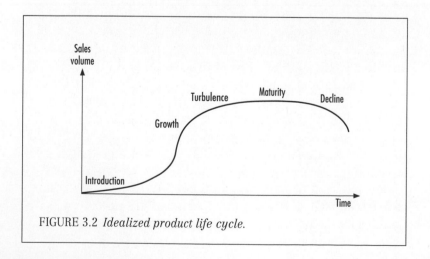

FIGURE 3.2 *Idealized product life cycle.*

Traditionally, the product life cycle charts the following five stages:

- Introduction
- Early Growth
- Late Growth
- Maturity
- Decline

Introduction

During a product's introduction, consumers may require significant information about the product to decide whether to include it as an alternative during purchase decision. Marketers use promotion, such as advertising, to achieve *top of mind status* with a product. This simply means that when a consumer thinks of a product category, top of mind status will determine which brand is most easily associated with a product. In the soft drink category, for example, three top of mind choices might be Coke, Pepsi, and Sprite. Thus, packaging (the fifth "P") in the introductory state should not only draw visual attention to the product to enhance top of mind status, but also to provide information about the product.

If the product meets a need unmet by any other product on the market, promotion efforts and packaging practices should focus on raising customer awareness and need for the product. Conversely, if a new product is within a market where the need for the type of product has already been defined, managers should focus advertising and marketing efforts on differentiating their product from others already on the market.

Product differentiation requires customers to be aware of the difference between the features of a product or service and the benefits of that product or service. In this context, a *product feature* is simply a characteristic that the product or service may have. This could range from weight to color to functionality. A *product benefit,* however, rests in the customer's perception of how a given product feature will benefit them. For example, how much a laptop computer weighs may be a feature, but being "lightweight" in the eyes of the customer may be a benefit. Close attention must be paid to discern exactly which of a product's features are perceived as benefits if new products are going to compete in well-established markets.

Early Growth

The second stage in the product life cycle is *early growth.* An increase in the rate of sales for a product usually marks the transition from the introduction phase to the early growth phase. Goods are produced in greater volume to meet greater demand, resulting in a cost benefit, or a reduction in cost results. Marketers aim to take advantage of these cost benefits, known as *economies of scale,* by passing on the cost savings to the consumer.

The early growth stage may also prompt a shift in the marketing effort away from general demand creation through need recognition towards more concentrated efforts on product differentiation. Typically, increased sales during this period are thought to be from market expansion rather than from stealing competitor's market share. Hence, the perceived threat of the new product or service by its competitors is minimal in the early growth stage. For example, sales of Internet-based television recording appliances, such as Tivo and Ultimate TV, result from customers buying the product in addition to a VCR, rather than instead of a VCR. Tivo and Ultimate TV advertising focuses on the differences between the two competing products, as well as between the appliances and a VCR, rather than on the need for the product.

Late Growth

A decline in the rate of sales growth—but not a decline in sales themselves—signals the *late growth stage.* In the late growth stage, market segments are easily identifiable, prompting product modification efforts to cater to these segments to maintain market share. Competitors tend to launch their strongest efforts to retain sales growth and market share during this period. Price also becomes a major basis for competition in addition to product variations. An example of a product in late growth stage in the United States is the personal digital assistants (PDAs) market/industry. Companies like Palm, Handspring, and Blackberry are constantly developing new features and applications to adapt to the decline in sales growth and to maintain market share.

Maturity

In the maturity stage, the product has been on the market long enough to develop a strong and loyal customer base.

Most sales in the maturity stage are to a base of repeat users. As a result, sales remain steady and are affected more by changes in the purchasing ability of the customer to buy the product than any addition of new customers to the base. Very little product modification occurs in the maturity stage, and most marketing efforts focus on packaging and promotions for the product rather than changing the product itself. The personal computer market in the United States is a good example of a product in the maturity stage. Although manufacturers add new software and Pentium processors, promotion and price drive sales for customers buying an additional computer, rather than their first PC.

The maturity stage is also marked by the phenomenon of *turbulence,*—the clear emergence of the dominant industry players and the elimination of minor players. Minor players are eliminated because they could not sell enough volume to achieve the economies of scale needed to stay competitive within the market. For the same reason, new players have difficulty entering mature markets. Distribution channels, such as stores and catalogs, also become a major focal point for continued success in a mature market; the more widely available a product is, the easier it is to purchase. In the personal computer market, companies like Dell, IBM, Gateway, and Compaq control the lion's share of the market. Texas Instruments and other former PC manufacturers have fallen by the wayside.

Decline

The final stage in the product life cycle is *decline.* During this stage, product sales begin to drop off, and the rate at which they decrease is directly related to the cause that precipitated the onset of the decline stage. If a new substitute product enters the market and renders the original product obsolete, product sales might decrease more sharply. Consider, as an illustration, the case of music CDs replacing tapes and LP records. If, however, there are more gradual changes in the original customer need, this condition might bring about a slower decrease in sales. For example, DVD players are moving at a slower rate to replace VCRs, partially because recording capability was not introduced until five years after the product came to market. Now that DVD manufacturers are including this feature, the decline in VCR sales will probably increase.

Once the decline stage is under way, microeconomic factors can precipitate an even more rapid deterioration. If demand for a product decreases, an excess supply can cause prices to drop. In addition, a decrease in demand also eliminates the economies of scale benefits the product once enjoyed, again making it less profitable (see Economics chapter). Since all managers battle with scarce resources, a product in the decline stage generally receives less marketing and the promotion dollars are allocated to fund a more profitable product. The combination of all these factors can increase the swiftness of the decline phase. For example, children's toys have a rapid life cycle. After sales of a toy begin to drop off, toy companies shift their efforts and advertising dollars to the season's hot toy, abandoning the slow seller. The product life cycle allows managers to read external signals to discern the phase of life of their products. Insight into where a product is on the life cycle enables marketing professionals to manage the current phase more effectively, as well as to plan ahead for upcoming phases. For these reasons, and many others, the product life cycle is one of the most common and long-lived tools used in marketing today.

Positioning and Branding

Although managers may easily identify a product's phase in the life cycle, and use the gap model to find the difference between their product's actual and perceived features, they often misjudge customers' perception of their product in comparison to its competitors. *Perceptual maps* provide a visual representation of where specific products fall within a category based on measures of what attributes a customer is seeking in a *product class,* suggesting how marketers should position the product. A *product category* is a subset of the product class. For example, soft drinks are a product category, and lemon-lime sodas (such as Sprite and 7 Up) are a product class. So, for example, a product manager for 7 Up might use a perceptual map to better understand how customers view 7 Up in relation to their perceptions of Sprite.

Perceptual maps are usually drawn on a simple X- and Y-axis structure, where either two or four dimensions of consumer's perceptions of a product's attributes can be captured. Information on consumer perceptions and preferences is obtained through marketing research and marketing survey techniques. For example, consumers may perceive Ford trucks as being more reliable than Chevy or Dodge trucks. The reality could be the opposite, but it is the consumer perception that is important. Statistical analyses of the data provide results, which are more scientific and more easily used for predictive purposes. Once the dimensions of consumer perception have been identified, a marketing manager can identify all products his or her company offers in relation to these dimensions, as well as assess the competition's product lines.

Figure 3.3 is an example of the perceptual map of the passenger automobile market. The X axis represents the perceived inverse connection between youth, responsibility, and functionality on the part of customers. The right side of the X axis denotes the most extreme perception that people equate sports cars with youthfulness because they are less functional and practical, and functionality and practicality are adult concerns. Marketing executives can use this information to promote sports cars as inspiring youthful feelings in their owners, thus appealing to those who may feel pressured by adult concerns and perceive that purchasing a sports car will make them feel young and carefree again.

The left side of the X axis denotes the other extreme customer sentiment, that a car with a higher degree of function-

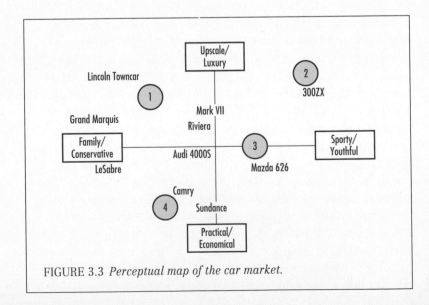

FIGURE 3.3 *Perceptual map of the car market.*

ality and less sportiness is the more responsible adult choice. Marketing professionals address these perceptions by appealing to a customer's sense of conservation, often through emphasizing a family orientation when presenting a car through advertising.

The Y axis represents the price variable associated with buying a car. The top of the Y axis represents luxury automobiles, known to be very expensive. The bottom of the Y axis represents value automobiles, known to be least expensive.

Marketers understand, through customer surveys, that these are the considerations most people weigh before buying a car. Most people want some combination of sportiness, luxury, functionality, and value for the dollars being spent. The combinations of these features that people choose, as represented by the cars they buy after expressing their portfolio of preferences, are plotted on the X and Y axes.

Using a perceptual map yields many benefits for the marketing person. It clues the marketing person in to customer perceptions and misperceptions about a product by visually displaying the consumer perceptions and allowing the marketer to compare it to reality. It facilitates successful product positioning, as the marketing person is now aware of what needs and preferences the customer is looking to satisfy and can use this information to highlight the features and benefits of his or her product that address the customer's concerns.

The perceptual map can also identify new product possibilities for a company, as it highlights areas of the market and indicates how successful products are in the eyes of the consumer. Perceptual maps can also prevent a company from making too many products within the same class, avoiding *cannibalization* within a single company's product line. Cannibalization occurs when consumers purchase a new product in lieu of purchasing another product from the same company. For example, when Coke introduced Diet Coke, many consumers purchased Diet Coke instead of Coke. The increase in overall sales, however, from consumers who bought Diet Coke instead of other brand name drinks, makes the decline in Coke sales worthwhile. Finally, perceptual maps ensure that marketers stay well acquainted with the needs and desires of their target markets.

Companies seeking to develop their *brand* also often use perceptual maps and focus groups to understand how their products are perceived in relation to similar products or brands on the market. According to the American Marketing Association, a brand is a "name, term, sign, symbol, or design or a combination of them intended to identify the goods and services of one seller or group of sellers and to differentiate them from those of the competition." Thus, while a brand is still a product, it is also one that adds other dimensions to differentiate it in some way from other products designed to satisfy the same need.[5] Popular brands for a vast array of products include: the Nike swoosh, Ralph Lauren's polo player, and Gateway's cow designs. Achieving the status enjoyed by the aforementioned brands is to say that those companies have high levels of *brand equity*. Marketing professionals have diverse opinions as to what exactly brand equity is, but for our purposes we'll use the definition David Aaker outlines in his book, *Building Strong Brands:* "Brand equity is a set of assets (and liabilities) linked to a brand's name and symbol that adds to (or subtracts from) the value provided by a product or service to a firm and/or that firm's customers."[6] Aaker goes on to delineate brand equity into four asset categories: (1), brand name awareness; (2) brand loyalty; (3) perceived quality; and (4) brand associations. In essence, it is what causes someone to buy the Advil brand ibuprofen even when they know a generic version has the exact same ingredients. Strong brand equity can mean more to a company than just trumping the competitor at the point of sale. Branding guru Kevin Keller provides a more specific and extensive list of the possible outcomes of building customer-based brand equity:

- Greater loyalty
- Less vulnerability to competitive marketing actions and crises
- Larger margins
- More elastic response to price decreases
- More inelastic response to price increases
- Increased marketing communication efficiency and effectiveness
- Possible licensing opportunities
- More favorable brand extension evaluations[7]

Given this definition, of course every manager is interested in building strong equity, but what are some of the successful methods? Keller views the construction of brand equity as dependent on three factors:

1. The initial choices for the *brand elements* or *identities* making up the brand. Brand elements include: brand name, logo, symbol, character, packaging, and slogan; not every element of a brand will be included in the plan to build brand equity. Apple has changed its slogan and packaging designs many times since the introduction of its first PC, but the apple symbol has remained a constant throughout.

2. The *supporting marketing programs* and the manner by which the brand is integrated into it. These programs include the marketing elements we have discussed throughout this chapter: product, price, distribution channels, and communications.

3. Other associations indirectly transferred to the brand by linking it to some other entity (e.g., the company, the country of origin, channel of distribution, or another brand). A good example of this was Volkswagen's recent reintroduction of the VW Beetle—while the company relied on its usual branding style for the product as a whole, it also only offered specific product colors and options via Web-based purchases.

The challenges of building brand equity across geographic boundaries, across product offerings, across diverse cultures and market segments also make it difficult to quantify and evaluate. However, marketers often use evaluative brand-related information to inform future strategic decisions and therefore have developed some indirect and direct methods for measuring their brand equity. Details of tracking systems, brand audits, and brand management systems are too detailed for this chapter but are readily available in the texts mentioned in the notes and resources accompanying this chapter. We mention them because if you are going to build brand equity that lasts over time, you will need to also implement a means by which to evaluate your original choices for each segment of your customer base. Of course, no matter how well you seek to build brand equity, if your product isn't priced correctly no one will want to buy it.

Price

If a company doesn't price its product or service correctly, it won't sell enough to allow the company to make a profit. The bottom line is that the success and longevity of a product hinges on how well the product sells. How well a product sells is directly related to how much it costs. Second only to the actual features and benefits of the product itself, the price of a product has the greatest influence on how it sells in the marketplace and how quickly it completes the product life cycle.

Marketing professionals use many strategies to determine the price of a product. One of the basic tenets of microeconomics is that a product should be sold at whatever price results when the revenue from selling one additional unit, called *marginal revenue,* is equal to the cost of producing one additional unit, called *marginal cost* (see Economics chapter for a more detailed explanation). Other strategies, however, may also determine a product's price.

A product's price should always fall between its cost and its perceived value to the customer. The cost of a product is the cost to design, manufacture, and deliver the product to the customer. Due to economies of scale, the cost of a product decreases as volume increases. Thus companies must know the approximate volume of sales when determining the cost of a product. Consider the product's cost the minimum price of a product.

The *perceived value* of the product is the price at which the customer is "indifferent"—(i.e., the price at which the customer may or may not buy the product). If the price is lower than the customer's perceived value, he or she will probably buy it. If the price is higher than the perceived value, he or she will not buy it. Thus the price must be high enough to cover costs, but lower than the perceived value. Consider the perceived value the maximum price of a product. A marketer's rule of thumb is to price the product midway between its cost and perceived value, giving half of the gap to the customer and the remainder to the company. Luxury goods, however, are usually priced much more closely to or at the perceived value, which we will discuss later in detail.

Perceived value of a product ties into a second important economic concept that affects pricing, *elasticity of demand.* As the perceived value of a product differs among consumers, they opt to buy or not to buy the product at different prices. Elasticity of demand numerically predicts how sensitive a product's sales volumes might be to changes in that product's price. Specifically, the elasticity of demand for a product is equal to the value of the marginal change in a product's sales brought on by a change in price, divided by the actual marginal change in price.

Elasticity of demand

$$= \frac{\% \text{ change in quantity of product demanded}}{\% \text{ change in price}}$$

Given these two considerations, marketers generally choose from one of the following four pricing strategies, or create some successive combination of these strategies.

Penetration Pricing

Marketers often use *penetration pricing* to introduce a new product. In a penetration strategy, marketers set the price of an item as low as possible to generate the greatest possible volume of sales for that product. A penetration strategy is generally used in lieu of product differentiation. For example, a company may find it difficult to show the benefits of a generic product, like sugar, over a competitor's. Thus, the company uses penetration pricing to motivate consumers to make their purchase decision based on price.

Perceived Value Pricing

Perceived value is a pricing strategy where marketers set the price to how valuable the customer believes the item to be, and hence how much the customer will pay for it. The gap between the cost to produce and the perceived value is irrelevant to this strategy. Because of this, it is most often used for luxury goods, like prestige fragrances. For example, the $65.00 price of a 3.5 oz. bottle of Calvin Klein cologne is in no way linked to the $4.50 it costs to manufacture the product.

Skimming Pricing

In a *skimming strategy*, marketers set the price of the new product as high as the market will allow. Once the population segment that is not price-sensitive has been saturated, or the product has reached almost all those consumers who were ever going to buy it, marketers progress to incorporate a different pricing strategy. One example of this phenomenon is the retail clothing industry. When clothes are originally available for purchase, they can only be purchased at full retail prices. Those consumers with a low elasticity of demand buy what they like with little regard for price. Once enough time has elapsed, the merchant puts the clothes on sale, reducing the price by degrees until it is low enough to meet the requirements of those who desire the clothes but have a higher elasticity of demand.

Target Return Pricing

Some companies measure the success or failure of a product based on the relationship of how much revenue, or in some cases profit, a product generates in relation to how much it costs to make the product. This measure is called *return on investment,* or ROI. A target return pricing strategy is commonly used within an ROI framework, as it allows the price of an item to be set with predetermined revenue and return figures in mind. The choice to use this strategy depends less on the product category and more on the general philosophy of the company making the product.

The strategy a firm uses to price a good or service can and does vary from firm to firm and from product to product within a firm. Clearly, marketing professionals weigh a whole host of considerations before choosing one strategy. Aside from the features and quality of the product itself, price is the single most powerful variable in determining the success or demise of a product. Today, beyond promotions and discounts, producers are able to use dynamic pricing strategies on the Internet to capture even greater profits. Dynamic pricing is a "real time" change in price based on customer preferences and past purchasing habits. The price of an airplane ticket has always changed depending on when a customer purchases it and how full the plane is. What dynamic pricing means is that because of recorded past spending habits, the retailer knows that a particular customer may be willing to pay more than another customer (as captured in a database) for that airplane ticket. Thus, the price shown to one customer will be more than the price shown to another customer. However, as was the case with Amazon.com, different prices for the same product can backfire if consumers become aware of it. Companies today are grappling with how to use dynamic pricing capabilities effectively. Web purchasing provides new challenges for pricing and every marketing strategy.

Promotion/Advertising

Almost every marketing strategy includes an advertising plan. Advertising is the best-known method for influencing and creating customer awareness of a product. Successful ad campaigns like "Got Milk?" or the humorous Budweiser frog television ads last in the minds of consumers long after the ads have been removed from daily view. As we know from the common look of Hewlett-Packard ads for printers or computers, advertising can be as much about raising overall brand awareness as it is one specific product. What is most important is that the ad catches the attention of the consumer, communicates key information, and is memorable.

Typically, a company will hire an advertising firm to further develop the advertising strategy for content, ad placement, and ad frequency. The *key message* of an advertisement is what the advertiser hopes the consumer will take away from reading the ad; basically, it is what the ad says. Advertisements are usually developed for one *target audience*—a specific demographic or subset of the market. The *positioning* of an ad is how the advertisement differentiates its product from other similar products on the market. The *placement* of an ad is what form of media it will take—billboard, magazine or newspaper print, radio, or television. Each of these options has different strengths and weaknesses depending on the product being advertised; people like to see what a new car looks like, but may better remember the product benefits of a new toothpaste from a radio ad. A cheaper, but popular option is the *banner ad*—advertisements on the Web, usually appearing as banners across the screen of your computer. The *frequency,* or *timing intervals* for the appearance of an advertisement will depend both on the amount of money dedicated to the campaign and whether the ad is one of many for the product.

Marketers similarly use promotions (coupons; buy one, get

one free) in addition to advertising to get consumers to try new products or switch from current choices. Database marketing coupled with the use of promotions can be a powerful tool to marketers—particularly late in a product's life.

Today, sophisticated databases provide advertisers information about consumer behavior, particularly regarding Web purchases. Consequently, depending on recent purchases, different banner ads may appear every time a customer logs into a particular search engine. Or, for example, Amazon.com suggests different books to every customer depending on what his/her past purchases have been. Technological advances in database marketing, high-tech special effects, and content delivery platforms like Palm Pilots have opened up whole new worlds for advertisers to meet their marketing objectives.

Packaging

Particularly in the maturity stage, marketers also use packaging techniques to create incremental sales by expanding the concept of packaging beyond the physical container of the product. *Product bundling,* for example, can increase sales of several products by selling them simultaneously. Clairol's Herbal Essences often packages a bottle of shampoo with a bottle of conditioner at a price less than purchasing each separately. Bundling makes both products more appealing to the customer, resulting in incremental sales. Clairol's cost savings from increased sales makes it worthwhile to decrease prices. Bundling can also increase sales where no physical product exists. For example, AT&T bundles its long-distance, wireless, and Internet services to its customers by providing discounts to customers who receive all three services. AT&T also increases customer convenience by offering combined billing for all three services. Thus AT&T not only gains incremental sales, but also cost savings by issuing one bill for three streams of revenue.

SUMMARY

Many leading firms see marketing as one of the most effective weapons for competing in today's business world. To have a market orientation, a firm must know its customers and be committed to serving their needs as they emerge, and change in all aspects of its operations. This is no small task.

The successful marketing professional must integrate scientific skills with human perception and intuitive talents. In this chapter, we outlined some of the basic tools available to marketing professionals to achieve this end, as well as highlighted some of the more important considerations marketers must balance. Ultimately, the true test of a marketing professional is his or her ability to understand the consumer base and manage to satisfy consistently the ever-changing consumer needs.

INTERNET RESOURCES

Ad Age Global (www.adageglobal.com). The site is an extensive source of marketing, advertising and media news, information, and analysis—providing daily international news, agency reports, and ranked listings of global marketers.

American Demographics: Marketing Tools (www.demographics.com). The American Demographics magazine site focuses on consumer trends and their impact on consumer marketing. The site offers an electronic archive of the monthly publication, featuring articles on topics including technological change, economic conditions, product segments, various markets, and any topic affecting consumers and the particular products and services they choose to buy.

American Marketing Association (www.marketingpower.com). Lets you track trends in the marketing profession through the site's Personalized Newsletter. Also enables you to develop new skills through an extensive series of Best Practices articles. A good source of new marketing job opportunities through the AMA Career Center.

MarketingProfs.com (www.marketingprofs.com). Self-promoted as "marketing know-how from professors and professionals," this site offers a range of articles and tutorials that are based on state-of-the-art thinking about marketing.

The Marketing Resource Center (www.marketingsource.com). Enables you to browse through over 40,000 market intelligence publications in its "Market Research" link. Reviews of popular marketing and business publications are also located under "Book Reviews." The site also keeps you informed with the latest business, marketing and web development software.

MARKETING CRITICAL REFERENCE MATERIALS

Aaker, David, V. Kumar, George Day. *Marketing Research,* 7th edition. New York: John Wiley & Sons, 2000.

Taking a "macro-micro-macro" approach toward communicating the intricacies of marketing research, this text is a thorough one. While dealing with the marketing research process, the authors adopt a decision-oriented perspective, which will help readers make decisions. As in other editions, the text covers the newest developments in marketing research methodology, discussing their limitations in addition to their potential.

Aaker, J. *Managing Brand Equity.* London: The Free Press, 1991.

The book distinguishes brands from products and explores factors that are inherent in the management of brand equity. Aaker indicates that while a product can be reproduced by a competitor, a successful brand is a distinguishing name or symbol.

Allan, Gerald B., and John S. Hammond, III. *Notes on the Use of Experience Curves in Competitive Decision Making.* Boston: Harvard Business School, 1975, pp. 1–12.

Synthesizes basic ideas concerning experience curves and their effective use in competitive analysis. The basis of the article is partly a result of the publications of The Boston Consulting Group. The article indicates that firms whose marketing and pricing strategies are geared to accumulating experience much faster than their competitors can often achieve significant cost advantages.

Capon, Noel. "The Product Life Cycle." *AMA Management Handbook,* 3rd edition. John J. Hampton, Ed. New York: AMACOM, 1994.

An explanation of the product life cycle which describes a given product's sales trajectory over time from introduction to decline. The application of the term "product" is identified as having four potentially distinct meanings: product class, product form, brand, and model. The different application of these terms influences the sales trajectories as a result of market potential factors and marketing strategy efforts, which are two separate but interacting sets of variables.

Kotler, Philip. *Marketing Management: Analysis, Planning, Implementation and Control,* Millennium edition, 2000.

This comprehensive marketing management text is used at many top business schools. The book is structured into five parts: understanding marketing management, analyzing marketing opportunities; developing marketing strategies; planning marketing programs; and managing the marketing effort. Hence, the text has an informative structure as it first presents marketing management and then analyzes marketing and its development, planning, and management.

Webster, F. E. *Market-Driven Management.* New York: John Wiley & Sons, 1994.

This book combines cutting-edge research (from the founder of the Industrial Marketing area) with the latest marketing advances in a wide range of industries worldwide. It offers a new approach to integrating the marketing concept with all phases of corporate strategy, structure, culture, as well as other functions such as R&D, finance, human resources, and corporate communications.

Organizational Behavior

Organizational behavior examines the effects that individuals, groups, and structure have on behavior within organizations. Not only can the application of organizational behavior principles improve an organization's effectiveness, but organizational behavior gives you, the manager, the information and knowledge you need to manage your workforce effectively. This field is often mistaken as a "soft" (and therefore less relevant) area of interest by MBA students focused on learning financial modeling techniques, but its importance can be clearly seen when we consider that the largest part of most companies' costs come from their labor force. Since the success of every initiative you undertake in an organization depends on the willingness of your workforce to implement it, understanding your organization's structure and patterns of behavior is crucial to success. The workplace is increasingly complex due to globalization, rapidly evolving technologies, and a more diverse workforce. The strategic use of a company's employees has never been more critical, and understanding the fundamentals of organizational behavior is the key to maximizing your organization's chances for success.

Organizational behavior covers human behavior in organizations—a huge field. However, it is usually broken down into three main areas, based on the level of analysis: (1) individual level elements (managing individuals), (2) group level elements (managing teams), and (3) elements of organizational structure (managing the organization).

INDIVIDUAL LEVEL OF ANALYSIS—MANAGING INDIVIDUALS

The study of individual aspects of human behavior has its roots in the field of psychology. From an organizational perspective, we are interested in explanation and prediction to help us manage productivity and commitment. The core of every organizational behavior course includes coverage of personality and attitudes, decision making, motivation, leadership, and power.

Personality and Attitude

Managers often blame "personality conflicts" for problems, or say of employees that "they just don't have the right attitude." This is an easy way out for most managers—we can't do anything about personality or attitudes (other than tell a person to change them), so we can feel secure in the knowledge that the low productivity is not our fault and that our employees would be effective if only they made the effort. However, a good manager can use personality differences to enhance the creativity and work of a division; a good manager can set things up so that people working for him or her have positive, constructive attitudes. Yes, there are personality conflicts and bad attitudes out there—the key is how well do you manage them? To manage something, you need to understand it.

Personality

People differ along many attributes and these differences in attributes make up their personality. Sixteen "traits" have been found to be generally steady and constant sources of behavior: extroversion, intelligence, emotional stability, dominance, conscientiousness, risk-aversion, sensitivity, trust, creativity, directness, confidence, controlling, relaxed, group-dependent, timid, and serious. When thinking about each of these traits in turn, it is easy to see that people who are strong in some traits will behave differently from people who are not so strong. In organizational behavior, several other attributes have been shown to be related to behavior in the workplace. These are self-esteem, locus of control, achievement orientation, machiavellianism, self-monitoring, risk-taking, and authoritarianism.

Why does all this matter? It matters because most of us tend to think that other people are like us, and do the same things for the same reasons. Most managers manage people using this principle. And yet, this does not work in the workplace. How many times have you expected one behavior from a person and actually seen something very different? This is where the difference in personality comes into play. If you are a manager who happens to have high self-esteem, you may expect your employees to be similar to yourself—and manage then accordingly. However, if one of your subordinates has low self-esteem, criticism from you could have a more powerful effect on him or her than you expect. You may think you are giving a mild reprimand, but the employee hears a major, negative piece of feedback, and his or her response is unlikely to be the one you expect. By understanding the differences between your employees, you can adapt your management style to be effective. With high-self-esteem people you can give direct, blunt, and negative feedback; to your low-self-esteem employees you may want to soft-pedal and coach to get the same results. Suddenly an incomprehensible response becomes a manageable behavior, once you understand its source.

One final point about personality: experts have questioned how much personality influences behavior, especially in the workplace. The big answer is that "it depends." If a person is in what is called a "strong" situation, where the situational cues are very powerful (for example, the traffic light is red), then we can predict their behavior regardless of personality most of the time (they will stop). However, if the situation is "weak," and the cues are ambiguous or unclear (for example, the light is out), then their behavior becomes more a result of their personality (more aggressive people will tend to drive through, more timid people will behave differently). Usually in the ambiguous, "weaker" situations personality begins to have a direct effect on workplace behavior. This has implications for managers: systems, guidelines, and behavioral rules can all create a strong situation, minimizing the impact of personal differences in the workplace, and leading to predictable behaviors.

Attitudes

What about those employees who have a "bad attitude"? Most of us believe that attitudes are pretty set, and that our attitudes control our behavior. That makes intuitive sense. However, research into cognitive dissonance has shown that attitudes are a lot more changeable than we used to think, and that in a lot of cases our behavior controls our attitudes. This means that you can change someone's attitude by changing their behavior.

Let's look at a simple example, such as when you give money to charity. Research shows that after people donate money to a charity, their attitude toward that charity is consistently more positive than it was before the donation. The act of giving money leads to a change in attitude. If you think about this, it does make sense: I have a certain image of myself—which may include disliking a certain charity. If I give money to that charity, I now have what the researchers call "dissonance"—I've just done something that goes against my attitudes and psychologically, I feel uncomfortable. To resolve this dissonance I can do several things: I can negate the donation by saying I was forced to give; I can stop giving to the charity; or I change my attitude by saying, "Well, the charity isn't that bad after all."

A knowledge of cognitive dissonance leads the manager to focus not on changing the attitude but on changing the behavior—which will then lead to a change in attitude. How do you change behavior? We'll talk more about that in the section on motivation, after we explore individual decision making.

Decision Making

Many managerial decision-making systems are based on the *rational optimizing model:* that people determine the need for a decision, identify the decision criteria, allocate weights to the criteria, develop the alternatives, evaluate the alternatives, and then select the best alternative in a rational, fact-based manner. As early as the 1950s, the validity of this principle was challenged by March and Simon, who saw that many decisions were in fact based on irrational processes and premises.[1] Intuitively, we know that very few people are perfectly rational in their decisions—we make a lot of choices based on emotion, on avoiding risk, on not losing face, and so on—so it is hardly surprising to discover that similar, nonrational elements enter into decision making in the workplace. Some elements that we will look at in this section include: escalating commitment, heuristics, selective perception, misunderstanding of probability, anchoring, and framing.

Escalating Commitment

Escalating commitment is an example of nonrational decision making. Let's say you have already invested a million dollars in a project—and it still isn't making money for your company. The rational thing to do is write off that money and start investing in a more profitable project. However, a lot of people would not make that decision. With thoughts like "We've spent so much on it now, we have to keep going," "It's bound to come good soon," or "If we back off after spending this much, we'll look foolish," good money can be thrown after bad. The most frequently cited example of escalating commitment is President Lyndon Johnson's decisions during the Vietnam war in the 1960s: despite clear information showing that bombing North Vietnam was having no effect on ending the war, his decision was to increase the rate of bombing. As a manager, you must avoid the temptation to prove your original decisions are right by throwing good resources into bad projects.

Heuristics

The effect of heuristics, another influence on decision making, is often misunderstood and thus not dealt with. *Heuristics* are rules of thumb that people evolve to help deal with the myriad of decisions they face in their everyday lives. If we went through the full rational optimizing decision-making model for every decision that we make, most of us would never get out of bed in the morning. We have developed numerous shortcuts that help us make decisions quickly and, usually, effectively. However, while these shortcuts originally helped us survive against predators, and now make our everyday lives easier, these heuristics can work against us in the workplace. Stereotypes are a classic heuristic: By basing our understanding of a whole group of people on one or two individuals we know, or on stories we have heard, we are able to make quick decisions about others. However, the accuracy of those decisions is unlikely to be very high. As a manager, be aware of the shortcuts you tend to use and only use them when it doesn't affect the quality of the decision.

Selective Perception

Selective perception is another shortcut we use: generally when we make a decision, we already have an option in mind. This *implicit favorite* then influences how we go about the decision-making process. If I favor flextime, I am likely to collect lots of examples of where it has been effective and had positive results. However, I am unlikely to collect information on cases where it hasn't worked. In some situations I may not even see or hear things that contradict my preferred view, and I certainly won't go actively looking for "disconfirming evidence": facts that may prove me wrong. Yet every scientist knows that the only way to prove something is to disprove it: You can never prove that all swans are white, as it is impossible for you to look at all swans, past, present, and future. You can, however, disprove the statement: one observation of a black swan proves that "not all swans are white."

In the workplace, if we suspect someone of poor performance, we will watch them closely—and, sure enough, we'll see evidence that they are poor performers, but how often do we actively look for the disconfirming evidence? Maybe that poor performance was a one-off, and they are generally good performers, but we will never know, because we are not looking for that information.

Misunderstanding of Probabilities

Misunderstanding of probabilities also leads to nonrational decisions. Let's take an example of a flight instructor, with two students. One of the students makes a very poor landing. The instructor punishes the student and threatens him with suspension if he "doesn't get his act together." On the next flight, this student does much better. The second student lands perfectly on her first attempt. The instructor praises her and holds her up as an example to the class, yet, on the next time around, her landing is much worse. The instructor then, from the evidence, assumes that praise makes people lazy: they don't try as hard, and punishment and threats are more effective in training pilots. What this instructor is forgetting is that he is basing all his assumptions on a sample of just one flight—and that generally, performance "regresses to the mean": on average, I may have a performance of, say, 6/10. I may have a "lucky" day—where I perform at 9/10—but this doesn't mean that 9/10 is now my standard performance. My next performance is far more likely to be closer to 6/10 than 9/10, whatever the instructor does. The only thing the instructor can do is train me so that, over time, my average performance comes up.

Anchoring

All good salespeople know that *anchoring* can work for or against you in decision making. Try this experiment: Ask two groups of 10 people how much they would pay a trainee secretary—tell the first group of 10 that you think the pay should be $10,000; but tell the second group of 10 that you think the pay should be $30,000. If you average the responses of the two groups, you will see that the second group's average is significantly higher than the first group's. Their decision was influenced by the amount you stated: the "anchor" was higher, so their average decision was higher. Marketers use this all the time when they offer discounts off recommended prices—people buy more than if the article was the same price but not discounted because they think they are getting a bargain compared with the higher, discounted, "anchor" price.

Anchoring doesn't just happen with numbers: it also happens with first impressions and reputations. Most people make judgments about others within a few minutes of meeting them—and these first impressions then act as an "anchor" for future behaviors and attitudes toward that person. In addition, if you hear about a person from others, what you hear can influence the way you behave toward that person when you meet him or her—your impression of the person is influenced and anchored by what you have heard about them. This, combined with the selective perception we talked about earlier, shows how important it is to have a good reputation in the workplace.

Framing

Framing is a matter of how information is presented. Think about this phrase: "Our cookies are 90 percent fat-free." Now think about it after reframing: "Our cookies are ten percent fat." Simply reframing how the information is presented leads to a very different feeling about the product and, probably, to a different decision.

Other common weaknesses in decision making are a tendency to "satisfice" (take the first workable option rather than seeking out the optimal alternative); a tendency to be risk averse (if you frame something in terms of losses, the decision is likely to go against you, if you frame it in terms of gains, you will get a positive decision); the halo effect (the tendency to assume that because someone has a good reputation in one area, they are right here too); and the effect of history: if the last decision a person made was right, we may assume the next one will be right too, or, if we have historically been good in one area, we may assume that we will continue to be good there without applying the full rational model to the decision.

Recently, the concept of "bounded rationality" has developed: that human beings are capable of being rational within limits. As a manager, the use of reframing, seeking out disconfirming evidence, and being aware of the factors influencing decision makers can increase the rationality and effectiveness of your decisions.

Motivation

Like finance, operations, and so many other MBA subjects, organizational behavior has equations. As a manager, the first equation you need to know is:

$$\text{Performance} = \text{ability} \times \text{effort}$$

Before you can even start talking about effort, you need to make sure that your employees have the skills and knowledge they need to do the job well. Without this, it doesn't matter how motivated they are; you still won't get high productivity because your people are unable to perform any more effectively. First, solve the ability part of the equation—then you are ready to move on to the effort, or motivation, element. If the ability part of the equation is the "can do" element, then motivation is the "will do" part: motivation can be described as the "will to work and exert effort even when there is resistance."

The simplest way to motivate people is to expect them to be motivated! The self-fulfilling prophecy works here as well as anywhere else: if you expect something of someone, your behavior reflects that expectation, and the person begins to behave that way. Our own behavior as managers can affect the behavior and performance of our employees.

Apart from this, there are many ways of looking at motivation that are useful to a manager. These fall into four main categories: (1) needs theories; (2) task theories; (3) reinforcement theory; and (4) calculative theories.

Needs Theories

Early work on motivation focused on drives of needs that people have, and how if work helps fulfill these needs, then people will exert more effort. Maslow's hierarchy of needs and McClelland's needs theory both take this approach. One thing all the needs-based theories have in common is that to use them effectively, you need to know what your employees' needs are.

Task Theories

Work design can have an effect on how motivated people are. If a job has skill variety, task identity and task significance, allows autonomy, and provides feedback, then employees are likely to feel that the work is meaningful and they will feel responsible and have knowledge of the outcomes of their work. This, in turn, leads to high internal motivation, high-quality work performance, and high satisfaction. This model has led to the redesign of work in many organizations—and its principles underlie the replacement of assembly line manufacture with other, more integrated approaches.

Related to the task, yet motivating in a different way, is the use of goal-setting. Research has shown that setting high but achievable goals encourages people to exert effort in trying to achieve them. One word of warning—goals only work if the people trying to reach them accept them, so you either need their participation in setting the goals, or need to do a good selling job to persuade them why the goals are relevant and reasonable. Remember: goals should be SMART (i.e., specific, measurable, attainable, relevant, and timely).

Reinforcement Theory

The basic principle of reinforcement theory is that behavior is a function of its consequences. If I think a certain behavior will lead to pleasant consequences, I am more likely to choose it. If I think a certain behavior will lead to unpleasant consequences, I am less likely to choose it.

Rewards and punishment are based on reinforcement theory, and an understanding of the theory could help explain why some of your rewards and punishments are not having the desired effects. If, as a manager, you can make sure that when someone works hard, the consequences are pleasant for them, then you are likely to have motivated employees. An example would be to simply acknowledge good performance and say "Thank-you," or to give added pay for good perform- ance. Conversely, if someone has done a poor job, and you don't want them to repeat it, you need to make sure that any pleasant consequences are withdrawn—don't say "Thank- you" for bad work.

This is not as straightforward as it seems. What if someone came to you with what you think is a good idea, and you say, "Great idea, write it up in more detail and I'll take it to the board"—some might think this is a pleasant consequence. But what if the person is already snowed under with work—the last thing he or she might want is another project on the plate, so the consequence is not pleasant. What ends up happening? The person stops coming to you with ideas. By punishing idea- generating behavior, by giving negative consequences, you have inadvertently stopped a behavior you may have wanted to encourage. For some people, punishment can be attractive as it guarantees attention and, often, notoriety. Thinking through the perception and consequences of the reinforcement is critical if you want to be an effective manager.

Timing is another important aspect of reinforcement. For punishment to be effective, it must be specific and immediate. However, for encouraging a behavior, intermittent reinforce- ment has the strongest effect. Gambling offers the best demonstration of this: if you won every time you gambled, or every fifth time (a fixed schedule of reinforcement), you would probably not find gambling as exciting as winning occasion- ally and unpredictably.

As a manager, if you want someone to develop a particular behavior, you can get them started with training and positive reinforcement every time you see them use that behavior. However, as we all know, if you constantly reinforce, people get satiated, and the "Thank-yous" and "Well dones" lose their power. This is when you switch to intermittent reinforcement to keep the behavior going.

Reinforcement theory looks at motivation as a reflex—like Pavlov's dog, we are the victims of our conditioning. There are approaches to motivation that explicitly take into account human thought processes and cognitive reasoning; these can be called *calculative theories.*

Calculative Theories

These theories assume that motivation is the outcome of a calculated (although often subconscious) process that people go through when presented with a situation.

In *equity theory,* people calculate their inputs and outputs and compare them to others' inputs and outputs. For example, if I think I am working harder than my colleague, yet I'm being paid the same, I may well reduce my inputs (effort) until I think we are "equitable." This has implications for organizations using fixed pay scales for jobs—how do you encourage people to perform better? Many companies respond with incentive schemes, or performance-related pay, but these have their own problems, as we'll see when we look at reward systems in the section on organizational-level elements. Equity theory can often explain why some people who used to be "high-flyers" crash—there comes a point when they realize that although they are working harder and smarter, their returns are the same as those of other people who are just passing the time at the office, so why bother?

Expectancy theory is another calculative way of looking at motivation. The second equation you need to know is:

$$F = E * I * V$$

F (the force of motivation) is equal to Expectancy (the belief that exerting the effort will lead to performance) times Instrumentality (the belief that the performance will lead to an outcome) times Valence (the value given to the outcome). The importance of expectancy theory is that it shows that there are several places where motivation can break down:

1. Does my effort lead to performance? I might be working flat out, but the equipment I'm using is just not good enough to do the job.

2. Does the performance actually lead to a desired outcome? I could be the best service technician you have ever had in the company, but however well I do my job, the customers complain that it takes too long to repair a machine because we don't have enough technicians to cover the territory, so I never get a good performance report—I end up demotivated.

3. How important is the outcome to me? I might be performing well—and it might really be possible for me to win the end-of-year sales bonus—but the amount is so small relative to my salary—and my peers will tease me for winning—so it just isn't worth the effort.

At each stage there could be personal or organizational reasons for the breakdown in motivation. One lesson from expectancy theory is that it is as important (and often easier) to remove the demotivators as to improve the motivators. You can pay a person as much as you like, but if any one of the three steps breaks down, you will not get any more motivation for your money.

Leadership

The definition of leadership is neither complete, nor yet agreed upon. For most people leadership is one of those things that they can't describe, but they know it when they see it. For now, we're going to use the definition of leadership as "the ability to influence people or groups toward one or more goals." From this definition, it seems that leadership belongs in the next section: at the group level of analysis. However, the history of leadership began with a very individual level look at what constitutes a leader. So that's where we'll start as well. In the research, there are three main types of theory: (1) trait theories; (2) behavioral theories; and (3) contingency theories.

Trait Theories

Early research into leadership focused on whether leaders and nonleaders had certain personality attributes. Are leaders born? Are there certain characteristics that leaders have and followers don't? This would make life easy: we would be able to identify leaders early on and make sure they took the leadership positions, a definite help for most companies. However, the research proved disappointing: while most leaders show certain traits (including high ambition, high energy, the desire to lead, honesty and integrity, self-confidence, intelligence, job-related knowledge, and high self-monitoring), the correlation between these traits and leadership are low. The trait approach also overlooks the role of followers, the role of the situation (remember we said that behavior depends on the situation), and does not make clear the causality: does confidence lead to being a leader, or does being a leader lead to confidence?

Behavioral Theories

In an advance on trait theories, researchers moved on to explore whether leaders displayed certain behaviors that made them effective. This was particularly interesting to trainers, since if we could discover the key behaviors, then we could train everybody to be a leader by teaching them the behaviors. The most famous studies in this area were the Ohio State studies, the University of Michigan studies, and Blake and Mouton's managerial grid.[2] All three of these studies showed that to be effective it was important for leaders to manage both the task and people elements of the job. However, another thing these approaches had in common was that while they provided a conceptual framework that is useful for many managers, they do not give us any answers we can directly apply to the workplace because they do not take the situation or rest of the group into account.

Contingency Theories

Called *contingency theories* because these theories say that the effectiveness of a behavior depends on the situation you are in, these are the theories most managers find most useful in the workplace. Five main theories here include: Fiedler's model,[3] Hershey and Blanchard's situational theory,[4] leader-member exchange theory, path-goal theory, and the leader-participation model (Vroom-Yetton). In all these models the effectiveness of various leadership styles depends on characteristics of the followers (their maturity, for example) as well as the situation. The key lesson is that the most effective leaders are able to "flex" their leadership style to match the group and the situation.

Any discussion of leadership would not be complete without looking at "substitutes for leadership." In some situations, certain factors define the requirements so clearly that leadership becomes superfluous. For example, professional associations often act as substitutes by providing universally accepted codes of conduct and standards of performance.

Power and Influence

Leadership has been defined as the ability to influence a group toward a goal; power is the ability to influence, period. There are three main areas to look at when we think about power. These are: the power, the role of dependency, and politics.

Where Does Power Come From?

French and Raven[5] are credited with the early attempts to describe where power comes from. They developed a list of five sources of power within organizations. These are: *coercive power,* which depends on fear; *reward power,* from the ability to give out things of value; *expert power,* or influence because you have special skills or knowledge; *legitimate power,* which you have because of your position in the company; and *referent power:* power you have because people admire and respect you. As a manager, think about where your power comes from: Coercive power relies on the fact that people fear you, and reward power is only effective so long as people value the rewards you have to offer. Legitimate power relies on your rank in the company hierarchy, and recent events such as white-collar downsizing have shown how quickly that can change for any level of management. Expert power lasts as long as no one else knows as much as you do. Referent power is the only source that seems maintainable—and referent power is the one source that seems to rely on interpersonal skills and an understanding of other people.

How can you use your power bases? By using power tactics. Tactics for influencing others include *reason* (use of facts and data); *friendliness* (use of social connections and appeal); *coalition* (getting support of others); *bargaining* (negotiating exchanges of favors); *assertiveness* (being direct, open, and firm in your needs); *higher authority* (gain support of upper levels for you plans); and *sanctions* (use of organizational rewards and punishments to induce compliance). Again, like the bases, the different tactics have different levels of acceptability, as well as some negative consequences that need to be thought through before you act.

The Role of Dependency

The key to power: The greater a person's dependency on you, the more power you have over that person. At first glance, a CEO seems like a very powerful person. However, CEOs are almost totally dependent on other people—so, in fact, their level of power is not very high. If you as a manager are dependent on other people's performance for your own performance review, then these other people have power over you, whether they know it or not. Dependency can increase if the "resource" you control is important, scarce, and nonsubstitutable. So, you can work to increase your power by either increasing other people's dependency on you or by reducing your dependency on others.

Politics

Often framed as negative, politics are a natural part of any organization. Having accepted that, what is a working definition of politics, and when are they functional or dysfunctional for an organization? Political behavior can be defined as "activities not required in your formal role, but that influence, or try to influence activities and resource distributions within the company." Such behavior can be in the interests of the company—or it can be in direct opposition to what is best for the organization: then it becomes dysfunctional, political behavior. Organizations are a social structure of human beings, with limited resources—and these factors combine to make political behavior almost inevitable. Political behavior tends to increase as resources become more constrained, and if the situations facing the company are more ambiguous, making rational optimizing decision-making difficult.

Other, individual factors can contribute to political behavior. People who score high on a characteristic called "machiavellianism" are more likely to show political behaviors than people who score low on this scale. In addition, people who are high self-monitors show a tendency to "politick." An extreme form of politicking, where people try to control the image others have of them, is called *impression management*— where most of a person's energy and time goes to managing impressions rather than doing work.

Much politicking is aimed at self-protection as much as at self-promotion, and defensive behaviors are often seen in organizations with high levels of political behavior. Defensive behaviors include: working to rule; passing the buck; playing dumb; stalling; scapegoating; escalation of commitment; and protecting turf and territory.

Although politics can be useful, more often they are dysfunctional for the organization. As a manager, be aware of why politicking increases, what political behavior looks like, and what to do to handle it when you see it.

GROUP LEVEL OF ANALYSIS

Some say that psychologists do not study groups because it's too hard—whereas organizational behavior researchers study groups because they have no choice. How many people in any organization truly work alone? To some extent every employee interacts with others, and increasingly companies are looking to teams, self-managed or otherwise, to increase creativity and/or productivity. At this level of analysis, organizational behavior includes: social influences, organizational factors influencing groups, and the group itself.

Social Influences

Most people are influenced by other people around them. If my colleagues all think the job is great, I am more likely to think so too—after all, they can't all be wrong, can they? The social information processing model argues that employees adopt attitudes and behaviors in response to social cues given by other people, including other employees, family, friends, and customers. Subtle comments about autonomy and job challenge have been shown to influence motivation and satisfaction levels of employees—so the social influence is very strong. This becomes particularly important when we start looking at what happens in groups.

In groups, one of the most powerful social influences is the drive to conformity. Most group members want to be accepted by the other people in the group, and to do this, many of us go along with group norms and decisions that we would otherwise disagree with. A classic example of group pressures toward conformity is the Asch experiment (see Glossary for details), where 35 percent of people gave the wrong answer rather than disagree with the rest of their group! This social pressure to conform is important in that it can lead to suppression of differences and disagreements, resulting in groupthink—where everyone goes along with a bad decision because no one wants to disagree. Pressure to conform is even greater where authority figures are involved.

Social Influences in groups are usually in the form of *norms*. Norms are acceptable standards of behavior that are shared—and enforced—by group members. A simple norm might be that we all arrive to meetings on time. If you are late, the group enforces its norm by starting without you, or by commenting on your lateness. Most norms are implicit—few groups actively discuss their norms. However, some evidence suggests that they should do so: if only to capture and deal with the norms that push for conformity rather than allowing disagreement and discussion of alternatives.

Some people in groups seem to go against the social influences of the group. First, there are the "social loafers," people who, because they are in a group where their individual contribution cannot be measured, sit back and let the rest of the group do the work. The level of loafing is directly tied to accountability, and in groups where it is clear to all members who is contributing what, and where there are sanctions for loafing, loafing is less of a problem.

Second, there are people who will continue to challenge the status quo and disagree, regardless of group pressure for agreement and conformity. These brave souls, who can ultimately play a role in leading the group to a high-quality outcome, often suffer a dire fate: they are labeled as "institutionalized deviants" and anything they say is dismissed as "coming from the person who always disagrees" rather than being examined as a sensible and important comment. This institutionalization is the group's way of not dealing with the lack of consensus, and it enables the group to take an easy path.

For a manager, there are two messages here: If you are managing a group, you need to encourage disagreement and make sure that if someone challenges the "agreed state of affairs" they are actively encouraged and not closed down; while as a group member, you need to make sure you don't end up an "institutionalized deviant."

How can you avoid this fate? First, build up your credibility with the group through contributing early on; second, be constructive with your suggestions, building where possible on other people's contributions rather than knocking them down; and third, build coalitions with other people in the group so that when you disagree, you are not alone.

A word of caution: Minorities in groups tend to be institutionalized more than other group members, so if you are the only engineer, the only woman, the only man—or the only anything in your group—you will have to take extra care in managing your role for the group to be effective.

Organizational Factors Influencing Groups

To understand groups, realize that they are part of a larger system—the organization—and so can be influenced by organizational factors. Richard Hackman's work[6] with teams in organizations has shown that organizational factors can explain a lot of group effectiveness. First, does the team have a "clear and engaging direction"? Do they know what they are trying to achieve and are they interested in achieving it? This links directly to the larger picture of organizational strategy—without a clear organizational strategy, it is unlikely that a team will have a clear and engaging direction.

Second, does the team have the "organizational context" to do a good job? This includes organizational reward and information systems as well as resource availability. A team, like an individual, has to see a clear link between performance and rewards (it's the expectancy theory all over again), and has to have the information they need to do their job in a timely fashion (getting sales figures a month after the event may be interesting, but it is of little use in planning tactics for the team). Many companies make the mistake of setting up teams to work on a project and not allocating resources. What kind of resources? Time, physical space, money—all are resources necessary to keep a group functioning effectively.

Third, does the organization have the coaching skills to develop the teams? Not every one of us can naturally work well in a team—we need to learn the teamwork as much as the technical side of our jobs. One major industrial company spent a lot of money putting its top managers through a high-level strategy development course, expecting that when they returned from the course, these managers would lead their own teams in developing strategies. However, the divisional teams produced very low quality decisions and failed to produce any usable strategies. What happened? The teams knew what they were supposed to do, but had no idea how to work toward their objective as a team. It is one thing to tell someone to "manage conflict"—but how do I do that? Management coaching is critical for the success of teams in organizations.

Over and above these factors that Hackman found, there are others: does the organizational culture support teamwork? If you put a team together but its members get criticized every time they get together for being away from their desks, the team is unlikely to be successful.

One last thing an organization can do to help groups be effective is to design the task so that it is interdependent. If the task can be done by individuals, then the time taken by group meetings and so on will lead to lower levels of perform- ance (imagine an assembly line with meetings every week to discuss objectives: unnecessary and costly). However, if the task is redesigned to be interdependent (Volvo's team-based car manufacture, or Xerox's teams of service technicians, jointly responsible for servicing a huge territory), then the meetings and time spent in group sessions directly improves the quality and quantity of work produced by the group.

The Group Itself

Characteristics of the group itself have a direct impact on the group's behaviors and performance. Specifically, group com- position, patterns over time, and interaction patterns all have an effect.

Group Composition

A lot of research has been done on the effects of group com- position performance. A basic requirement for the group is that its members have the mix of skills, knowledge, and resources to do the task. If the group has to do financial analyses, make sure that people in it have the knowledge and skill to perform the necessary calculations.

One dimension that has been looked at in depth is whether the group should be heterogeneous or homogenous. Homoge- nous groups seem to have advantages in being able to reach decisions faster, but heterogeneous groups may offer the ben- efit of bringing more alternatives to the table and so generat- ing better quality decisions. Recent work in the area of top management teams has suggested that the benefits of homo- geneity and heterogeneity are contingent on other things: If the external environment is turbulent, and experiencing rapid change, then a top team that is homogeneous has advantages for the company, whereas when the environment is stable, a top team that is heterogeneous is best.

From a manager's point of view, the risks of a homogenous team are clear: groupthink and lack of breadth of options.

However, to manage a heterogeneous team successfully, the members must be able to handle the heterogeneity to minimize the "process losses" and capitalize on the "process gains" of the group. This suggests that it is not the heterogeneity *per se* that is the issue: Rather it is a matter of how the group manages its members and their differences effectively. Often, one of the best methods for minimizing friction from heterogeneity is a directive from higher authorities that cross-team and diverse solutions will be celebrated.

As earlier discussions of "institutionalized deviants" suggested, an individual from what is a minority group in your firm may find his or her contribution restricted, either by virtue of the majority's inclination to disregard ideas different from their own or by virtue that the minority feels his or her opinion will not be valued. So, when you are putting a group together, it is usually a good idea to include more than one minority from any minority group. For example, it may be better to have two women or two engineers rather than what might otherwise be just one dissenting voice. Of course, it's also true that two members of any minority group may not agree with another, and that additional diversity may add to the entire team's learning as well as best address the firms' intended task.

Patterns Over Time

In the 1960s, a five-stage model of how groups developed over time became popular. In this model, the first stage is *forming,* a time of uncertainty and exploration into group purpose, behavior, and structure; then comes a *storming* stage, where large amounts of conflict emerge about leadership, roles, and task. From this stage, the group moves into the *norming* stage, when close relationships develop and group cohesiveness increases. The fourth stage is *performing:* now the group can get down to the business at hand and begin producing output. The final stage, *adjourning,* occurs when the immediate task is complete and before the next project is received, or in "wrapping up" a temporary group.

While this model is intuitively appealing, there is little evidence to show it is what really happens in groups. Its main usefulness is in reminding managers that conflict is a necessary part of the evolution of groups: A group with no conflict is unlikely to produce high-quality work.

More recent work has followed the life of groups as they worked and has led to the development of the *punctuated equilibrium* model of group development. This model suggests that, once formed, groups settle into norms and behaviors very quickly and stay in those patterns for a while. About halfway through the project, the group will experience a "midpoint" transition, where its members are likely to rethink their structure, norms, and processes. From this time on, the new patterns stay in place until the project is complete. The implications of this model are that if you want to intervene in a group's dynamics or work processes, you have two chances— at the start, and at the midpoint. A manager can create midpoints by imposing deadlines and asking for milestone reports and outputs.

Interaction Patterns

Managing groups is different than managing individuals in that you are not just dealing with people, but also with how they interact. Key interactions that a manager needs to understand, and help the team learn to handle are: conflict management, negotiations, giving feedback, and sharing information. All of these are elements of interpersonal communication, and most team members will tell you that the most important thing teams need to learn is how to listen. But let's take a quick look at the specifics of these group interactions:

Conflict Management.   Research shows that a group with high task-related conflict will perform well, but a group with high relationship-based conflict will do poorly. Your teams need to be able to distinguish disagreement about how we do the task from disagreement about how we are getting along. Also realize that not all of us handle conflict in the same way, so training in conflict skills such as listening and assertiveness usually helps groups to be more effective.

Negotiations.   Fisher and Ury's classic work[7] on negotiating applies as much to intragroup interactions as it does to between-party negotiations. Groups that bog down in positional bargaining and try to "cut up the pie" tend not to do as well as groups that look for the interests of the different group members and use these to move toward integrative bargaining, creating new solutions.

A classic example of the difference between these two approaches is the story of the two women who wanted the last orange in the store. They quickly agreed to cut the orange in half, as that seemed fair. However, if they had asked why each wanted the orange, they would have found out that while one wanted the juice to drink, the other wanted the peel for a recipe. Each could, in fact, have had 100 percent of what she wanted if the two had taken the time to learn each other's interests in the orange. Groups that search for win-win rather than win-lose solutions to disagreements are likely to last longer.

Giving Feedback.   There are times in every group when one person doesn't agree with or like how another person is behaving. What if every time I try to put an idea forward, another person interrupts me? I'm going to be frustrated and probably end up being angry at that person—not good news for the group trying to do its job. The skill of giving feedback to people about their behavior in a low-conflict way is valuable to all groups. Effective feedback is immediate, specific, and focuses on behaviors, not judgmental statements. It also emphasizes the effect the behavior is having on the group's work performance. After all, if a behavior bothers you but it doesn't affect the work of the group, then it's more a matter of you learning to live with it, isn't it?

Sharing Information.   One of the most important things in groups is sharing information. The main benefit of a group is the breadth of knowledge and experience it has available for problem solving. However, as earlier discussions have indicated, just because something is the sensible and rational thing to do doesn't mean that it always happens. Social influences, politics, and/or conflict can all limit the amount and quality of information sharing that takes place. One tip is to centralize the information the group has so that everyone can see it—and make sure that the group has a norm of new information being encouraged and seen as helpful, rather than being seen as disruptive. One thing that often happens is that information is heard, but misunderstood. Getting group members into the habit of paraphrasing information received is an easy and effective way of checking that the information received is the same as the information sent.

After all this discussion of difficulties with groups, you may be wondering why do organizations bother? The simple answer is to cut costs. An interdependent, supportive team is often more productive than a selection of individuals. Many companies are actively looking to teams to reduce management layers and increase productivity in all types of work.

An important thing for a manager to remember about groups is that it is not who's in the group that matters so much as how they interact—and that could be a matter of group composition (ability, knowledge, functional expertise), organizational conditions (is there a clear direction? is the team rewarded for team performance rather than individual achievement? are the resources available for the team to work effectively?) and coaching (can the team members handle disagreements effectively? do they have the interpersonal skills needed to work as a group?).

ORGANIZATIONAL LEVEL OF ANALYSIS

One mistake many managers make is to underestimate (or ignore completely) the effect that the structure and systems of the organization have on how people behave. Our discussions of individual and group behavior have probably given you lots of ideas as to how many aspects of an organization can have unintended consequences—one reason why this section is shorter than the others, we have already covered a lot of the material. It is important as a manager to think in a systems way (holistically) before attributing performance problems to either the individual or group level.

Four main areas to think through are: the structure of the organization, the culture of the organization, the management systems and practices operating in the organization, and change management.

The Structure of the Organization

Basic organizational structure has three components. The first is *complexity:* To what extent are activities broken up? The second is *formalization:* How much are rules and procedures used? And the third is *centralization:* To what extent is decision making kept at a central headquarters unit? All these factors have been shown to influence organizational behavior.

High complexity means work is broken down and is thus easy to control and monitor, but tends to lead to employees missing the "big picture." Low complexity, usually resulting in a "flat" organization, can give rise to high intrinsic motivation, but places huge demands on communication and time. High formalization can lead to highly predictable behaviors (creating a constantly "strong" situation), but it can also reduce innovation and create strong pressures for conformity. Low formalization allows innovation, but makes it difficult to produce consistency, or to measure performance objectively. High centralization gives an organization tight controls and good information on the rest of the division, as well as ensuring that all divisions are working to a common strategy. However, the low autonomy experienced by the divisions and employees may cause other problems for motivation and performance. High decentralization allows local responses to customers and a large amount of autonomy to divisional managers, but reduces the control and influence that the central organization has for producing a consistent strategy across the board.

One classic way of looking at organizational structure is the *mechanistic/organic* dichotomy. A *mechanistic* structure is characterized by high complexity; high formalization; a limited, mostly downward information network; and high-level decision making—the typical "pyramid" organization. An *organic* structure is low in complexity and formalization; has a comprehensive, free-flowing information network; and has highly participative decision making. These two structures clearly have very different consequences for the behavior of the people working in them.

Almost all organizations are broken into work divisions. These work divisions are set up in many different ways—by function, by geographic location, by product, by process, by customer—or a combination of any of these (a matrix structure). Which structure is best depends on what your company does and how it does its work. The thing to remember is that people will tend to identify with their "in-group," and that communication across divisions will need to be actively managed.

Informal systems evolve within each division, leading to other divisions being viewed as "different" and therefore not as valuable. As a manager, you need to be aware of this and be prepared to actively manage across-division information flows, communications, and the interaction between the divisional cultures, especially when the tasks are highly interdependent.

The Culture of the Organization

For most people organizational culture is something they cannot define but will recognize when they see it. It can perhaps best be defined as the set of informal rules, relationships, and norms that determine what is acceptable and unacceptable behavior within the organization. Organizational culture can often have a more powerful influence on behavior than the formal structures and systems. If you view the organization as a very large group, then all the factors we discussed in the group level of analysis section can apply at the organizational level with respect to the informal systems in operation. An example of how the informal culture can undermine the intentions of your formal systems is the role that peer pressure plays in performance: however great the incentive pay, however good the reward system, if the culture has norms of low effort and low performance, then that is what you will get.

A manager needs to pay as much attention to the *informal organization* as to the formal structure and systems. Management by walking around, by listening, and by keeping in touch with the "grapevine" all help you to collect information on this element of the organization. Culture can be managed: modeling and reinforcing certain behaviors can set a different tone, and in many organizations you will see many different "subcultures" operating, showing how different managers can develop different informal systems—whether they intend to or not.

Management Systems and Practices

Within an organization, the management systems also have consequences for organizational behavior. In particular, decision-making systems and human resource management systems have strong effects.

Decision-Making Systems

How are decisions made in your company? Are they made on an ad hoc, intuitive basis, or are they based on facts and information? Are the decisions made top-down, or is decision making participative? How are decisions evaluated? The answers to all these questions have effects on how people in your organization behave.

If company decisions are made on a nonrational basis, then your employees are likely to do the same. It is difficult to persuade people to follow a time-consuming, rational model if no one else in the company is doing it and there is little support for the time and effort it takes. In addition, how likely am I to put together a closely reasoned report to send to senior management, investing time and energy, if I know that their decision is going to be based on intuition or politics?

Participation in decision making has been shown to improve motivation and job satisfaction and reduce turnover and absenteeism. Top-down directives may be quick and easy, but they may miss some critical points that only the people on the front-line know. Don't get confused though: participation does not mean democracy; top management is still ultimately responsible for the decisions an organization makes.

Whether decisions are evaluated will also have an effect on how much effort people put into the decision in the first place—remember, motivation is related to the belief that effort leads to an outcome. If decisions aren't evaluated, then how can there be positive outcomes related to my effort?

Human Resource Management Systems

Recruitment and selection, career development, and reward and recognition systems have crucial impacts on motivation and performance.

Although much of what we have discussed in this chapter suggests that it is behavior that is important rather than personality, there is one area where personality assessment is used a lot: in recruitment. The important thing for both company and employees is that there be a "fit" between what the company needs and what the employee wants. If an employee is highly authoritarian, he is unlikely to feel comfortable and perform well in a "flat" organization. Recruiting and selecting the right people on the basis of skills, knowledge, and "fit" is critical to developing performance enhancing cultures and a satisfied workforce.

Career development can act as a reward to most people: and a lack of opportunity to move upward and onward can be a huge demotivator for employees. It is also critical that promotions are seen as being based on performance rather than on politics. Employees often see political promotions as being outside their control, whereas if performance is the basis of promotion, then motivation to perform well is increased.

If you think back to most of the motivation theories, the outcomes of behavior are important to the effort exerted. If I get rewarded for a behavior, I'll probably keep doing it; if I'm punished, I'll stop (most of the time). Many reward systems are left over from a company's early days and do little to encourage the behaviors the company wants to see in the workplace.

As a simple example, a piece-rate pay system should encourage people to work harder and produce more—but can end up with the people paying so much attention to quantity that quality suffers. "Performance based compensation" sounds like a great idea—until you realize that everybody's efforts are focused on getting a good review, and making a good impression at review time, rather than on producing high-quality work all year round. Try to remember that rewards aren't just about money: employees can perceive promotion opportunities, benefits, and many other aspects of the job as rewards. Many companies are capitalizing on this by using flexible benefit packages rather than standard reward systems.

One last point on rewards: if you have a team, working on a team task (i.e. it is an interdependent task) then you need to make sure the rewards are also interdependent, or you will be encouraging individual competition rather than team support.

Change Management

One of the areas where the knowledge of organizational behavior is making its biggest contribution is that of *change management*. Understanding why people behave the way they do includes understanding why they resist change and how that resistance might be overcome. It has been said that there is nothing new about effective change management: it is simply effective management with a new name. This is, indeed, close to the truth. Applying the principles of organizational behavior, the role of needs, motivation, social influences, and structure and systems will usually result in effective change implementation.

SUMMARY

If you only take three points away after reading this chapter, they should be:

1. How people behave is contingent upon individual, group, and organizational factors. You need to explore and understand these to understand why a person is behaving a certain way.

2. "Thinking things through" is critical. Otherwise your actions may well have unintended, dysfunctional consequences.

3. Organizational behavior is the *systematic* study of human behavior in organizations. There is nothing soft about it; it is probably the hardest subject on the MBA curriculum to truly master. Ask any manager.

Finally, managing people without understanding organizational behavior is like trying to fly without understanding aerodynamics—it can be done, but not very well.

INTERNET RESOURCES

ASTD (www.astd.org). ASTD, a premier professional association, provides information, research, analysis, and practical information on the fundamentals of performance technology, performance improvement interventions, and strategies for training design.

Journal of Computer-Mediated Communication (jcmc.huji.ac.il). A resource covering both information systems and organization behavior; articles focus primarily on technology, yet still offer strong organizational behavior overtones and deal with issues pertinent to the topic.

Society for Industrial and Organizational Psychology (www.siop.org). Home page for the SIOP, working to enhance performance in organizational and work settings by promoting the science, practice, and teaching of industrial-organizational psychology.

The Society for Organizational Learning (learning.mit.edu). MIT's site for organizational learning includes a useful "Idea Exchange" providing good information of various organizational behavior topics.

Workforce Magazine (www.workforce.com). A useful site that provides weekly information on various human resources issues relevant to organizational behavior, such as work attitudes, rewards, telecommuting, and recruitment.

ORGANIZATIONAL BEHAVIOR CRITICAL REFERENCE MATERIALS

Books

Argyris, Chris. *On Organizational Learning.* Cambridge, MA: Blackwell Publishers, 1993.

This book focuses on organizational learning with emphasis on detecting and correcting errors that are or could be embarrassing to members of the organization. Each chapter has been published previously in a journal or book. The ideas presented are illustrated with actual interventions that integrate the ideas into practice.

Blake, Robert Rogers. *The Managerial Grid III: A New Look at the Classic That Has Boosted Productivity and Profits for Thousands of Corporations Worldwide.* Houston: Gulf Publishing Company, 1985.

This book creates an actual managerial grid with the vertical side charting the concerns for people (1 being low, 9 being high) and the horizontal side charting the concerns for productivity (1 being low and 9 being high). Points (1,1), (1,9), (9,1), (9,9) and (5,5) on the grid are each discussed in terms of motivation, managing conflict, behavioral elements, management practices, consequences, how to recognize the particular style of management being discussed, behavior, suggestions for change, and a summary.

Champy, James. *Reengineering Management: The Mandate For New Leadership.* New York: Harper Business, 1995.

Champy's first book, *Reengineering the Corporation,* focused on reengineering the doings of the workplace and caused a partial revolution in reengineering efforts. In this new book Champy tries to further the revolution he began with a new tactic—reengineering the *manager.*

Galbraith, Jay, Diane Downey, and Amy Kates. *Designing Dynamic Organizations: A Hands-On Guide for Leaders at All Levels.* New York: AMACOM, 2001.

An essential handbook citing the essential steps of organizational design. *Designing Dynamic Organizations* poses critical questions on how to configure organizational structure to maximize corporate success.

Hackman, J. Richard. *Groups That Work (and Those That Don't): Creating Conditions for Effective Teamwork.* San Francisco: Jossey-Bass, 1990.

This book examines how work groups function. It links descriptive accounts of specific work groups with theoretical concepts, providing insights helpful to those who form, lead, serve as part of, or conduct research on work groups.

Hackman, Lawler, and Porter. *Perspectives on Behavior in Organizations.* New York: McGraw-Hill, 1983.

This book discusses the behavior of organizations. Each section contains papers written by various scholars in the particular subject matter. The six broad and main sections covered are: individuals and organizations, development of individual-organization relationships, design of work and reward systems, interpersonal and group processes, intergroup and structural factors, and leadership and organizational change.

Handy, Charles B. *Understanding Organizations.* New York: Oxford University Press, 1993.

The book is broken down into two clear and helpful sections. The first describes the concepts of organizations (motivations to work, roles and interactions, leadership, power and influence, workings of groups, and cultures of organizations). The second section focuses on the applications of these concepts (the people of organizations and their development, the work of the organization—and its design, politics and change, being a manager, and the future of organizations).

Kanter, Rosabeth Moss. *The Change Masters: Innovation for Productivity in the American Corporation.* New York: Simon and Schuster, 1983.

This book focuses on the importance of people in making a corporation work. It explains how individual people can contribute to an entire corporation's success. It encourages the idea that a lot of little changes, made by individuals, can add up to produce a large change within a company. The book also stresses how environment is an important factor in fostering progressive thinking and stimulating ideas. The differences between those companies that nurture a creative environment and those that do not are discussed.

Kotter, John P. *The New Rules: How to Succeed in Today's Post-Corporate World.* New York: The Free Press, 1995.

This book tracks the experiences of 115 Harvard MBAs from the class of 1974. It looks at each of their experiences to see how they have, or have not, adjusted to the rapidly changing workplace of the last 20 years. The book focuses on the importance of being aware of globalization, being flexible, and not relying on conventional career paths. It stresses moving away from big businesses and instead branching out on one's own into small business and entrepreneurship. Furthermore, it emphasizes the importance of not just managing, but leading, and doing so with a competitive drive and a desire to constantly learn and grow.

Kouzes, James M., Barry Z. Posner, and Tom Peters. *The Leadership Challenge.* New York: Jossey-Bass, 1996.

Using actual case studies and survey questionnaires, *The Leadership Challenge* provides guidance on all aspects of leadership dynamics. Readers learn about behaviors—dubbed by Kouzes and Posner as the "Ten Committments of Leadership"—that enable ordinary people to accomplish extraordinary things at all levels of leadership within the work environment. Animated, individual cases bring this guide to rewarding organizational behavior and leadership to life.

Lorsch, Jay W. *Handbook of Organizational Behavior.* Englewood Cliffs, NJ: Prentice-Hall, 1987.

This book provides managers, students, and teachers of management with a brief but thorough set of references pertaining to the organizational behavior field. It centers on the way people actually behave in organizations and why they behave in that particular manner. The history and growth of the field is discussed in the first three sections (general overview, organizational behavior and underlying disciplines, and organizational behavior and methodologies). The last three sections deal with the many different uses and functions of organizational behavior in different settings (organizational behavior at various systems levels, managerial issues, and organizational behavior in nonbusiness settings).

Pfeffer, Jeffrey. *Managing with Power: Politics and Influence in Organizations.* Boston: Harvard Business School Press, 1992.

This book deals with the control and use of power from a managerial prospective. It covers power in organizations, sources of power, strategies and tactics for employing power effectively, and power dynamics (how power is lost and how organizations change). It explains positive and negative uses of power and management with the use of real-life examples.

Steers, Richard M. *Introduction to Organizational Behavior.* Glenview, IL: Scott, Foresman, 1984.

This is a textbook meant to introduce students to the fundamentals of organizational business. It is separated into five parts: the work setting, individual behavior, group behavior, people at work (use of applied topics), and predictions for the future. Throughout the text there are real-life examples from various workplaces, and case studies and exercises are given at the end of each chapter.

Journals

Academy of Management Executive. Ada, OH: The Academy of Management.

This quarterly publication contains academic papers that cover relevant issues in management for the near term. The academic papers are written specifically for managers as a primary audience. Each issues also contains a section of book reviews.

The Academy of Management Review. Mississippi State, MS: Academy of Management.

This quarterly publication covers the organizational sciences in a global forum. The divisions and interest groups of AMR are very broad, ranging from business policy and strategy to women in business. Each topic is presented in purely theoretical, academic papers written by leading scholars. Along with the many different divisional topics being discussed in each issue, academic books are also reviewed.

Economics

Traditionally, the study of economics includes two major disciplines:

1. *Macroeconomics,* which is the study of business forces on a national or global level
2. *Microeconomics,* which is the study of the business dynamics that affect economic behavior on a firm level

The first part of this chapter presents a discussion of key concepts in macroeconomics, and describes how managers can use this information to make better business decisions. The second part of this chapter presents and explains key concepts in microeconomic theory, and then concludes with a discussion of microeconomic business analyses.

MACROECONOMICS

Macroeconomics attempts to measure and understand relationships governing overall economic activity, such as income, output, and the relationships among diverse economic sectors. By developing such measures and an understanding of them, governments attempt to influence the world economy. In the United States, the economist with the most influence on the economy is the chairman of the Federal Reserve Board. The Federal Reserve Board (commonly known as the "Fed") controls the nation's monetary policy, regulates banks, and seeks to maintain the financial stability of the United States. The goal is to control the growth of the U.S. economy, known as *economic expansion,* and minimize shrinkage of the economy, known as *recession.* One might think the economy should grow as quickly as possible. However, a rapidly growing economy results in inflation, which can subsequently lead to deep recession. The Fed controls the growth of the U.S. economy by raising and lowering interest rates and engaging in other monetary activities. The chairman bases decisions on an analysis of economic indicators.

LEADING ECONOMIC INDICATORS

The Fed and company managers alike use *economic indicators* to get a feel for trends within an economy or to predict economic activity related to a particular industry. Although 11 recognized leading economic indicators exist, this chapter will focus on the 4 that are most commonly used in business.

1. Gross domestic product (GDP)
2. Employment statistics
3. Personal income
4. Industrial production

Gross Domestic Product

Gross domestic product, or GDP, is the most comprehensive measure of a country's economic activity. GDP measures economic activity from the perspective of the total income generated by different entities within an economy as well as by measuring the total expenditures of those entities. Thus, GDP sets up a fundamental macroeconomic equation where the sum of income generated from domestic sources equals the sum of the expenditures generated by the same domestic sources, such that:

$$GDP = C + I + (X - M) + G$$

In this equation, C represents *consumer goods,* I represents *investment goods,* $(X - M)$ represents exports less imports (or net exports) and G represents government spending. This equation measures the sum of all expenditures from these sources, or the sum of all income from these sources. In the case of the *income application,* GDP can be presented as a market value, or adjusted for inflation.

Because a change in GDP has many economic and business-related implications, business managers use GDP values to get a feel for overall economic conditions and for prevailing trends in the business environment. A consistently increasing GDP, for example, indicates that an economy is healthy and expanding. Managers often perceive a GDP increase as a predictor of an accompanying increase in the demand for goods and services within an economy. This might have the positive effect of increasing business revenues and creating more jobs. During the 1990s the United States experienced a period of unprecedented economic expansion, leading to the lowest unemployment rates in U.S. history.

Managers looking at GDP values could, however, perceive a potential economic expansion in terms of having potentially negative effects if demand exceeds the current supply, or if capacity within a market has already been fully utilized and cannot expand to meet the new production levels. In recent decades Asian economies have suffered from a fully utilized economy.

If the GDP decreases two quarters (of the year) in a row, the economy is in recession. A recession indicates that there may be an accompanying decrease in demand for goods and services within an economy. Managers often respond to a recession by minimizing expenses, which sometimes includes eliminating jobs and cutting production. Moreover, managers will often cut jobs *in anticipation* of a recession. This was visible most recently in 2001, when managers responded to a slowing in the growth of the economy by cutting hundreds of thousands of jobs. Expansions and contractions in the economy are a natural part of the *economic cycle,* also known as the *business cycle.* The economic cycle is the long-term pattern of alternating periods of economic growth (expansion) and decline (recession), characterized by changing leading economic indicators.

Employment Statistics

Employment statistics measure how much of the available labor capacity of a country is being used. In the United States, the Bureau of Labor Statistics compiles data and publishes

The Employment Situation report every month. This report focuses on changes in payroll employment, broken down by industry. While the report captures data on the number of payroll jobs available and the number of those jobs occupied, it makes an implicit assumption of one person per job. The report does not make any provision for measuring the number of persons who hold more than one job.

Managers use employment data in several ways across many industries. In the simplest terms, managers use employment data to project levels of disposable income, which affects a consumer's willingness and ability to make purchases. Managers may also use *The Employment Situation* report to get information on average wages paid by industry.

An even more sophisticated managerial application of employment data involves predicting the response of The Federal Reserve Bank to changes in employment. As the setter of interest rates, the Fed pays close attention to employment data as an indicator of upcoming economic trends. For example, the Fed might interpret a steep drop off in employment from one month to another in such a way that it responds by lowering interest rates. Clearly, any change in interest rates immediately and profoundly affects the financial services industry because these rates directly affect financial institutions' borrowing rates. A manager in the financial services industry would be better able to take advantage of an interest rate change if he or she had anticipated it. Furthermore, because lower interest rates make borrowing money cheaper, the Fed lowering interest rates motivates companies to borrow capital to make investments. These investments create jobs. Thus the Fed can use interest rates to influence the overall economy, not just the financial services industry.

Personal Income

The third indicator, personal income, tracks how people earn income as well as how they spend it. As a result, the Personal Income report, while far less timely than the Employment report, is thought to be a better indicator of spending power within an economy and is widely used by managers in consumer products industries to gauge future spending patterns of consumers at large.

The Bureau of Economic Analysis generates *The Personal*

Income and Consumption reports. This agency identifies the primary uses of income, such as personal tax payments, consumption spending, interest payments, and personal savings. The primary sources of income are wages and salaries, income from other labor, proprietor's income, rental income, personal dividend income, interest income, and net transfer payments. *Net transfer payments* are monies given by the government to its citizens. For example, social security taxes are collected from citizens and then "transferred" to other citizens in the form of social security income.

Industrial Production

The fourth indicator is industrial production. The Federal Reserve Board tracks the production of all intermediate and finished goods, including utilities, produced in the United States. The Fed responds to changes in the economy's output of goods as an indication of a strengthening or weakening of the economy overall, and changes interest rates accordingly. The industrial production data, however, reflects production of goods only, and does not include any measure of production of services such as hotel labor, customer service, or the like. Thus, as the number of service-oriented positions within the labor market has increased, the Industrial Production Indicator has become a less predictive, though still key, economic indicator.

Other Economic Indicators

Other economic indicators include the consumer confidence index, the consumer price index (CPI), the producer price index (PPI), unemployment, housing starts and permits, and the National Association of Purchasing Management Diffusion (NAPM) index. Depending on a manager's industry or particular concern, different economic indicators can be used to predict upcoming trends in the economy, or in a specific industry. Finally, the *overall* prediction of The Fed's next change in interest rates may itself be seen as an indicator. When interest rates move as predicted, the market rarely reacts. An unexpected change, however, can lead to a melee on Wall Street. Thus you should understand and track not only the previously mentioned indicators, but the Fed itself.

THE FEDERAL RESERVE BANK SYSTEM

The Federal Reserve System, or the Central Bank of the United States, consists of 12 Federal Reserve banks, 7 members of the Board of Governors of the Federal Reserve System, and 12 members of the Federal Open Market Committee (FOMC). The members of the FOMC include the 7 members of the Board of Governors, the president of the Federal Reserve Bank of New York, and the presidents of 4 other Federal Reserve banks. Within the Federal Reserve system there is also the Federal Reserve Council and approximately 5,000 member commercial banks. This number of commercial banks represents approximately 40 percent of all commercial banks in the United States. While it is not a requirement for a commercial bank to be a member of the Federal Reserve System, all commercial banks are subject to the rules and regulations handed down by the Fed.

As discussed earlier, the Federal Reserve's aim is to regulate the growth of the economy. Specifically, it regulates the amount of money in the economy, called *monetary aggregates*. Enough money must be available for borrowing to ensure sufficient credit expansion to foster economic growth. There must not, however, be so much growth as to cause inflation or to disrupt the orderliness of the financial markets. The Fed controls U.S. monetary policy primarily through the use of three policy-making instruments. These tools include (1) controlling open market operations, (2) setting interest rates, and (3) dictating reserve requirements. As a more in-depth discussion of interest rates will follow, we will address the issue of reserve requirements first. The term *reserve requirements* refers to the amount of funds that a member bank must have on hand as some percentage of the total deposits of that bank. The Fed dictates what this percentage is. The Fed also controls the federal funds rate, or the interest rate that American banks who have funds in excess of the requirements dictated by the Federal Reserve can use to make overnight loans to banks whose funds do not meet the levels dictated by the Fed.

The last responsibility of the Fed is to set the prime lending rate. While commercial banks and other lending agencies can offer lending rates higher than that offered by the Fed, these rates are generally expressed as *prime plus* rates. To appreciate the significance of interest rates and the influence they have on the economy, one must understand how interest rates affect the overall money supply and economy.

The Money Supply–Monetary Aggregates

The Fed identifies three different components of the overall money supply:

1. *M1.*   This is the narrowest category, consisting of only currency, checks, demand deposits, and traveler's checks. Of all the categories, M1 has the highest liquidity.

2. *M2.*   This category includes all M1 money, but also includes savings, deposits under $10,000, money market deposit accounts, money market mutual account balances, overnight repurchase agreements, and overnight Eurodollar deposits (which are deposits in U.S. dollars held in foreign banks, not to be confused with Euros as a currency).

3. *M3.*   This category contains all M2 but also includes term deposits for repurchase agreements (very short-term Treasury loans to dealers collateralized with bonds), and Eurodollar deposits, as well as dealer-only money market funds.

The supply of these aggregates available to the public is monitored through the joint activities of the Federal Reserve and the commercial banks. Commercial banks make the decision to extend credit to a particular individual or company based on the amount of capital they have to lend. The Fed determines the reserve rates the banks must maintain on outstanding deposits, thereby reducing the amount of capital available to that bank to lend to credit customers.

Money Supply and Demand

The Fed has the power to change interest rates. Manipulating interest rates helps control the available money supply. If interest rates are high, customers may prefer to save money rather than spend it, increasing the available reserves the commercial banks have to work with. Yet the banks, who must pay the interest on these outstanding deposits, must find customers who want to borrow funds so that the bank can earn enough interest revenue to cover depositor interest payments and, hopefully, have funds left over in the form of profits.

Interest rates also affect the demand for money. Economic activity can be viewed as a series of transactions, where money is the vehicle on which these transactions are based. A great deal of economic activity, or a high number of transactions, increases the demand for money. For example, if the number of new homes being built increases, the number of mortgage transactions increases. This can also lead to an increase in borrowing by construction companies to buy more equipment. Wood and textile suppliers may also borrow to expand their operations. Thus the initial transaction, the building of a new home, leads to many further transactions that require money, thereby increasing the demand for money.

The IS/LM Curves: Managing Supply and Demand

The federal government, via the Fed, changes the money supply in an attempt to control the country's economic condition. An increase in the money supply will decrease the cost of money (i.e., borrowing rates, mortgage rates, etc.) and therefore increase the demand for money. Prices and wages, however, take a long time to react to changes in the money supply. Thus, in the short term, the Fed can increase demand without affecting prices. This is known as *Keynesian economics,* which summarizes the complicated relationship between money supply, demand, and output in an economy through the use of IS/LM analyses. IS/LM analysis (see Figure 5.1) graphically shows how changing the money supply will affect the economy.

The *investment and savings curve* (IS) represents the different combinations of total output and interest rates such that the total quantity of goods produced equals the total number of goods demanded, or those combinations of output and interest rates that achieve market equilibrium. Simply put, it is the curve on which the supply of goods equals the demand for goods. Remember that GDP is the total value of all final goods and services produced by a country over a period of time. This is the supply of goods produced by the country. Goods not consumed in the home country are exported, and excess demand results in the importation of goods. Thus the IS curve is inextricably linked to both GDP and demand for goods.

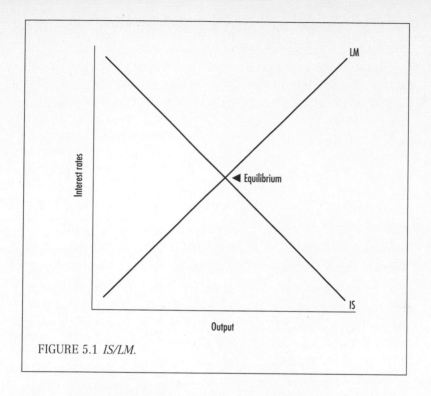

FIGURE 5.1 *IS/LM.*

The *LM curve,* on the other hand, represents the combinations of total output and interest rates such that the total amount of money demanded equals the quantity of money supplied, or those combinations of output and interest rates that achieve money-market equilibrium. L is a function representing the demand for money and M is the money supply. Simply put, the LM curve is where the supply of money equals the demand.

Taken together, the IS/LM curves intersect at a point (point x, as labeled on the chart) that indicates the equilibrium levels for aggregate output as well as for interest rates such that both goods market equilibrium and money market equilibrium are achieved and maintained. Thus the IS/LM curve indicates where goods, and money available to purchase these goods, are in equilibrium. Moreover, the IS/LM analysis illustrates the inextricable relationship between interest rates, the money supply, and GDP. This framework is a powerful tool for understanding the key elements of macroeconomics.

MICROECONOMICS

As mentioned previously, the study of macroeconomic relationships assists managers in making business decisions in relation to the overall economy. The study of microeconomics, however, can assist managers in making decisions on a firm-specific level.

Microeconomic analyses can help a manager make the most efficient use of the limited resources under his or her management by predicting the relationship between supply and demand. Further, microeconomic principles can be used to set production levels to maximize revenues, minimize costs, and determine appropriate prices for products and services.

Supply and Demand Curves

In microeconomics, the term *supply* refers quite literally to the amount or quantity of a product available for consumption in a given market. The term *demand,* however, is a measure of how much a consumer wants a product, expressed as a function of how much that consumer is willing to pay for the product.

Supply and demand curves (see Figure 5.2) are graphic representations of each function in relation to the other. More simply put, a supply curve expresses the behavior of the supply function, where quantity serves as the independent or X axis, and price serves as the dependent or Y axis. Across these axes, the supply curve is an increasing function. This represents the desire of firms to sell more (and thereby make greater quantities of product available) when prices are high than when prices are low.

The demand curve also expresses the behavior of the demand function across the same axes. This behavior, however, is opposite in nature, as demand is represented by a decreasing function. This means that when there is a lesser quantity of a product available, people are willing to pay more for it. When a product is available in abundant supply, people will pay less for it.

The point of intersection of these two curves represents the price and quantity amounts when a given market is in equilibrium, or when supply equals demand. From this point, a manager can evaluate the outcomes of changes in supply and the corresponding effects on price, and vice versa for a particular product.

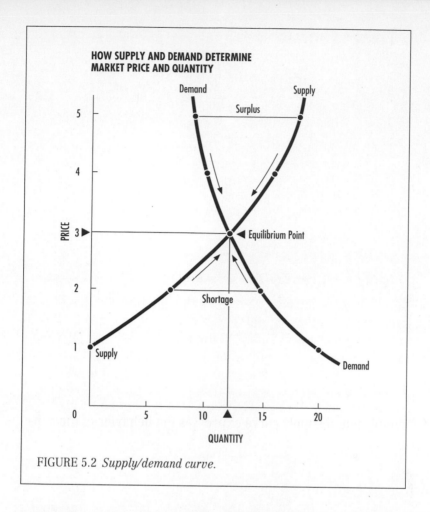

FIGURE 5.2 *Supply/demand curve.*

Revenue, Cost, and Profit Equations

Managers can also use microeconomic tools to assess the maximum and minimum values for revenue, cost, and profit equations. To understand these relationships, however, one must understand what components make up these three equations.

Revenue, simply put, is all the money a firm makes before any expenses are taken out. In other words, revenue is equal to the number of units of product sold, times the price each unit is sold for. In its simplest form:

Revenue = price × quantity sold

Clearly, this equation increases in complexity for firms that produce more than one product, but the general principle remains the same.

Cost equations are slightly less straightforward than their revenue counterparts. Total cost equations consist of *variable costs,* or costs that change depending on how many units a firm produces, and *fixed costs,* which do not change with production. An example of a variable cost would be material expenses, while an example of a fixed cost would be a company's rent. Thus, in its simplest form:

Total cost = variable cost × quantity sold + fixed costs

Profit equations measure what a firm makes after it covers its costs of production. This translates to a firm's revenues less its costs, or:

Profit = (price × quantity sold)

– [(variable costs × quantity sold) + fixed costs]

For example, suppose a New York City hot dog stand paid $20 each day to rent the equipment and space on the street. If the stand charges the customer $5 for each hot dog and pays $3 for the raw materials (uncooked hot dogs and buns) involved in producing each hot dog, then the hot dog stand must sell 10 hot dogs to breakeven (breakeven is where profits equal zero):

$$0 = (\$5 \times 10) - [(\$3 \times 10) + 20]$$

$$0 = \$50 - [30 + 20]$$

$$0 = \$50 - \$50$$

If the hot dog stand sells more than 10 hot dogs, the incremental profit on each additional hot dog sold will be $2, as the fixed costs have been covered ($5 – $3 = $2). Alternatively, the price of the hot dogs could be raised to increase profits. If the price goes up, however, the stand may sell fewer hot dogs, as people opt for the $3 hot sausage available down the street. Thus, as the price of hot dogs increases, the demand will decrease. This brings us to our next concept.

Elasticity of Demand

Elasticity of demand refers to the change in behavior of buyers when there is a change in the price of a product. More specifically, elasticity of demand is calculated as:

Elasticity of demand

$$= \frac{\text{\% change in quantity of product demanded}}{\text{\% change in price}}$$

Under the most basic conditions, the supply and demand curves presented show that buyers are directly sensitive to price, such that the lower the price of an item, the greater the quantity of the item the buyers are willing to purchase, and vice versa. There are conditions, however, when the relationship of price to quantity is not so direct, nor is selling fewer units of a product necessarily a negative outcome. For example, the price of some luxury items increases proportionally to their scarcity. Thus producing fewer of the luxury good can be more profitable than producing more.

Consider the revenue equation:

$$\text{Revenue} = \text{price} \times \text{quantity}$$

Every manager's objective is to maximize revenue. The concept of demand elasticity means that an incremental increase in price does not necessarily result in an identical decrease in the quantity sold, where the net change in revenue is zero. An incremental increase in price, while it might prompt a decrease in demand, can prompt a lesser decrease incrementally, resulting in an overall increase in revenue. For example, returning to the hot dog stand, let's suppose we sell 40 hot dogs a day at $5, but only 37 hot dogs a day at $7. Although the volume decreases, the profit increases from $120 to $128.

40 hot dogs at $5	37 hot dogs at $7
120 = ($5 × 40)	128 = ($7 × 37)
− [($3 × 40) + 20]	− [($3 × 37) + 20]
120 = $200 − [60 + 20]	128 = $259 − [111 + 20]
120 = $200 − $80	128 = $259 − $131

While the concept of elasticity is a useful one, it simply isn't time-efficient for managers to randomly choose prices for products until revenue is maximized. Fortunately, there is a more scientific way to optimize profit.

Optimization

The concept of *optimization,* or the practice of maximizing revenues and profits while minimizing costs, rests on the idea of *marginal analysis*. Marginal analysis seeks to balance the cost of producing one more item (marginal costs) with the revenue gained from selling one more item (marginal revenue). Reconsider the plight of the manager who wants to maximize revenues for a specific product. Ideally, the manager wants to find the right combination of price and quantity so that when they are multiplied, they yield the highest revenue possible. Since trial and error is not an option, how can this be done?

Suppose for a minute that trial and error *was* an option. The manager's strategy might be to increase the price of a product by one dollar each week and note the corresponding effect on quantity sold and overall revenue. Effectively, the manager would be evaluating the corresponding change in revenue for every one unit change in price. If the current price of the product is lower than the market will bear, then increasing the price will yield a positive change in revenue. If the manager overdoes it and sets the price of the product too high, the change in revenue will be negative. From this, it stands to reason that the manager will know when he or she has hit the right price when the change in revenue is neither positive nor negative. This is the heart of marginal analysis.

Maximizing Revenue

Performing marginal analyses enables managers to find the right combination of price and quantity that maximizes revenue without trial and error. This is done using calculus, but the concept is straightforward. Both marginal revenue and marginal costs can be graphed to a curve, called the *marginal function*. The curve uses price as the independent variable on the Y axis and quantity as the dependent variable on the X axis. Marginal revenue (or cost) is maximized when the curve reaches its maximum point.

At the curve's maximum point, its slope equals zero (the change in Y is given a one unit change in X). At that point, calculus lends that the first derivative of the function of the curve also equals to zero. Thus you can find marginal revenue by taking the first derivative of the total revenue function and solving for the quantity, which made marginal revenue equal to zero. For example:

$$\text{If total revenue (TR)} = 120Q - 3Q^2$$

where Q is quantity sold, and

$$TR = P \times Q,$$

then

Marginal revenue (MR) $= 120 - 6Q$

and marginal revenue would be optimized where

$$120 - 6Q = 0,$$

or

$$Q = 20$$

Minimizing Costs

Managers also use techniques of optimization to find levels of production that minimize total costs. Recall that:

Total cost = variable costs + fixed costs,

or

$$TC = AQ + C$$

where Q is quantity and A and C are constants. In marginal analysis, only terms that contain variables get differentiated on. Thus, the marginal cost function (MC) represents the transition of variable costs to marginal costs, where the marginal cost associated with a given unit represents the additional cost of producing the next unit. Setting the marginal cost equation to zero and solving for a Q value minimizes total costs.

Maximizing Profit

The last critical value that managers want to maximize is profit. Recall that:

Profit $(\pi) = TR - TC,$

or

$$P \times Q - (AQ + C)$$

Finding the values for which the marginal profit function equals zero optimizes profit. Taking the first derivative of the profit function requires taking the first derivatives of the revenue and total cost functions respectively, such that:

$$M\pi = MR - MC,$$

or

$$MR = MC$$

This final equation is one of the founding rules and neatest applications of microeconomics for real-world managers. It states that profit is maximized when a company produces a level of output such that the incremental revenue earned on producing the next unit is equal to the incremental cost incurred of producing the next unit. Since producing one unit more would result in the company incurring an incremental cost greater than the incremental revenue benefit from selling that unit, the company should limit production to the number of units that makes its marginal profit equation equal to zero.

SUMMARY

Business managers use macroeconomics, or the study of how the economy behaves in the aggregate, to understand and predict how changes in the overall economy may affect the success of the businesses they run. Managers can draw inferences about the economy in terms of the general business climate, or they can assess how specific changes in fiscal or monetary policy will drive trends in a particular industry.

Microeconomics, or the study of the dynamics of the firm, can also be used to aid managers in making critical business decisions on a daily basis. More specifically, managers can use their understanding of supply and demand to predict business changes. In addition, managers can use marginal analysis to target optimum levels of production to maximize revenues and profits while minimizing costs.

When used in conjunction, macro- and microeconomic concepts allow a manager to understand, predict, and manage market forces to a company's benefit. Otherwise, a company is left to manage in the aftermath of what it could not capitalize on in the forefront.

INTERNET RESOURCES

The Dismal Scientist (www.dismal.com). The Dismal Scientist covers over 80 economic releases from over 15 countries to provide you with global economic analyses and data.

Economy.com (www.economy.com/default.asp). A useful gateway to a number of valuable economic research tools, including the Dismal Scientist and Research@Economy.com, a comprehensive source for professional economic research with hundreds of analytical and statistical reports covering a wide range of industry, macroeconomic, regional, and international topics.

Forbes Global News (www.forbes.com/global). Global news provided by Forbes.com, this site analyzes worldwide current events and discusses how they will directly impact international businesses and global markets. A subsection of the Forbes home page, the site is updated daily.

Foreign Affairs Magazine: Economics, Trade and Finance (www.foreignaffairs .org). The Economics, Trade, and Finance section of the magazine is published by the Council of Foreign Relations and provides summaries and previews of upcoming articles.

New York Times (www.nytimes.com). A good source for the latest economic happenings around the world and particularly for interesting op-ed pieces on economics.

ECONOMICS CRITICAL REFERENCE MATERIALS

Board of Governors of the Federal Reserve System. *The Federal Reserve Bulletin.*

One of three most important sources of officially compiled data, this is the main source of data on money, banking, credit conditions, and additional U.S. financial sector indicators. *The Federal Reserve Bulletin* consists of three main sections: articles on aspects of financial economy or on monetary policy, legal notices of changes in banking regulations, and monetary and financial indicator statistics in tabular form.

Buchholz, Todd G., and Martin Feldstein. *New Ideas from Dead Economists: An Introduction to Modern Economic Thought.* New York: Penguin USA, 1999.

Using vibrant anecdotes and an accessible tone, *New Ideas* surveys economic thinking of the past several centuries while relating age-old principles to modern events such as communism's fall and the Asian financial crisis. The book acts as an animated guide to contemporary issues of our shifting world economy, using the insightful wisdom of the great economists of the past.

Council of Economic Advisors. *The Economic Report of the President*

One of the three most important sources of officially compiled data. *The Economic Report of the President* is published annually and consists of approximately 300 pages of analysis and discussion on the U.S. macroeconomy. There are an additional 100 pages of tables presenting annual data on a range of U.S. economic factors for the post–World War II period.

Dornbusch, Rudiger, and Stanley Fischer. *Macroeconomics,* 4th Edition, Englewood Cliffs, NJ: Prentice-Hall, 1998.

This comprehensive macroeconomics text is utilized by various top business schools. Its development of theory is supported by case studies and diagrams. It is a good source for a broad overview of macroeconomics or as a reference for greater detail on a specific subcomponent of macroeconomics.

Friedman, David. *Hidden Order: The Economics of Everyday Life.* New York: Harper Business, 1996.

Friedman's book is an application of economic principles to daily life. He masterfully uses economics to understand and explain people's behavior on a daily basis and what action they will likely follow in the future. *Hidden Order* is an unfolding of witty examples to demonstrate strategies for various economic decisions. Some examples are: driving in rush-hour traffic; negotiating the best job offer; choosing the right career; buying the best car at the lowest price. Friedman gives new meaning to the concept of applied economics as he integrates economics into the decision-making processes of people's daily lives.

Galbraith, John Kenneth. *A Journey Through Economic Time.* New York: Houghton Mifflin Company, 1994.

Galbraith traces the course of the history of capitalism in an international context from the late eighteenth century through the 1990s. *A Journey Through Economic Time* effectively conveys the central core of economic life in the progression of the decades. With titles such as The Crash,

The Great Depression, The New Deal, The Second War, and The Good Years, the book is structured so that each chapter addresses a specific point in the history of economics. It is a valuable source for demonstrating the progression of economics throughout the last century and offers a distinct historical perspective of the dynamics of economics.

Heilbroner, Robert. *The Worldly Philosophers: The Lives, Times, and Ideas of the Great Economic Thinkers*. New York: Touchstone Books, 1999.

This historical look at economics succeeds in providing great insights of our present world. In his attempt to explain how a capitalist society functions, Heilbroner spans all of the great economic minds from Adam Smith to Karl Marx. The book's concluding chapter shifts from an analysis of the past to speculation on the future; Heilbroner hypothesizes that a "scientific" strain of economics is overtaking the social and political pillars of economics, and calls on his readers to combat this increasing trend.

Keynes, John Maynard. *The General Theory of Employment, Interest and Money*. New York: Harcourt Brace & Company, 1964.

This is the critical book which changed previous conceptions held by economists as to the working of the capitalist system and, as a result, established Keynesian economics. The effects of this work have been called the "Keynesian Revolution" as it reshaped economic theory by modernizing business cycle theory and establishing the framework for modern macroeconomic analysis. Keynes' work has a profound historical influence, and the importance of his thinking serves as the basis for classic economic theory today.

Pindyck and Rubinfield. *Microeconomics*. New York: Macmillian, 1992.

This text used by top business schools presents a comprehensive approach to microeconomics. The book incorporates microeconomic theory and applies these principles to specific examples. It is a good text for learning or honing details of microeconomics.

U.S. Commerce Department. *The Survey of Current Business*.

One of the three most important sources of officially compiled statistics, this is the primary publication through which the Commerce Department presents economic and business data. The monthly publication consists of three parts: white pages in the front containing articles and supporting tables on various aspects of aggregate economic activity; yellow pages present tables of data and charts that show the business cycle behavior of 250 key economic indicators that have cyclical characteristics; and blue pages consisting of tables covering most aspects of general business activities and specific industry measures.

Young, Philip K. Y., and John J. McAuley. *The Portable MBA in Economics.* New York: John Wiley & Sons, Inc., 1994.

Designed for managers and entrepreneurs to hone their working knowledge of economics and apply it effectively to their respective businesses. *The Portable MBA in Economics* covers both macro- and microeconomics and demonstrates their interrelationship and how both are applied to the daily interworkings of business. The book incorporates insights from experts at top business schools and demonstrates concepts with real-world examples and case studies. It is an invaluable source for expanding and solidifying economic knowledge and then applying that information to improve business performance.

Accounting

A sound accounting process provides accurate information for improved internal decision making and creates a concise representation of the business's operations to outside constituencies. This chapter will focus on accounting's role in both the production of financial information for internal purposes and in its dissemination to outside interested parties. Although the dot.com boom of the 1990s led many to believe that traditional accounting measures were no longer relevant in valuing a company, many of the bankruptcies of the dot.com crash could have been easily predicted by reviewing the companies' financials. Whether you're using accounting data to decide about investing in a company, or to make changes in your own company, a fundamental understanding of accounting has become more, not less, important as a result of the Internet revolution.

TYPES OF ACCOUNTING

Companies engage in three types of accounting:

1. Managerial accounting
2. Financial accounting
3. Tax accounting

Managerial and financial accounting are most relevant to the businessperson (see Table 6.1). Tax accounting, although critical to minimizing taxes to maximize the bottom line, is best left to certified public accountants (CPAs), as it provides the least realistic view of a company's financial condition.

In short, financial accounting is used to prepare standard statements of financial information for use by the public. Managerial accounting, however, is used at the discretion of the company, solely for internal purposes.

MANAGERIAL ACCOUNTING

We begin with a look at managerial accounting, one of the primary informational resources for a company. It produces information that helps workers, managers, and executives in organizations make better decisions about a company's

TABLE 6.1 CHARACTERISTICS OF FINANCIAL AND MANAGERIAL ACCOUNTING

	Financial Accounting	Managerial Accounting
Audience	External: stockholders, creditors, tax authorities	Internal: workers, managers, executives
Purpose	Report on past performance to external parties; contracts with owners and lenders	Inform internal decisions made by employees and managers; feedback and control on operating performance
Timeliness	Delayed; historical	Current, future-oriented
Restrictions	Regulated; rules driven by generally accepted accounting principles and government authorities	No regulations; systems and information determined by management to meet strategic and operational needs
Type of Information	Financial measurements only	Financial, plus operational and physical measurements on processes, technologies, suppliers, customers, and competitors
Nature of Information	Objective, auditable, reliable, consistent, precise	More subjective and judgmental; valid, relevant, accurate
Scope	Highly aggregate; report on entire organization	Disaggregate; inform local decisions and actions

products, processes, and customers. It also provides economic and performance information to business insiders, such as employees, middle managers, and senior executives. Traditionally, most managerial accounting information has been financial in nature. However, the areas of coverage in modern managerial accounting processes have expanded recently to encompass operational or physical (nonfinancial) information, such as quality and process times, as well.

Because companies use managerial accounting information to meet their specific decision-making needs, they have significant discretion in the design of their managerial accounting process. Thus, it is less rule-driven than financial accounting. For example, the information from a managerial accounting process should help employees understand how to improve the quality, lower the cost, and increase the responsiveness of their operations for customer needs. Therefore, managerial accounting students learn about the decision-making process and informational needs of an organization, not about rules and journal entries.

Measures and assessments of the economic condition of an organization—the cost and profitability of the business's products, services, customers, and activities—are available only from managerial accounting processes. Managerial accounting information also measures the economic performance of decentralized operating units, such as business units, subsidiaries, divisions, and departments. These measures of economic performance provide a link between the overall strategy of the hierarchical organization and the execution and implementation of the strategy by various operating entities. Managerial accounting information is also one of the means by which employers can assess the performance of employees, middle managers, and executives. Employees can use the results to learn from their past decisions and to improve performance.

Ultimately, organizations succeed and prosper by designing cost-efficient products and services that customers value. They produce these products and services and distribute them to customers with efficient operating processes. Finally the organization's outputs are marketed and sold effectively to customers. Although an organization's managerial accounting information cannot by itself create success in these important activities, inadequate and inaccurate information from managerial accounting processes can lead a company and its decision makers to encounter severe operating and financial difficulties. An effective managerial accounting process creates considerable organizational value by providing timely and accurate information about the activities required for success in today's increasingly competitive environment.

Functions of Managerial Accounting

Managerial accounting information serves four functions, including (1) operational control, (2) product costing, (3) customer costing, and (4) management control. Table 6.2 summarizes the important objective of each function.

The demand for managerial accounting information differs, depending on the level of the organization. At the line level, where raw materials or purchased parts are converted into finished products or where services are performed for customers, information is needed primarily to control and improve operational efficiency. That is how the organization provides a quality product at the lowest possible cost. Relevant information here is diffuse and frequent; it is more physical and operational than financial and economic. As we move higher in an organization, where supervisory work is performed and decisions about products, services, and customers are made, information may be received less frequently but is more aggregate and strategic. Information at this level is used primarily to convey a broad picture of the organization; to provide a more complete assessment of the business; and to

TABLE 6.2 FUNCTIONS OF MANAGERIAL ACCOUNTING INFORMATION

Operational Control	Provides feedback information about the efficiency of tasks performed
Product and Customer Costing	Measures the costs of resources used to produce a product or service and to market and deliver the product/service to customers
Management Control	Provides information on the performance of managers and operating units.

identify potential problem areas if some aspect of operations differs from expectations.

The information needs at higher organizational levels include summaries of transactions and events that occur at the individual employee or customer level. Here, more financial information is necessary so that managers can assess the profitability of events occurring at the operational level of the organization. At the highest level of the organization, the information is even more strategic and less frequent. Much more of the information is now financial, with only a few key operational variables or value-drivers used to report on important success factors for the organization. Thus, managerial accounting information must be customized to meet needs at each level of an organization.

Role for Activity-Based Cost (ABC) Processes

Activity-based costing (or ABC, as it is frequently called), championed by Professor John Shank of the Tuck School of Business, is now being introduced in many manufacturing and service organizations to overcome the inability of traditional cost processes to accurately assign overhead costs. According to Professor Shank, companies have spent years and millions of dollars trying to develop accounting systems that nevertheless have incorrectly distributed costs, especially indirect and fixed costs. With many manufacturing companies now having overhead costs 5 or 10 times as large as their direct labor costs, managerial accounting processes that allocate overhead based on direct labor may lead to large distortions in the costs assigned to an organization's products and customers.

ABC processes are designed to avoid arbitrary allocations and subsequent cost distortions by assigning the costs of organizational resources to the activities being performed by the resources. Then, activity costs are assigned to the products, services, and customers that are creating the demand for or benefiting from the activities being performed. Consequently, the cost of purchasing is assigned to the items purchased, the cost of designing products is directly assigned to the newly designed products, and the cost of assisting customers is assigned to the individual customers.

Improvement of Operational Control Processes

The traditional product costing process was not the only managerial accounting process that became inadequate in the new competitive and technological environment. Operational control processes, with their detailed periodic summaries of financial performance, were slow in forwarding summary reports and were not adequately linked to nonfinancial databases, such as inventory and logistics. Consequently, corrective actions were not taken on a timely basis and were made with incomplete information.

As a result, companies have implemented enterprise resource planning (ERP) systems to integrate their financial information with their logistics, inventory, orders, and often with human resources information systems (HRIS). Thus information has evolved from aggregated monthly or weekly reports to real-time, online, and disaggregated (reporting on the resources used for each individual job, not the sum of all resources used for all jobs performed during a month). The net result was that new processes did adequately identify the source(s) of favorable and unfavorable performance.

Real-time ERP systems also replaced monthly performance reports of many operating departments that had become filled with cost allocations, so that managers were being held accountable for performance that was neither under their control nor incurred by their operations. ERP systems allow flexible reporting such that managers are held accountable for only that which is under their control. The costs of corporate- or factory-level resources, such as the heat and lighting in the building or the landscaping outside, are allocated to individual departments even though the departments are not directly responsible for these costs. Their incurrence can be traced to the actions taken at the individual departments.

Employee Empowerment: Sharing Financial Information

Among the myriad of new and interesting changes under way in providing relevant and timely information to assist employees in their quality and process improvement activities is an expanded role for financial information: quantities of inputs used, time required to complete a task, and quality of work accomplished. Combining financial information with operating or nonfinancial information using an ERP system, of course, becomes even more important to employees as they participate in quality and process improvement activities. Employees also benefit from the provision of cost and expense information about the resources they are using. For example, they can decide whether to bear the cost of replacing the tooling in a machine so that the output has more consistent quality. As employees modify and redesign processes, they should be concerned not only with improving cycle times, quality, yields, and productivity, but also with reducing the cost of completing work. For this purpose, innovative organizations now share financial information with operators to enable them to:

- Identify the opportunities for significant cost reduction
- Identify opportunities for innovation
- Set priorities for improvement projects
- Make trade-offs among alternative ways to improve operations
- Evaluate proposed investments to improve operations
- Assess the consequences of their improvement activities

Thus, another new and important theme in managerial accounting is the role such information can provide to employees for their problem-solving and continuous improvement activities. This approach stresses the use of financial and nonfinancial information to inform local decision making and de-emphasize the traditional role for cost accounting information to control operator performance.

FINANCIAL ACCOUNTING

While management accounting is focused primarily on internal processes, *financial accounting* is concerned with the reporting and communication of a business's economic information to external stakeholders: shareholders, creditors (such as bankers and bondholders), regulators, and governmental tax authorities. Publicly held companies must prepare and report financial statements every quarter and also must file detailed reports annually as well as whenever there is a significant event (as defined by law). There are, of course, common rules that all businesses must follow in reporting their financial information. Companies must prepare their financial statements according to rules known as generally accepted accounting principles (GAAP), which are created by the Financial Accounting Standards Board (FASB) and enforced by the Securities and Exchange Commission (SEC) in the United States, and by governmental tax agencies. As a consequence, financial accounting tends to be a rule-driven discipline, and financial accountants use detailed rules and procedures to generate a business's required financial statements. The benefit of such a process is that the economic performance of many different businesses is relatively easy to compare. Thus you can use financial statements to analyze a company's performance over time and to compare it to other companies.

Principal Financial Statements

Individuals external to a company most frequently use financial statements that appear in the firm's annual report to shareholders. The annual report to shareholders typically includes a letter from the firm's CEO or president summarizing operating and financial activities of the past year and assessing the firm's prospects for the coming year. The section of the annual report containing the financial statements includes the following:

1. Balance sheet
2. Income statement
3. Statement of cash flows
4. Notes to the financial statements, including various supporting schedules
5. Opinion of the independent certified public accountant

The Balance Sheet

The balance sheet (see Figure 6.1 for a sample balance sheet from Timberland, a U.S. shoe and apparel company), also called the "*statement of financial condition,*" is an accountant's snapshot of the firm's value. In short, the balance sheet shows everything the company owns as well as everything the company owes to outside parties. A banker may look at a balance sheet to determine the firm's creditworthiness. A supplier may be more interested in the amount owed to suppliers—"accounts payable." This may indicate the general promptness

Assets

	($ in thousands)	
	2000	**1999**
Current assets		
Cash and equivalents	$114,852	$196,085
Accounts receivable, net of allowance for doubtful accounts of $5,825 in 2000 and $4,910 in 1999	105,727	78,696
Inventory	131,917	114,673
Prepaid expense	13,717	9,890
Prepaid income taxes	15,547	15,297
Total current assets	381,760	414,641
Property, plant, and equipment	150,462	130,425
Less accumulated depreciation and amortization	(76,817)	(75,019)
Net property, plant, and equipment	73,645	55,406
Excess of cost over fair value of net assets acquired, net	15,848	17,533
Other assets, net	5,058	5,731
Total assets	$476,311	$493,311

Liabilities and Stockholders' Equity

	2000	**1999**
Current liabilities		
Accounts payable	$ 49,437	$ 33,247
Accrued expense		
Payroll and related	34,311	30,570
Other and interest	41,976	35,038
Income taxes payable	19,349	13,500
Total current liabilities	145,073	112,355
Long-term debt	—	100,000
Deferred income taxes	8,975	8,588
Excess of fair value of acquired assets over cost, net	5,512	—
Stockholders' equity		
Preferred stock, $.01 par value; 2,000,000 shares authorized; none issued	—	—
Class A Common Stock, $.01 par value (1 vote per share); 60,000,000 shares authorized; 39,833,928 shares issue at December 31, 2000 and 37,276,710 shares issued at December 31, 1999	398	187
Class B Common Stock, $.01 par value (10 votes per share); convertible into Class A shares on a one-for-one basis; 15,000,000 shares authorized; 7,932,900 shares issued at December 31, 2000 and 9,351,396 shares issued at December 31, 1999	79	47
Additional paid-in capital	109,756	82,755
Deferred compensation	(4,373)	(3,658)
Retained earnings	403,972	282,209
Accumulated other comprehensive loss	(7,292)	(4,151)
Less treasury stock at cost; 8,151,039 shares at December 31, 2000 and 5,342,698 shares at December 31, 1999	(185,789)	(85,021)
Total stockholders' equity	316,751	272,368
Total liabilities and stockholders' equity	$476,311	$493,311

FIGURE 6.1 *Sample Balance Sheet: Timberland Company*

of payments to its suppliers. Many users of financial statements, including managers and investors, want to know the true value of the firm. This is not found on the balance sheet because many of the true resources of the firm do not appear on the balance sheet: good management, proprietary assets, favorable economic conditions, and so on. These factors all add value to the firm, but will generally not appear as an "asset" on the firm's balance sheet.

The balance sheet is prepared on a particular date, as if the firm were momentarily frozen. It has two sides: on the left are the *assets,* and on the right the *liabilities* and *stockholders' equity.* The balance sheet states what the firms owns and how it is financed. The accounting definition that underlies the balance sheet is

$$\text{Assets} \equiv \text{liabilities} + \text{stockholders' equity}$$

We have put a three-line equality in the balance equation to indicate that it must always hold, by definition. The stockholders' equity is therefore defined to be the difference between the assets and the liabilities of the firm. In principle, equity is what the stockholders would retain after the firm discharged its other financial obligations.

Assets

An asset is something of economic value that can be exchanged for cash. For example, the money in your wallet, the money in your checking account, your car, and your home are all assets. These assets are *tangible assets* because they physically exist. All of a company's tangible assets, such as bank deposits, buildings, and inventory are included as assets in the balance sheet. For an asset to appear on the balance sheet, its value must be measurable. In the United States, GAAP requires that tangible assets appear on the balance sheet at their cost to the company, known as the *historical value, carrying value,* or *book value* of the asset. This may mislead readers of financial statements who mistakenly assume a firm's assets are recorded at true market values. *Market value* is the value or price at which buyers and sellers are willing to trade their assets. For example, assume you purchase an antique for $10 and sell it 10 years later on eBay for $200. The antique would be on your "balance sheet" at the book value of $10 for 10 years while the market value of the antique was growing to $200. The new purchaser of the antique will place it on his or her balance sheet with a book value of $200, because that's what he or she paid for it.

Depreciation is an expense subtracted from the book value of an asset to account for the decline in the value of the asset to general wear and tear or obsolescence over a period of time. Thus the value of many tangible assets on a balance sheet is the book value less depreciation. Land is the only physical asset that is not subject to depreciation under GAAP. Cash and cash equivalents are not subject to depreciation. For example, although the money in your bank account does not "depreciate" over time, your car is subject to depreciation, as using it makes it worth less. In a corporate example, if a company purchases a factory for $50,000, it will initially appear on the balance sheet as a $50,000 asset. At the end of the year, however, the value of the asset will be less, due to wear and tear. Thus the $50,000 asset may now appear on the balance sheet as being worth only $48,000 if the depreciation of the asset is estimated to be $2,000. Depreciation will be discussed in more detail later in this chapter.

There are also *intangible assets*. These are assets with no physical presence, such as corporate reputation, brands, trademarks, patents, management expertise, and research. Intangible assets created within a company do not currently appear on the balance sheet in the United States (they do, however, in the United Kingdom) because it is too difficult to measure their value accurately. Thus if a company does research and gains a patent, the patent does not appear on the balance sheet. If a company purchases a patent from another company, however, the value is known (the purchase price) and the patent appears on the balance as an asset called "goodwill." *Goodwill* is the amount the purchase price exceeds the value of the tangible assets purchased. For example, if you buy a company whose factories are worth $150,000 and pay $200,000, the $50,000 difference is goodwill. The goodwill could be a brand, a strong reputation, a trademark, or management expertise. Regardless of the type of intangible asset, it should give you a competitive advantage, making it worth the $50,000.

Accounting Liquidity

Accounting liquidity refers to the speed and certainty with which assets can be converted to cash. *Current assets* are the most liquid class of asset and include cash as well as those assets that the firm expects to convert into cash within a year, such as money markets and demand deposits. *Accounts receivable* is the amount of the firm's sales not yet collected from customers. This is generally due to the sale of merchandise on credit to customers. *Accounts receivable* are generally collected within one year and are therefore considered a current asset. *Inventory* consists of raw materials to be used subsequently in production, work in process, and finished goods. *Fixed assets* are the least liquid class of asset. *Tangible fixed assets* include items such as property, plant, and equipment. These assets do not convert to cash from normal business activity, and they are not usually used to pay expenses, such as payroll. However, the activities they perform within the firm are designed to generate cash for the firm. For example, the construction of a new manufacturing plant is designed to increase productive capacity. Other fixed assets are not tangible. Intangible assets, as discussed earlier, have no physical existence but can be very valuable.

The more liquid a firm's assets are, the less likely the firm is to experience problems meeting short-term obligations. Thus, the probability that a firm will avoid financial distress can be linked to the firm's liquidity. However, liquid assets frequently have lower rates of return than fixed assets; for example, cash generates no income for the firm. The more a firm invests in liquid assets, the more it sacrifices an opportunity to invest in more profitable investment projects. Thus, a firm's liquidity position often involves a trade-off between the likelihood of financial distress and the loss of foregone investment activities.

Debt versus Equity

Liabilities are obligations of the firm that require a payment of cash on specific dates in the future. Many liabilities involve legal contractual obligations to repay a predetermined amount and interest over a particular period. Thus, liabilities are debts and frequently require cash payments on the interest or principal of the debt. These payments are known as *debt service*. Failure to repay on a timely basis places the firm in default. Stockholders' equity represents an ownership claim against the firm's assets. Generally speaking, when the firm borrows, it gives the bondholders a priority claim on the firm's cash flow stream. Bondholders can sue the firm if the firm defaults on its contractual obligation. This may lead the firm to declare bankruptcy. Stockholders' equity is the residual or remaining difference between the firm's assets and liabilities:

$$\text{Assets} - \text{liabilities} \equiv \text{stockholders' equity}$$

This is the stockholders' ownership share in the firm expressed in accounting terms. The accounting value of stockholders' equity increases when retained earnings are added or new shares are sold. Stockholder's equity increases when the firm decides to retain part of its earnings instead of paying them out as dividends.

The Income Statement

The *income statement,* or *statement of operations,* measures performance over a specific period of time, usually reported on a quarterly and an annual basis. The accounting definition of income is

$$\text{Revenue} - \text{expenses} \equiv \text{income}$$

Unlike the balance sheet, which is a snapshot at a point in time, the income statement (see Figure 6.2 for an example of Timberland's income statements) shows financial transactions over a period of time.

The income statement includes several essential pieces of information. The *operations section* reports the firm's revenues and expenses from its principal business operations. Among other things, the nonoperating section of the income statement includes provision for all of the firm's financing costs, such as interest expense. Usually a second section reports as a separate item the amount of income taxes. The last item on the income statement is the *bottom line,* or *net income.* Net income is frequently expressed per share of outstanding common stock, that is, earnings per share.

	($ in thousands)		
	2000	**1999**	**1998**
Revenue	$1,091,478	$917,216	$862,168
Cost of goods sold	582,966	524,114	519,329
Gross profit	508,512	393,102	342,839
Operating expense			
Selling	258,081	219,545	195,688
General and administrative	65,129	55,321	50,876
Amortization of goodwill	1,130	1,685	1,685
Total operating expense	324,340	276,551	248,249
Operating income	184,172	116,551	94,590
Other expense (income)			
Interest expense	5,648	9,342	9,538
Other, net	(8,128)	(3,449)	(1,942)
Total other expense (income)	(2,480)	5,893	7,596
Income before income taxes	186,652	110,658	86,994
Provision for income taxes	62,528	35,411	27,838
Net income before extraordinary item	$ 124,124	$ 75,247	$ 59,156
Extraordinary item—loss on debt extinguishment, net of tax benefit of $1,071 (see Note 3)	2,126	—	—
Net income	$ 121,998	$ 75,247	$ 59,156
Earnings per share before extraordinary item			
Basic	$ 3.09	$ 1.75	$ 1.29
Diluted	$ 2.91	$ 1.70	$ 1.26
Earnings per share after extraordinary item			
Basic	$ 3.04	$ 1.75	$ 1.29
Diluted	$ 2.86	$ 1.70	$ 1.26
Weighted-average shares outstanding			
Basic	40,119	42,895	45,698
Diluted	42,647	44,355	47,035

FIGURE 6.2 *Income Statement for Timberland Company*

When analyzing an income statement, one should keep in mind three concepts:

1. GAAP
2. Noncash items
3. Time and costs

GAAP and Accrual-Based Accounting

One of the many rules dictated by GAAP (Generally Accepted Accounting Principles) is the matching principle, under which revenues are matched with expenses. This concept requires recognizing revenue when earned and expenses when incurred. Thus, income is reported when it is earned, or accrued, whether cash has been received (for example, when goods are sold for credit, sales and profits are reported). Revenue is reported on a firm's income statement when the earnings process is virtually completed and an exchange of goods or services has occurred. Therefore, items such as the unrealized appreciation in owning property will not be recognized as income on the firm's income statement. This provides an alternative for managers to smooth income by selling appreciated property at their discretion. Companies seek to have steady growth and may use "smoothing" to manipulate earnings from year to year to avoid dramatic increases or decreases in earnings. This creates the illusion of stability for the company. For example, if the firm owns property that has doubled in value, then, in a year when its earnings from other businesses are down, it could raise overall earnings by selling the property.

Noncash Items

The market value of an asset depends upon its ability to generate future inflows of cash. However, cash flow is not reported on an income statement. This is because several *noncash items* are reported as expenses against revenues. But these items do not affect cash flow. The most important noncash item is *depreciation*. Depreciation represents an accountant's estimate of the cost of equipment used during that time period in the production process. For example, suppose an asset with a five-year life and no resale value is purchased for $5,000. The $5,000 cost must be expensed over the useful life of the asset, although the firm actually incurs the full expense at the time of purchase. If straight-line depreciation is used, there will be five equal charges of $1,000 of depreciation expense each year. From a finance perspective, the cost of the asset is the actual negative cash flow incurred when the asset is acquired (that is, $5,000 *not* the accountant's smoothed $1,000-per-year depreciation expense). Depreciation does have a cash flow effect, however. This is because depreciation is deductible for corporate income tax purposes.

Another common noncash expense is *deferred taxes*. Accounting income and taxable income are often different and the tax expense projected based on the accounting income is often greater than the actual taxes paid, resulting in a deferral of a portion of the tax expense, "deferred taxes." If taxable income is less than accounting income in any given year, it will exceed accounting income in the future. Consequently, taxes that are not paid today must be paid at some point in the future, and hence they represent a liability of the firm. This liability shows up on the balance sheet of the firm as *deferred tax liability*. From a cash flow perspective, however, deferred tax is not a cash outflow.

Time and Costs

Think of future time as having two distinct parts, the *short run* and the *long run*. The short run is that period of time in which certain equipment, resources, and commitments of the firm are fixed. It is, however, long enough for the firm to vary its output by using more labor and raw materials. The short run is not a precise period of time that will be the same for all industries or even all firms within the same industry. However, all firms making decisions in the short run have some *fixed costs,* that is, costs that will not change because of the fixed commitments. Examples of fixed costs are interest payments, overhead expenses, and property taxes. Costs that are not fixed are *variable*. Variable costs change as the output of the firm changes. Some common examples are raw materials and employee wages.

Although costs are considered fixed in the short run, in the long run, all costs are variable. Financial accountants therefore do not distinguish between variable costs and fixed costs. Instead, accounting costs usually fit into a classification that

distinguishes *product costs* from *period costs.* Product costs
are the total production costs incurred during some particular
period and are reported on the income statement as *cost of
goods sold.* Production costs would normally consist of items
such as raw materials, direct labor, and manufacturing overhead. Both variable and fixed costs are included in product
costs. Period costs are costs that are allocated to a time
period. Those are usually referred to as selling, general, and
administrative expenses. An example of a period cost would
be the rent on the corporate headquarters.

Statement of Cash Flows

The emphasis in accounting income statements is the determination of the net income of the firm. Perhaps the most
important item that can be extracted from financial statements, however, is the firm's actual *cash flow.* Cash flow is
generally related to *accounting profit,* which is simply net
income as reported on the income statement, but it is not the
same. Although companies with relatively high accounting
profits generally have relatively high cash flows, the relationship is not always perfect. Therefore, investors are concerned
about cash flow projections as well as accounting profit projections.

Since the value of any asset, including a share of stock,
depends on the cash flow produced by the asset, managers
should act to maximize the cash flow available to its providers
of capital (stockholders, bondholders, etc.) over the long run.
A business's cash flow is equal to cash from sales, minus cash
operating costs, minus interest charges, and minus taxes.
Before we proceed further, however, we need to revisit *depreciation,* which is an operating cost, but not a cash outlay.

Remember that depreciation is an annual charge against
income, which reflects the estimated dollar cost of the capital
equipment used up in the production process. For example,
suppose a machine with a life of 7 years and a zero expected
salvage value was purchased in 2002 for $210,000. This
$210,000 cost is not expensed in the purchase year; rather, it
is charged against production over the machine's seven-year
depreciable life. If the depreciation expense were not taken,
profits would be overstated, and taxes would be too high.
So, the annual depreciation charge is deducted from sales

revenues, along with such other costs as labor and raw materials, to determine taxable income. However, because the $210,000 was actually expended back in 2002, the depreciation charged against income in 2003 through 2009 is not a cash outlay, as are labor or raw materials charges. Depreciation is a noncash charge, so it must be added back to net income to obtain the cash flow from operations.

Firms can be thought of as having two separate but related sources of organizational value: *existing assets,* which provide current profits and cash flows, and *growth opportunities,* which represent opportunities to make new investments that will eventually increase future profits and cash flows. The ability to take advantage of growth opportunities often depends on the availability of the cash needed to buy new assets, and the cash flow from existing assets is often the primary source of the funds used to make profitable new investments. This is another reason why both investors and managers are concerned with cash flows as well as profits.

Net working capital is defined as current assets minus current liabilities. The values of current assets and current liabilities are on the balance sheet. The statement of cash flows uses the change in net working capital from year to year. Net working capital is positive when current assets are greater than current liabilities. In this case, the cash that will become available from assets over the next year exceeds the cash that must be paid out. The net working capital of the Timberland Co. was $237 million in 2000 and $303 million in 1999.

Year	Current assets ($ millions)	−	Current liabilities ($ millions)	=	Net working capital ($ millions)
2000	382	−	145	=	237
1999	415	−	112	=	303

In addition to investing in fixed assets (i.e., capital spending), a firm can invest resources in net working capital. This incremental investment is called the *change in net working capital.* The change in net working capital is the difference between the net working capital in the previous year and the net working capital in the current year. In the case of Timberland, the change in net working capital is $237 − $303, or −$66 million. The change in net working capital is usually positive in a growing firm. Hence, the difference must be financed with some long-term source of capital, such as debt or equity. Thus, looking at the change in net working capital in isolation, one would assume Timberland did not experience growth in 2000 and did not need additional financing.

Cash flow is not the same as net working capital. For example, increasing inventory requires use of the firm's cash. Because both inventories and cash are current assets, this investment does not affect net working capital. In this situation, an increase in a particular net working capital account, such as inventory, decreases cash flow.

Similar to the relationship that the value of a firm's assets is equal to the value of the liabilities and the value of the equity, the cash flows from the firm's assets (that is, its operating activities), CF(A), must equal the cash flows to the firm's creditors, CF(B), and equity investors, CF(S):

$$CF(A) \equiv CF(B) + CF(S)$$

The first step in determining a firm's cash flow is to calculate the cash flow from operations. As can be seen in the statement of cash flows for Timberland (see Figure 6.3), operating cash flow is the cash flow generated by business activities, including sales of goods and services.

For our purposes, it is useful to divide cash flow into two classes: (1) *operating cash flows* and (2) *other cash flows*. Operating cash flows arise from normal operations, and they are, in essence, the difference between sales revenues and cash expenses, including taxes paid. Other cash flows arise from the issuance of stock, from borrowing, or from the sale of fixed assets. Our focus here is on operating cash flow.

Operating cash flow can differ from accounting profits (or net income) for three primary reasons:

1. All the taxes reported on the income statement may not have to be paid during the current year, or, under certain circumstances, the actual cash payments for taxes may exceed the tax figure deducted from sales to calculate net income.

2. Sales may be on credit, and hence not represent cash.

3. Some of the expenses (or costs) deducted from sales to determine profits may not be cash costs. For example, depreciation is not a cash cost.

	($ in thousands)		
	2000	**1999**	**1998**
Cash flows from operating activities:			
Net income	$121,998	$ 75,247	$ 59,156
Adjustments to reconcile net income to net cash provided by operating activities:			
Deferred income taxes	137	(714)	(35)
Depreciation and amortization	19,291	24,410	18,199
Loss (gain) on disposal of property, plant and equipment	(131)	396	1,303
Extraordinary item	2,126	—	—
Tax benefit from stock option plans	12,600	2,500	2,300
Increase (decrease) in cash from changes in working capital:			
Accounts receivable	(24,419)	(2,687)	(2,781)
Inventory	(10,479)	15,817	11,637
Prepaid expense	(1,104)	1,679	1,112
Accounts payable	14,120	10,144	5,083
Accrued expense	7,681	15,290	(9,975)
Income taxes	(507)	(4,301)	459
Net cash provided by operating activities	141,313	137,781	86,458
Cash flows from investing activities:			
Acquisition of Asian Distributor business	5,237	—	—
Proceeds from sale of property, plant and equipment	—	81	97
Additions to property, plant and equipment	(35,444)	(20,094)	(20,683)
Other, net	(2,169)	(3,701)	(1,245)
Net cash used by investing activities	(32,376)	(23,714)	(21,831)
Cash flows from financing activities:			
Extinguishment of debt	(100,000)	—	—
Extraordinary item	(2,126)	—	—
Common stock repurchases	(101,718)	(71,670)	(16,223)
Issuance of common stock	15,359	4,828	3,844
Net cash used by financing activities	(188,485)	(66,842)	(12,379)
Effect of exchange rate changes on cash	(1,685)	(3,029)	870
Cash and equivalents at beginning of year	196,085	151,889	98,771
Cash and equivalents at end of year	$114,852	$196,085	$151,889
Supplemental disclosures of cash flow information:			
Interest paid	$5,863	$ 9,165	$9,378
Income taxes paid	55,471	40,848	27,336

For the Years Ended December 31, 2000, 1999, and 1998

FIGURE 6.3 *Consolidated Statements of Cash Flows, Timberland Company*

Thus, operating cash flow could be larger or smaller than accounting profits during any given year.

Operating cash flow reflects tax payments, but not financing, capital spending, or changes in net working capital. Accountants calculate operating cash flow by starting with the net income found on the income statement. They then add back any noncash expenses, such as depreciation, and determine the change in net working capital. This total shows the amount of cash brought into the business from the operations of the firm.

Cash Flow from Investing Activities

Cash flow from investing activities involves changes in capital assets: acquisition of fixed assets and sales of fixed assets (i.e., net capital expenditures). Property, plant, and equipment are considered fixed assets. The net change in fixed assets equals sales of existing fixed assets minus the acquisition of new fixed assets. The result is the cash flow used for capital spending.

Total cash flows generated by the Timberland's assets are the sum of

Operating cash flow	141,313
Capital spending	(32,376)
Additions to net working capital	(14,708)
Total cash flow of the firm	94,229

Cash Flow from Financing Activities

Cash flows to and from creditors and owners include changes in equity and debt. The total outflow of cash of the firm can be separated into *cash flow paid to creditors* and *cash flow paid to stockholders.* Creditors are paid an amount generally referred to as *debt service.* Debt service consists of interest payments plus any repayments of principal (that is, retirement of debt).

An important source of cash flow is from selling new debt. Thus, an increase in long-term debt is the net effect of new borrowing and repayment of maturing obligations plus interest expense. Timberland's net working capital is not increasing and it has not sold new debt, but has retired old debt. Thus one would assume the business is not expanding.

Cash Flow Paid to Creditors ($ thousands)	
Interest	$ 5,863
Retirement of debt	100,000
Debt service	15,863
Proceeds from long-term debt sales	0
Total	$ 15,863

Cash flow of the firm also is paid to the stockholders. It consists of paying dividends plus repurchasing outstanding shares of stock (shares of stock not owned by the company itself) and issuing new shares of stock.

Cash Flow to Stockholders ($ thousands)	
Dividends	$ 0
Repurchase of stock	101,718
Cash to stockholders	101,718
Proceeds from new stock issue	(15,359)
Total	$ 86,359

Several important observations can be drawn from our discussion of cash flow:

1. Several types of cash flow are relevant to a complete understanding of the firm's financial situation. *Operating cash flow,* defined as earnings before interest and depreciation minus taxes, measures the cash generated from operations not counting capital spending or working capital requirements. It should usually be positive; a firm is in trouble if operating cash flow is negative for a long time because the firm is not generating enough cash to pay operating costs. *Total cash flow* of the firm includes adjustments for capital spending and additions to net working capital. It will often be negative. When a firm is growing rapidly, expenditures on accounts receivable and fixed assets can be higher than cash flow receipts from sales.

2. Net income is not cash flow. The net income of the Timberland Company in 2000 was $122 million, whereas cash flow was $126 million. The two numbers are not usually the same. In determining the economic and financial condition of a firm, cash flow is more relevant.

FINANCIAL STATEMENT ANALYSIS

The objective of this section is to illustrate how to rearrange and interpret information from financial statements that we have discussed previously in this chapter. Financial ratios provide information about five areas of financial performance:

1. *Solvency*—the ability of the firm to meet its short-run obligations

2. *Activity*—the ability of the firm to control its investment in assets

3. *Financial leverage*—the extent to which a firm relies on debt financing

4. *Profitability*—the extent to which a firm is profitable

5. *Value*—the value of the firm

Financial statements do not directly provide the preceding five measures of performance. However, management can constantly evaluate how well the firm is doing, and financial statements can provide this kind of useful information. The financial statements of the Timberland Company, which appeared in the previous section provide the information for the examples that follow. (Values are given in $ millions.)

Short-Term Solvency

Ratios of *short-term solvency* measure the ability of the firm to pay its current bills. To the extent a firm has sufficient liquid financial resources, it will be able to avoid defaulting on its financial obligations and, thus, avoid financial distress. *Accounting liquidity* measures short-term solvency and is often associated with the firm's net working capital position. You may remember that current liabilities are debts and financial obligations that are due within one year. The primary source from which the firm will pay these debts is its current assets.

The most widely used measures of accounting liquidity are the *current ratio* and the *quick ratio.*

Current Ratio

To find the current ratio, divide current assets by current liabilities. For the Timberland, the figure for 2000 was:

$$\text{Current ratio} = \frac{\text{total current assets}}{\text{total current liabilities}} = \frac{381.8}{145.1} = 2.63$$

If a firm is experiencing financial and liquidity problems, it may not be able to pay its bills (accounts payable) on time or it may need to negotiate an extension and/or an increase in its bank credit (notes payable). As a consequence, current liabilities may rise faster than current assets and the current ratio may fall. This may be an indication of impending financial difficulty. A firm's current ratio should be calculated over several years for a historical perspective, and it should be compared to the current ratios of other firms with similar operating activities. Generally, the similar firms are those found in the same industry. We see here that Timberland, 2.63 current ratio appears to signal that they have more than enough (2.63 to be exact) in their current assets to cover their current liabilities, suggesting that business is going well. However, it is important to note that for this ratio, and many of the others that follow, firms can manipulate situations to change the ratios. These practices are particularly common when companies are reporting their numbers to analysts. Since they want their ratios to look as strong as possible, they may conserve cash, delay payments, or use write-downs to hide what otherwise may be interpreted as a signal of declining business.

Quick Ratio

The quick ratio is computed by subtracting inventories from current assets and dividing the difference (called *quick assets*) by current liabilities:

$$\text{Quick ratio} = \frac{\text{quick assets}}{\text{total current liabilities}} = \frac{249.8}{145.1} = 1.72$$

Quick assets are those current assets that can be most easily and quickly converted into cash. Inventories are generally regarded as the least liquid current assets. Many financial analysts believe it is important to determine a firm's ability to pay off current liabilities without relying on the sale of inventories. Moreover, since a firm carries its inventories on its balance sheet at cost, a fire sale may bring in less cash than the balance sheet might otherwise indicate. Referring to our example here, Timberland's 1.72 Quick Ratio suggests their current assets were not inflated by high inventory levels, and that they still have a strong position in their ability to pay off current liabilities with liquid current assets.

Activity

Ratios of activity are constructed to measure how effectively the firm's assets are being managed. The level of a firm's investment in assets depends on many factors, such as seasonal, cyclical, and industry considerations. How can the appropriate level of investment in assets be measured? One sensible starting point is to compare assets with sales for the year to arrive at turnover. The idea is to find out how quickly assets are used to generate sales.

Total Asset Turnover. The total *asset turnover ratio* is determined by dividing total operating revenues for the accounting period by the average of total assets. The total asset turnover ratio for the Timberland Company for 2000 was

$$\text{Total asset turnover} = \frac{\text{total operating revenues}}{\text{total assets (average)}}$$

$$= \frac{1{,}091}{485} = 2.25$$

$$\text{Average total assets} = \frac{476 + 493}{2} = 485$$

The ratio measures how efficiently a firm is utilizing its assets. If the asset turnover ratio is high, the firm is using its assets effectively in generating sales. If the ratio is low, the firm may not be using its assets efficiently and shall either increase sales or eliminate some of the existing assets. One problem in interpreting this ratio is that it is maximized by using older assets because their depreciated accounting value is lower than newer assets. Also, firms with relatively small investments in fixed assets, such as retail and wholesale trade firms, tend to have high ratios of total asset turnover when compared with firms that require a large investment in fixed assets, such as manufacturing firms. Thus, industry differences must be carefully considered in assessing the asset turnover ratio. For our Timberland example, it appears that given their total asset turnover ratio of 2.25, they are efficiently using their assets to generate sales. However to best interpret this, we would need industry comparisons as well as historical numbers for Timberland.

Receivables Turnover.   The ratio of *receivables turnover* is calculated by dividing sales by average receivables during the accounting period. If the number of days in the year (365) is divided by the receivables turnover ratio, the average collection period can be determined. Net receivables are used for these calculations. The receivables turnover ratio and average collection period for the Timberland Company are

$$\text{Receivables turnover} = \frac{\text{total operating revenues}}{\text{receivables (average)}}$$

$$= \frac{1{,}091}{92} = 11.8$$

$$\text{Average receivables} = \frac{106 + 79}{2} = 92$$

$$\text{Average collection period} = \frac{\text{days in period}}{\text{receivables turnover}}$$

$$= \frac{365}{11.8} = 30.8 \text{ days}$$

The receivables turnover ratio and the average collection period provide some information on the success of the firm in managing its investment in accounts receivable. The actual value of these ratios reflects the effectiveness of the firm's credit policy. If a firm has a liberal credit policy, the amount of its receivables will be higher than would otherwise be the case. However, sales would presumably be higher as well. One common rule of thumb that financial analysts use is that the average collection period of a firm should not exceed the time allowed for payment in the credit terms by more than 10 days. A long average collection period may indicate customers are not repaying on a timely basis. Timberland's average collection period of 30.8 days, assuming a credit term period of

30 days (a common standard), suggests that their customers are timely in paying their bills to Timberland and that Timberland operates an efficient collections program.

Inventory Turnover

The ratio of *inventory turnover* is calculated by dividing the cost of goods sold by average inventory. Because inventory is stated in historical cost terms, it must be divided by cost of goods sold instead of sales (sales include a margin for profit and are not comparable with inventory). The number of days in the year divided by the ratio of inventory turnover yields *the ratio of days in inventory.* The ratio of days in inventory is the number of days it takes to get goods produced and sold; it is called *shelf life* for retail and wholesale trade firms. The inventory ratios for the Timberland Company are

$$\text{Inventory turnover} = \frac{\text{cost of goods sold}}{\text{inventory (average)}} = \frac{583}{123} = 4.7$$

$$\text{Average inventory} = \frac{132 + 115}{2} = 123$$

$$\text{Days in inventory} = \frac{\text{days in period}}{\text{inventory turnover}} = \frac{365}{4.7} = 77 \text{ days}$$

The inventory ratios measure how quickly inventory is produced from raw materials and sold to customers. They are significantly affected by, among other things, the production technology of goods being manufactured. It takes longer to produce a 747 airplane than a pint of Ben & Jerry's ice cream. The ratios also are affected by the perishability of the finished goods. A large increase in the ratio of days in inventory could suggest an excessive buildup of high inventory of unsold finished goods, or a change in the firm's product mix to goods with longer production periods. Clearly, a high ratio can serve as a warning that requires further investigation. The best way to use these numbers is in comparison within industries and to compare with historical numbers within a firm. For our Timberland example, the method of inventory valuation can also materially affect the computed inventory ratios. Thus, financial analysts should be aware of the different inventory valuation methods and how they might affect the ratios.

Financial Leverage

Financial leverage is related to the extent to which a firm relies on debt financing rather than equity. Measures of financial leverage are used in determining the probability that the firm may default on its debt contracts. The higher a firm's debt level, the more likely it is that the firm could become unable to fulfill its contractual obligations. Too much debt can lead to a higher probability of financial distress.

On the positive side, debt is an important form of financing, and provides a significant tax advantage because interest payments are tax deductible. Dividends and share repurchases are not tax deductible.

Debt Ratio

The *debt ratio* is calculated by dividing total debt by total assets. We can also use several other ways to express the extent to which a firm uses debt, such as the debt-equity ratio and the equity multiplier (that is, total assets divided by equity). The debt ratios for the Timberland Company for 2000 were

$$\text{Debt ratio} = \frac{\text{total debt}}{\text{total assets}} = \frac{160}{476} = 0.33$$

$$\text{Debt} - \text{equity ratio} = \frac{\text{total debt}}{\text{total equity}} = \frac{160}{317} = 0.5$$

$$\text{Equity multiplier} = \frac{\text{total assets}}{\text{total equity}} = \frac{476}{316} = 1.5$$

And all of these numbers suggest that while Timberland carries some debt, its assets and equity are large enough that it remains in a healthy financial position. Debt ratios provide information about the relative protection for creditors from insolvency and the ability of firms to obtain additional financing for potentially attractive investment opportunities. However, debt is carried on the balance sheet simply as the unpaid balance. Consequently, no adjustment is made for the current level of interest rates (which may be higher or lower than when the debt was originally issued) or risk. Thus, the accounting value of debt may differ substantially from its market value. Some forms of debt may not appear on the balance sheet at all, such as pension liabilities, lease obligations, or guarantee for subsidiary debt.

Interest Coverage

The ratio of *interest coverage* is calculated by dividing earnings (before interest and taxes) by interest. This ratio emphasizes the ability of the firm to generate enough income to cover interest expense. This ratio for the Timberland Company in 2000 was:

$$\text{Interest coverage} = \frac{\text{earnings before interest and taxes}}{\text{interest expense}}$$

$$= \frac{181}{5.6} = 32$$

The ratio of interest coverage is directly related to the ability of the firm to pay its ongoing interest obligations. However, it would probably make sense to add depreciation to income in computing this ratio and to include other financing expenses, such as payments of principal and lease payments. These adjustments would provide a better measure of the cash available to repay all of the firm's current financial obligations.

A large debt burden is a problem only if the firm's cash flow is insufficient to make the required debt service payments. This is related to the uncertainty of future cash flows. Firms with predictable cash flows are frequently said to have more *debt capacity* than firms with high, uncertain cash flows. We see this is the case with Timberland, because their interest coverage ratio is 32. Therefore, it may be useful to calculate the variability of the firm's cash flows. One possible way to do this is to calculate the standard deviation of cash flows relative to the average cash flow. Note, however, that this is done using historical information while it is really the variability of future earnings that matters to creditors.

Profitability

Accounting profits are the difference between revenues and costs. Unfortunately, there is no completely unambiguous way to know when a firm is profitable. At best, a financial analyst can measure current or past accounting profitability. Many business opportunities, however, involve sacrificing current profits for future profits. For example, all new products require large start-up costs and, as a consequence, produce low initial profits. Thus, current accounting profits can be a poor predictor of true future accounting profitability. Another problem with accounting-based measures of profitability is that they ignore risk. It would be false to conclude that two firms with identical current profits were equally profitable if the risk of one was greater than the other.

An important conceptual problem with accounting measures of profitability is they do not give us a benchmark for making comparisons. Thus, profitability measures are important to understand but difficult to rely upon.

Profit Margin

Profit margins are computed by dividing profits by total operating revenue. Thus they express profits as a percentage of total operating revenue. The most important margin is the *net profit margin.* The net profit margin for the Timberland Company for 2000 was:

$$\text{Net profit margin} = \frac{\text{net income}}{\text{total operating revenue}} = \frac{122}{1091} = 11\%$$

$$\text{Gross profit margin} = \frac{\text{earnings before interest and taxes}}{\text{total operating revenues}}$$

$$= \frac{181}{1091} = 16\%$$

In general, profit margins reflect the firm's ability to produce a project or service at either a low cost or a high price. Profit margins are not direct measures of profitability because they are based on total operating revenue, not on the investment made in assets by the firm or the equity investors. Different industries will have distinctly different profit margins. For example, the PC industry has shifted more towards a commodity business, shrinking profit margins. Timberland's net profit margin at 11 percent was within the range for the retail industry, where price is often how firms compete. However, here again it is extremely important to compare the profit margin with historical company data and within the context of any other changes (like a decrease in operating costs) that may effect it.

Return on Assets

One common measure of managerial performance is the ratio of income to average total assets, both before tax and after tax. These ratios for the Timberland Company for 2000 were:

$$\text{Net return on assets} = \frac{\text{net income}}{\text{average total assets}} = \frac{122}{485}$$

$$= 0.25 \ (25\%)$$

$$\text{Gross return on assets} = \frac{\text{earnings before interest and tax}}{\text{average total assets}}$$

$$= \frac{181}{485} = 0.37 \ (37\%)$$

Thus, for each dollar of Timberland assets, the management of Timberland earned 37 cents before payments to the suppliers of capital. Using this number over time, we can assess a management team's ability to generate profits. However, this is a somewhat limited perspective since it does not take into consideration the costs of financing.

One of the most interesting uses of the return on assets (ROA) measure is to see how some financial ratios can be combined to produce ROA. The Du Pont system emphasizes that ROA can be expressed in terms of the profit margin and asset turnover. The basic components of the system are as follows:

$$\text{ROA} = \text{profit margin} \times \text{asset turnover}$$

$$\text{ROA(net)} = \frac{\text{net income}}{\text{total operating revenue}}$$

$$\times \frac{\text{total operating revenue}}{\text{average total assets}}$$

$$0.25 = 0.11 \times 2.25$$

$$\text{ROA(gross)} = \frac{\text{earnings before interest and taxes}}{\text{total operating revenue}}$$

$$\times \frac{\text{total operating revenue}}{\text{average total assets}}$$

$$0.37 = 0.17 \times 2.25$$

Firms can increase ROA by increasing profit margins or asset turnover. Of course, competition limits their ability to do both simultaneously. Thus, firms tend to face a trade-off between turnover and margin.

It is often useful to describe financial strategies in terms of *margins* and *turnover*. Suppose a firm selling specialized electronic equipment is considering providing its customers with more liberal credit terms. This action will probably decrease asset turnover (because receivables would increase more than sales). This suggests that the margins will have to increase to keep ROA from declining.

Return on Equity

This ratio (ROE) is defined as net income (after interest and taxes) divided by average common stockholders' equity, which for the Timberland Company for 2000 was:

$$\text{ROE} = \frac{\text{net income}}{\text{average stockholders' equity}} = \frac{122}{295} = 0.41 \ (41\%)$$

$$\text{Average stockholders' equity} = \frac{317 + 272}{2} = 295$$

The most important distinction between a firm's ROA and ROE is due to financial leverage. To see this, consider the following breakdown of ROE:

$$\text{ROE} = \text{profit margin} \times \text{asset turnover} \times \text{equity multiplier}$$

$$= \frac{\text{net income}}{\text{total operating revenue}} \times \frac{\text{total operating revenue}}{\text{average total assets}}$$

$$\times \frac{\text{average total assets}}{\text{average stockholders' equity}}$$

$$0.41 = 0.11 \times 2.25 \times 1.65$$

Based upon these calculations, it would appear that financial leverage always increases ROE. Actually, this occurs only when ROA exceeds the interest rate on a firm's debt obligations. For Timberland, the shareholders' return on equity was 41 percent, which is greater than the 25 percent return on assets because of the financial leverage, or risk, that the shareholders undertook. The return on equity ratio is another means by which investors can evaluate a firm and its management team, particularly with regard to its financing decisions.

Payout Ratio

The *payout ratio* is the proportion of net income paid out in cash dividends. For the Timberland Company, it is zero, as no dividends were paid in 2000. Let's assume for the sake of calculation, however, that the Timberland Company paid $6,100,000 in dividends.

$$\text{Payout ratio} = \frac{\text{cash dividends}}{\text{net income}} = \frac{6,100}{121,998} = 5\%$$

Had the Timberland Company paid $6,100,000 in dividends, the *retention ratio* for the Timberland Company would have been:

$$\text{Retention ratio} = \frac{\text{retained earnings}}{\text{net income}} = \frac{115,898}{121,998} = 95\%$$

Retained earnings = net income – dividends

The Sustainable Growth Rate

One ratio that is very helpful in financial analysis is called the *sustainable growth rate.* It is the maximum rate of growth a firm can maintain without increasing its financial leverage and using internal equity only. The precise value of sustainable growth can be calculated as

Sustainable growth rate = ROE × retention ratio

For the Timberland Company, ROE is 41 percent. The retention ratio, had the Timberland Company paid $6,100,000 in dividends, would be 95 percent, so we can calculate the sustainable growth rate as

Sustainable growth rate = .41 × (.95) = 39%

The Timberland Company can expand at a maximum rate of 39 percent per year with no external equity financing or without increasing financial leverage if it paid the dividend. As the Timberland Company's actual dividend payout was zero, its actual sustainable growth rate is equal to its ROE of 41 percent.

Market Value Ratios

As our previous discussion indicates, we can learn many things from an analysis of a firm's balance sheets and income statements. However, one important measure of a firm's value that cannot be found on an accounting statement is its *market value*.

Market Price

The *market price* of a share of common stock is the price that buyers and sellers establish when they trade the stock. The *market value* of the common equity of a firm is the market price of a share of common stock multiplied by the number of shares outstanding.

Sometimes the words *fair market value* are used to describe market prices. Fair market value is the amount at which common stock would change hands between a willing buyer and a willing seller, both with knowledge of the relevant facts. Thus, market prices provide an assessment of how investors value the true worth of the assets of a firm. In an efficient stock market, market prices reflect all relevant facts about firms, and thus market prices reveal the true value of the firm's underlying assets. Thus, a stock price provides an important indication of how investors assess the operating and financial policies adopted by management.

Price-to-Earnings (P/E) Ratio

One way to calculate the *P/E ratio* is to divide the current market price by the earnings per share of common stock for the latest year. The P/E ratios of some of the largest firms in the United States, Japan, and Germany are as follows:

P/E RATIOS
2000

United States		Japan		Germany	
Exxon	16	Nippon Telegraph & Telephone	31	Allianz Holding	tbd
General Electric	34	Toyota Motor	33	Bayer	16
Coca-Cola	37	Tokyo Electric Power	tbd	Siemens	18

As can be seen, some firms have high P/E ratios (Nippon Telegraph & Telephone, for example) and some firms have low
ones (Exxon). The price of a stock (P) should be equal to the
current value of the future cash flows. Thus firms with high
P/E ratios are often growing firms, as the market expects
future cash flows to be much larger than current earnings.
Firms with low P/E ratios are often in low-growth industries.
Comparing P/E ratios across industries may not be particularly useful, as different industries tend to have dramatically
different mean P/E ratios.

Dividend Yield

The *dividend yield* is calculated by annualizing the last
observed dividend payment of a firm and dividing by the current market price:

$$\text{Dividend yield} = \frac{\text{dividend per share}}{\text{market price per share}}$$

The dividend yields for several large firms in the United
States, Japan, and Germany are:

DIVIDEND YIELD (%) 2001

United States		Japan		Germany	
Exxon	2.5	Nippon Denko Co.	0.6	Allianz Holding	0.9
General Electric	1.6	Toyota Motor	0.9	Bayer	4.4
Coca-Cola	1.5	Tokyo Electric Power	1.5	Siemens	2.7

Dividend yields are related to the market's perception of
future growth prospects for firms. Firms with high growth
prospects will generally have lower dividend yields.

Market-to-Book (M/B) Value and the Q Ratio

Making *value ratio* is calculated by dividing the market price
per share by the book value per share.

The market-to-book ratios of several of the largest firms in
the United States, Japan, and Germany are:

MARKET TO BOOK
2000

United States		Japan		Germany	
Exxon	4.0	Nippon Telegraph & Telephone	1.5	Allianz Holding	tbd
General Electric	9.0	Toyota Motor	1.9	Bayer	1.4
Coca-Cola	11.5	Tokyo Electric Power	tbd	Siemens	2.1

USES AND LIMITATIONS OF RATIO ANALYSIS

As noted earlier, ratio analysis is used by three main groups: (1) *managers,* who employ ratios to help analyze, control, and thus improve their firms' operations; (2) *credit analysts,* such as bank loan officers or bond rating analysts, who analyze ratios to help ascertain a company's ability to pay its debts; and (3) *stock analysts,* who are interested in a company's efficiency and growth prospects.

While ratio analysis can provide useful information concerning a company's operations and financial condition, it does have limitations that require caution and judgment. Some potential problems are:

1. Many large firms operate different divisions in different industries, and this makes it difficult to develop a meaningful set of industry averages for comparative purposes. Therefore, ratio analysis is more useful for small, narrowly focused firms than for large, multidivisional ones.

2. Most firms want to be better than average, so merely attaining average performance is not necessarily good. As a target for high-level performance, it is best to focus on the industry leaders' ratios.

3. Inflation may have badly distorted firms' balance sheets— recorded values are often substantially different from "true" values. Further, since inflation affects both depreciation charges and inventory costs, profits are also affected. Thus, a ratio analysis for one firm over time, or a comparative analysis of firms of different ages, must be interpreted with judgment.

4. Seasonal factors can also distort a ratio analysis. For example, the inventory turnover ratio for a toy company will be

radically different if the balance sheet figure used for inventory is the one just before versus just after the close of the Christmas season. Using monthly averages for inventory (and receivables) when calculating ratios such as turnover can reduce this problem.

5. Firms can employ techniques to make their financial statements look stronger. As an example, a company might borrow on a two-year basis on December 28, 2002, hold the proceeds of the loan as cash for a few days; and then pay off the loan on January 2, 2003. This economically meaningless transaction improved the firm's current and quick ratios and made the year-end 2002 balance sheet look good. However, the improvement was strictly temporary. One week later the balance sheet was back at the old level.

6. Different accounting practices can distort comparisons. As noted earlier, inventory valuation and depreciation methods can affect financial statements and thus distort comparisons among firms. If one firm leases a substantial amount of its productive equipment, then its assets may appear low relative to sales because leased assets often do not appear on the balance sheet. At the same time, the lease liability may not be shown as a debt. Therefore, leasing can artificially improve both the turnover and the debt ratios.

7. It is difficult to generalize about whether a particular ratio is "good" or "bad." For example, a high current ratio may indicate a strong liquidity position, which is good, or excessive cash, which is bad (because excess cash in the bank is a nonearning asset). Similarly, a high fixed assets turnover ratio may denote either a firm that uses its assets efficiently or one that is undercapitalized and cannot afford to buy enough assets.

8. A firm may have some ratios that look "good" and others that look "bad," making it difficult to tell whether the company is, on balance, strong or weak. However, statistical procedures can be used to analyze the net effects of a set of ratios. Many banks and other lending organizations use statistical procedures to analyze firms' financial ratios, and, on the basis of their analyses, classify companies according to their probability of getting into financial trouble.

Ratio analysis is useful, but analysts should be aware of these problems and make necessary adjustments. Ratio analysis conducted in a mechanical, unthinking manner is misleading, but used intelligently and with good judgment, it can provide useful insights into a firm's operations.

SUMMARY

The field of accounting is a complex and challenging component of any business organization. Accountants are responsible for accurately and concisely summarizing many crucial aspects of a firm's operations for a variety of internal and external constituencies. Thus, the challenge is to provide information that reflects the changing dynamics of the modern business organization. As the nature of competition and the information needs of decision makers continue to evolve, the field of accounting will continue to change in a responsible manner.

INTERNET RESOURCES

Accountingweb (www.accountingweb.com/). Stay on top of daily accounting news stories and keep abreast of current trends and issues with the site's free weekly e-mail newswires. Explore lots of "what-if" scenarios with the help of financial calculators, and study new practice management ideas that have emerged.

IMA (www.imanet.org). The IMA is the leading professional organization devoted exclusively to management accounting and financial management. Statements on management accounting (SMAs) present the views of IMA regarding management accounting issues in reports—some of which can be downloaded from the web. Studies analyze the continued evolution of the accounting and finance profession.

Management Accounting Quarterly (www.mamag.com). An online archive of quarterly issues of the magazine dating back to Fall 1999; grapples with the most current and pertinent management accounting issues.

Rutgers Accounting Web (accounting.rutgers.edu/index.html). A gateway to every accounting-related topic imaginable, from associations to an accounting research directory.

ACCOUNTING CRITICAL REFERENCE MATERIALS

Atkinson, Anthony A. et al. *Management Accounting.* Englewood Cliffs, NJ: Prentice Hall, 1995.

Management Accounting is an inviting, colorful textbook that introduces students to the new role for management accounting and control information in organizations. The text focuses on organizational activities, and there is an emphasis on real-world examples. Topics include management accounting (information that creates value), managing activities, cost concepts, cost behavior, budgeting for operations, basic product costing systems, two-stage allocations and activity-bases costing systems, pricing and product mix decisions, process and activity decisions, capital budgeting, planning and control, financial control, compensation and behavioral and organizational issues in management accounting and control system design.

Choi, Frederick D.S. *Handbook of International Accounting.* New York: John Wiley & Sons, 1991.

The *Handbook of International Accounting* is helpful for anyone interested in the international aspects of accounting, reporting, and control. The text consists of 30 articles in 8 different topical sections. Each article is written by different leading academics and practicing businessmen. All of the Big-Six accounting firms contributed articles to the book and all of the contributing academics have had experience as consultants in their given fields.

Crouhy, Michel, Robert Mark, and Dan Galai. *Risk Management.* New York: McGraw-Hill Professional Publishing, 2000.

The bailout of Long-Term Capital Management and the Enron debacle have increased awareness of risk management and have led to new developments in research, techniques, and theories in the field. Given the high stakes in today's business world, with financial dealings in the billions (e.g., derivatives), it's clear why risk management has become a buzzword on the Street. *Managing Risk Management* provides a comprehensive description and analysis of modern risk management, including regulatory aspects, organizational issues, and tools to control and manage different kinds of risks: market risk, credit risk, and operational risk. The book also discusses structuring and managing the risk management function in a firm;

practical measurement issues in the field; and risk management in financial as well as nonfinancial institutions.

Gates, Sheldon. *101 Business Ratios: A Manager's Handbook of Definitions, Equations, and Computer Algorithms: How to Select, Compute, Present, and Understand Measures of Sales, Profit, Debt, Capital, Efficiency, Marketing, and Investment.* Scottsdale, AZ: McLane Publications, 1993.

101 Business Ratios is mostly directed toward managers of small and medium-sized businesses. The book is divided into two major parts. The first part introduces the reader to ratio analysis and then describes 101 specific measures, as well as formulas for their computation. The second section focuses on the use of these ratios (how to find the input numbers, how to calculate the ratios, and how to present them). The book also contains a glossary of technical terms, a list of ratios, a list of input statistics, a usage table, and suggestions for acronymic naming of variables and stock market ratios.

Horngren, Charles T. *Introduction to Financial Accounting.* Englewood Cliffs, NJ: Prentice Hall, 1988.

Introduction to Financial Accounting is a textbook meant to provide students with the essentials of financial and managerial accounting. It is for introductory courses and assumes the reader has no prior knowledge of accounting. The text consists of three major sections: (1) fundamentals of accounting; (2) some major elements of financial accounting; and (3) some financial reporting perspectives. Problems and cases can be found throughout the text.

Huefner, Ronald J. *Advanced Financial Accounting.* Chicago: Dryden Press, 1986.

Advanced Financial Accounting is a textbook intended to teach students some of the more advanced accounting topics. Topics covered in this text are: entity concept and personal financial statements, partnership accounting, fiduciary accounting, home office and branch accounting, business combinations and consolidated financial statements, segment and interim reporting, the Securities and Exchange Commission (SEC) and its role in financial accounting and reporting, accounting for international operations and government and nonprofit organizations. Exercises and problems are found throughout the text.

Kieso, Donald E. *Intermediate Accounting.* New York: John Wiley & Sons, 1989.

Intermediate Accounting is a lengthy textbook intended to give students an in-depth study of traditional financial accounting topics and accounting valuation and reporting practices. Examples from actual businesses are used to help students further understand the theories and practices. The text is divided into six main parts: (1) financial accounting functions and basic theory; (2) assets—recognition and measurement; (3) liabilities—recognition and measurement; (4) stockholders' equity, dilutive securities, and investments; (5) issues related to income measurement; and (6) preparation and analysis of financial statements.

Shank, John K., and Vijay Govindarajan. *Strategic Cost Management: The New Tool for Competitive Advantage.* New York: The Free Press, 1993.

This award-winning book, published in seven languages, presents a point of view in which issues of cost and profit are seen in their strategic context, rather than as topics in accounting methodology. Concepts such as value chain, activity costing, cost of quality, competitor costing, and balanced scorecard are described, illustrated, and evaluated.

Stickney, Clyde P. *Financial Accounting: An Introduction to Concepts, Methods, and Uses.* Fort Worth, TX: Dryden Press, 2000

Financial Accounting is a textbook that was created to help students understand the basic concepts of financial statements and to train them in accounting terminology and methods. The text has 16 chapters in four major sections: (1) overview of financial statements (2) accounting concepts and methods (3) measuring and reporting assets and equities (4) and synthesis. Problems and cases based on financial statement data are at the end of most chapters.

Stickney, Clyde P. *Financial Reporting and Statement Analysis: A Strategic Perspective.* Fort Worth, TX: Dryden Press, 1999

Financial Reporting and Statement Analysis is a textbook that hopes to teach students the analysis of financial statements by performing the analysis on actual companies. The text explains the important concepts, and analytical tools, and then applies them to the financial statements of Coca-Cola and Pepsi. Each chapter also contains problem sets that are based on the financial data of actual companies.

Wiley GAAP 2002: Interpretations and Applications of Generally Accepted Accounting Principles 2002. New York: John Wiley & Sons, 2001.

This is a standard used by accountants in need of up-to-the-minute GAAP coverage. This authoritative, comprehensive resource thoroughly studies and analyzes all generally accepted accounting principles (GAAP) set forth in the pronouncements of the Financial Accounting Standards Board. Wiley GAAP 2002 also contains AICPA Accounting Standards Executive Committee statements of positions. All pronouncements are explained with relevant terminology and practice-oriented, real-world examples. With examples, illustrations, and user-friendly practice tips.

Finance

Understanding corporate finance is not only integral to the successful operation of any business, but it is also key to understanding the specifics of how a firm's strategies have been prioritized and how its managers have used their available options to attain any specific goals. This is important information for you as an investor, as a potential employee, or as a competitor. For a manager within any firm, understanding corporate finance means understanding your financial options and limitations, as well as possessing a holistic understanding of the effect some financial decisions can have on your firm's value. Recent years have been filled with great complexities of change and activity within the corporate finance realm: the internet boom's high valuations and initial public offerings, financial restructurings, derivatives, and bankruptcies. In this chapter, then, we will focus on a discussion of financial management within the modern business corporation.

First, as an overview, let us look broadly at the field of finance. This field consists of three interrelated areas:

1. Money and capital markets. *Money markets* are the markets for debt securities that must be repaid within one year. *Capital markets* are the markets for debt securities that repay beyond one year, and for equity shares. *Equity shares* can be one of two types: *preferred stock* or *common*

stock. Common stock represents an ownership of a corporation; common shareholders are entitled to receive distributions of corporate earnings or assets after all other capital claimants have been paid. Preferred stock is a type of stock whose holders receive priority over common shareholders in the payment of dividends. Usually, however, dividend payments to preferred shareholders are fixed.

2. Investments. *Investments* focus on the decisions of individual and institutional investors as they choose securities for their portfolios. Successful investing requires an analysis of the potential risks and rewards of individual securities, and the ability to combine securities profitably in a portfolio. Most institutions and individuals will hire investment professionals to provide information and advise them in their investment decisions. Well-known examples of investment brokers include Merrill Lynch and Charles Schwab.

3. Financial management. *Financial management* describes the actual management of a firm in terms of investments, raising money, and managing cash inflow and outflow. Within most firms, this role is carried out by a Chief Financial Officer and, depending on the size of the firm, an entire department of financial analysts.

We focus here on financial managers because their decisions directly influence the value of their firms. They seek to increase their firm's value by making intelligent decisions in three important areas. First, financial managers choose which long-term investment projects the firm should undertake; this is referred to as the *capital budgeting decision*. Second, they raise the money needed to finance investment projects; this is referred to as the *financing decision*. Third, they determine how the firm's cash position and other short-term financial affairs (e.g., inventory policy or credit extension decisions) should be managed; these are referred to as the *net working capital* and *cash management decisions*. Because finance provides quantified values for the operating policies and business strategies of a firm at any specified point in time, it also is often used as an objective means for assessing the success or failure of past decisions.

FINANCIAL GOALS OF THE MODERN CORPORATION

In this chapter we assume that a financial manager's primary goal is maximizing shareholder wealth, which is equivalent to maximizing the price of the firm's common stock. Managers should, of course, establish and pursue other objectives as well. For example, managers also are interested in their own personal welfare, in their employees' welfare, as well as their reputation among key constituencies. Still, for the reasons we describe throughout this chapter, *share price maximization* is one of the most important goals for corporations. Moreover, share price maximization creates the most value for managers and shareholders seeking to pursue additional objectives.

Shareholders own the firm and elect the board of directors, which then appoints the corporation's management. Management, in turn, is supposed to make decisions that are in the best interests of all the shareholders. Later in this chapter, we discuss the most important decisions that managers make to achieve this objective. We know, however, that because the stock of most large corporations is widely held by a large number of shareholders, managers of large corporations have a great deal of autonomy. Because most corporations have a large number of owners (shareholders), each with a relatively small ownership of the corporation, managers could be tempted to pursue goals other than stock price maximization. For example, managers of a large, well-established corporation might decide to work just hard enough to keep stockholder returns at a "reasonable" level and then devote the remainder of their efforts and resources to higher executive salaries, or to other activities or expenditures that don't necessarily increase the firm's stock price.

Unfortunately, no one outside the firm can easily determine whether a particular management team is continually striving to maximize shareholder wealth or is merely attempting to keep shareholders satisfied while pursuing their own personal goals. For example, how can we tell whether employee or community benefit programs are in the long-run best interests of the shareholders? Similarly, was it really necessary for Walt Disney to pay its chairman Michael Eisner, more than $200 million in the mid-1990s to obtain and reward his services, or was this just another example of a manager taking advantage of shareholders?

Obviously we do not have definitive answers to these critical questions. However, managers of firms operating in markets subject to intense competition from other corporations will be forced to undertake actions that are reasonably consistent with shareholder wealth maximization. If they depart too far from this objective, they risk being removed from their jobs by their own board of directors, or through a hostile takeover or a proxy fight.

A *hostile takeover* is the acquisition of one company by another despite the opposition of management, while a *proxy fight* involves one group trying to gain management control of a corporation by getting shareholders to vote a new management group into place. Both actions are more likely to occur and succeed if a firm's stock price is low, so to retain their jobs, managers try to keep stock prices as high as possible. Successful hostile takeovers and proxy fights often result in the dismissal of top management from their jobs. Therefore, while some managers may be more interested in their own personal welfare than in maximizing shareholder wealth, the threat of losing their jobs motivates them to try to maximize stock prices. Many of the most spectacular takeover contests during the past two decades were precipitated by the conflict of interest between managers and shareholders. A crucial task for any modern-day manager is to manage corporate resources efficiently to achieve all of his or her objectives. Throughout the remainder of this chapter, we describe and develop a basic understanding of how a successful manager can make sound financial decisions.

WHAT IS FINANCIAL MANAGEMENT?

Thus far, we have suggested that the financial manager should act to increase the value of the shareholders' investment in the firm. But thousands of people are employed in a large company. Each individual considers his or her own personal interests as well as that of the shareholders. Modern corporate finance deals not only with the financial objectives of the firm, but also with the selection of appropriate reward and penalty systems to ensure that each member of the organization works toward the same objective.

Think of the company's net revenue as a pie divided among a number of claimants. These include the management and the employees as well as the lenders and shareholders who have put up the money to establish and finance the continuing operations of the business. The government is a claimant, too, since it gets to tax the profits of the enterprise.

All these claimants are bound together in a complex web of contractual relationships, alliances, and understandings. For example, when banks lend money to the firm, they insist on a formal, legal contract that specifically lists the interest rate and repayment dates, plus some additional restrictions (called *covenants*) on dividends or further borrowing in the future. Such a contract serves as a binding legal restriction on the future actions of the firm. Realistically, however, it is impossible to devise reasonable restrictions to cover every possible future event. So the explicit, legal contracts are often supplemented by implicit or explicit understandings. For example, managers understand that in return for a high salary they are expected to work hard on behalf of shareholders and not to divert corporate resources for their own personal benefit.

What enforces this type of understanding? Can we expect financial managers always to act on behalf of the shareholders? Most shareholders can't afford to spend their time monitoring every action of the manager to ensure that sound decision-making practices are being followed.

Various institutional arrangements have developed through time in an effort to help align managers' and shareholders' interests. Consider the following two examples:

1. Managers are subject to the scrutiny of specialists. Their actions are monitored by the board of directors and reviewed by banks; banks keep an eagle eye on the progress of firms receiving loans. Today, institutional investors are also very active at seeking information in an attempt to ensure that a firm is being managed with the best interests of the shareholders in mind.

2. Managers are motivated by incentives schemes, such as stock options, which pay off big if stock prices increase but are worthless if they do not.

These observations are not meant to suggest that all corporate life is a sequence of conflicts. It isn't, because practical corporate finance has gradually developed a variety of solutions to reconcile personal and corporate interests—to keep everyone working together to increase the value of the whole pie, not merely the size of each person's slice.

Nevertheless, the financial manager must stay alert to potential problems caused by conflicts of interest. We, too, have to think about potential conflicts to understand fully why takeovers occur, why lending contracts restrict dividend payouts, or why companies sometimes prefer to issue bonds that investors can convert to shares. We discuss some of these arrangements in more detail in the following section.

The Balance-Sheet Model of the Firm

Suppose we take a financial snapshot of the firm at a single point in time. The snapshot should contain a summary of all of the investment and financing decisions made by a firm throughout its relevant history. This information is contained in a firm's balance sheet (see the Accounting chapter for a more in-depth discussion of the balance sheet), which shows where and how the company raised its money and how it has spent it. Figure 7.1 shows a graphic conceptualization of the balance sheet that will help introduce you to corporate finance.

The assets of the firm are on the left-hand side of the balance sheet. Assets represent how a firm has spent its time and money, and are usually categorized as either current or fixed. *Fixed assets* are those that will last a long time, such as a building. Some fixed assets are *tangible,* such as machinery and equipment. Other fixed assets are *intangible,* such as patents, trademarks, and the quality of management. The other category of assets, *current assets,* comprises those that have short lives, such as inventory or accounts receivable. The products that your firm has made but has not yet sold are part of its *inventory.* Unless you have overproduced, the products will eventually be sold. At that time, one asset (inventory) will be converted into another (cash).

Before a corporation can invest in an asset, it must obtain funding, which means that it must raise the money to pay for the investment. Many firms obtain funding from a variety of different sources. The right-hand side of a firm's balance sheet sometimes summarizes the outstanding different types of financing the firm has used, and hence we often observe a number of sources rather than just a single provider. A firm

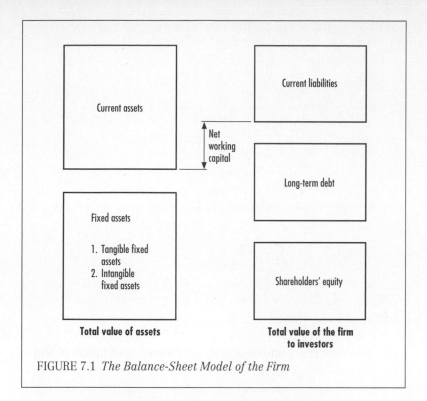

FIGURE 7.1 *The Balance-Sheet Model of the Firm*

will issue (sell) pieces of paper called *debt* (loan agreements) or *equity shares* (stock certificates). Debt obligations are owed to creditors, and the shareholders are the debtors. Typically, however, shareholders have the right of limited liability, which means they are not personally responsible for repaying the firm's credit obligations. Therefore, lenders base their loan decisions on the basis of their assessment of the corporation's ability (and willingness) to repay its credit obligations. Liabilities, like assets, are long-lived or short-lived. A short-term loan or debt obligation is called a *current liability. Short-term debt* represents loans and other obligations that must be repaid within one year. *Long-term debt* is debt that does not have to be repaid within one year. *Shareholders' equity* represents the difference between the value of the assets and the debt of the firm. These are the claims held by the owners of the corporation. In this sense it is considered a residual claim on the firm's assets. That is, shareholders get paid only after all other financial obligations of the firm have been satisfied.

From the balance-sheet model of the firm it is easy to see why financial management can be thought of as answering the following three questions:

1. In what long-lived fixed assets should the firm invest its financial resources? This question concerns the left-hand side of the balance sheet. Of course, the nature of the business the firm has chosen to operate in typically determines the type and proportions of assets the firm needs. We use the terms *capital budgeting* and *capital expenditure* to describe the process of committing investment capital and managing expenditures on long-lived assets. An example would be whether Ben & Jerry's should build a new manufacturing plant to meet the expected increase in demand for its ice cream products.

2. How should the firm raise the cash necessary to finance its capital expenditures? This question concerns the right-hand side of the balance sheet. These decisions establish the firm's *capital structure,* which represents the proportions of the firm's financing from current and long-term debt and equity. Continuing with our Ben & Jerry's plant expansion decision, if the management decides to proceed with its planned capital expenditure, should it issue debt or equity to finance the project?

3. How should short-term operating cash flows be managed? This question concerns the upper portion of the balance sheet. Depending on the industry in which a firm operates, there may be a mismatch between the timing of cash inflows and cash outflows during its operating cycle. Furthermore, neither the amount or the timing of operating cash inflows and outflows are known with certainty. Financial managers must establish policies and procedures to manage the temporary shortfalls (or excess inflows) in cash flow. Short-term management of cash flow is described by a firm's *net working capital* position. Net working capital is defined as current assets minus current liabilities. From a financial perspective, the short-term cash flow problem comes from the mismatching of cash inflows and outflows. It is the subject of short-term finance. Decisions such as how much inventory to carry, and how much customer credit should be extended are typical problems addressed here.

Capital Structure

Sometimes it is useful to think of the firm as a pie. The size of the pie will depend on how well the firm has made its investment decisions. After a firm has made its investment decisions, the value of its assets (e.g., its buildings, land, and inventories) is determined.

Financing arrangements determine how a firm's value is divided among the various entities that have provided funding for the corporation. The persons or institutions that buy debt from the firm are called *creditors*. The holders of equity shares are called *shareholders*. In terms of our "firm-as-a-pie" analogy, financing arrangements determine how the pie is sliced. Creditors and shareholders are entitled to slices, and the size of those slices depends on how well the firm makes its investment decisions as well as how much money each initially contributed to the firm.

The firm then determines its capital structure. The firm might initially have raised the cash to invest in its assets by issuing more debt than equity. Subsequently it might consider changing that mix by issuing more equity and using the proceeds to invest in new projects or to buy back some of its debt. Financing decisions like the latter can often be made independently of the original investment decisions. The decisions to issue debt and equity should be thought of as primarily affecting how the pie is sliced. They can, however, also affect the size of the pie itself. Thus, a creative financial manager can affect value through both investing and financing activities.

Figure 7.2 provides a pictorial representation of this discussion. The size of the pie is the value of the firm in the financial markets, and it reflects investors' understanding of the investing and financing activities of the firm. We can describe the value of the firm, V as consisting of two parts,

$$V = B + S$$

where B is the value of the debt and S is the value of the equity. The pie diagram illustrates two different ways of slicing the pie (i.e., financing the firm): 50 percent debt and 50 percent equity, and 25 percent debt and 75 percent equity. The way the pie is sliced could affect its value. If so, the goal of the financial manager will be to choose the optimal financing

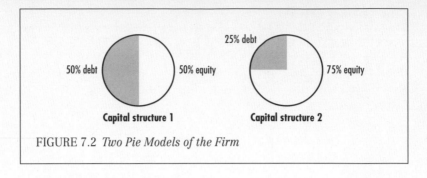

FIGURE 7.2 *Two Pie Models of the Firm*

arrangement that makes the value of the pie—that is, the value of the firm, *V*—as large as possible.

THE ROLE OF THE MODERN FINANCIAL MANAGER

In large firms, the finance function is usually associated with a top officer of the corporation, generally a vice president and chief financial officer, and some lesser officers and employees. The treasurer and the controller each report to the chief financial officer, and both have well-defined areas of responsibility within the firm. The treasurer is responsible for handling short-term (daily) cash flows, making capital-expenditure decisions, and recommending financial plans to raise funds from external sources. Typically, these decisions are projected over a three- to five-year time horizon. The controller handles the accounting responsibilities, which include tax management and planning, cost and financial statement accounting, and information systems.

As we've already stated, the most important job of a financial manager is to create value from the firm's capital budgeting, financing, and working capital management decisions. Financial managers create value in two general ways:

1. The firm acquires assets that generate more cash for the firm than they cost.

2. The firm sells stocks and bonds and other financial instruments that raise more cash than they cost in terms of expected future payments.

Thus, in both cases, the firm creates more cash flow than it uses to increase value. The cash flow paid to bondholders and shareholders of the firm should be higher than the cash flows put into the firm by the bondholders and shareholders. To see how this works, we can trace the cash flows from the firm to the financial markets and back again.

The interaction of the firm's financial decisions with the financial markets is illustrated in Figure 7.3. The arrows in Figure 7.3 trace cash flow from investors in the financial markets to the firm and back again. Consider first the firm's financing activities. To raise money the firm sells debt and common stock to investors in the financial markets. This results in cash flows from the financial markets to the firm (A). This cash is invested in the investment activities of the firm (B) by the firm's management. The cash generated by the firm (C) is paid to shareholders and bondholders (F). The shareholders receive cash in the form of dividends or share repurchases; the bondholders who loaned funds to the firm receive interest payments and, when the initial loan is repaid, principal. Not all of the firm's cash is paid out. Some is retained to repay the firm's future financial obligations or reinvested in new assets (E), and some is paid to the government as taxes (D).

Over time, if the cash paid to shareholders and bondholders (F) is greater than the cash raised in the financial markets (A), value will be created.

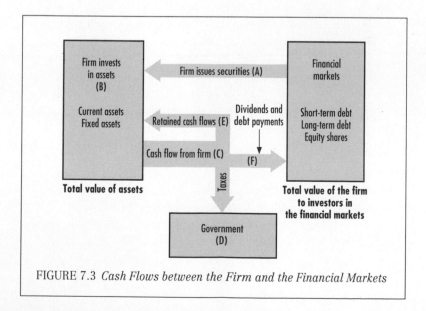

FIGURE 7.3 *Cash Flows between the Firm and the Financial Markets*

While this process may seem quite straightforward, the best financial managers must actively coordinate a wide variety of activities within the firm to ensure consistency of objectives. Here are some specific activities that the financial manager participates in to maximize the value of the firm:

1. *Forecasting and planning.* The financial staff interacts with officers and employees from other departments such as marketing, engineering, and production to project the firm's future plans and to assess the impact of those plans on the firm's financial health.

2. *Major investment and financing decisions.* A successful firm usually has rapid growth in sales, which requires investments in plant, equipment, and working capital. The financial manager determines the most efficient sales growth rate and helps to decide on the specific assets to acquire as well as the best way to finance those assets. For example, should the firm finance with debt or equity, and if debt is used, should it be long term or short term? Ultimately, a financial manager must convey that there's a big difference between profitable and unprofitable growth, no matter how fast sales are increasing.

3. *Coordination and control.* The financial staff also interacts with other officers and employees to ensure that the firm's operating and financing plans are implemented as efficiently as possible. All business decisions have financial implications, and all managers—financial and otherwise—need to understand this principle. For example, marketing decisions affect sales growth, which in turn affects investment and working capital requirements. Thus marketing decision makers must be able to understand how their actions affect (and are affected by) factors such as the availability of funds, inventory policies, receivables policies, and plant capacity utilization.

4. *Dealing with the financial markets.* The financial staff interacts with the money and capital markets to communicate the rationale behind its investment decisions. Every firm affects and is affected by the general financial markets—it is where funds are raised, where the firm's securities are traded, and where its investors are either rewarded or penalized. Because a firm's stock price is an

informative indicator of how well the firm's operating and financing plans are working as well as how investors view those plans, it is closely monitored by both investors and managers. This direct link between management decisions and stock prices also provides the firm with real-time feedback on the corporation's overall strategy.

In summary, financial managers make decisions regarding which assets their firms should invest in, how those assets should be financed, and how the firm should manage its existing resources and future opportunities. If these responsibilities are performed well, financial managers help maximize the value of their firms, and also maximize the long-run welfare of other corporate stakeholders such as customers who buy products from the corporation, suppliers who provide productive inputs for the firm, and employees who work for the company.

MANAGEMENT DECISIONS AND SHAREHOLDER VALUE

A firm's financing decision always reflects some view about the current status and future outlook of the capital markets. For example, suppose a firm chooses to finance a major expansion program by issuing debt. The financial manager first considers the terms of the debt issue and determines what price is fair. In addition, the manager has to determine whether the firm's shareholders are better or worse off by issuing additional debt to finance the firm's operating activities. Both of these decisions require a deep understanding of the capital markets and how corporate borrowing affects the value of a firm's shares.

Understanding how the capital markets function is the same thing as understanding how investors value financial assets. New theories during the last two decades have been developed to explain how investors price stocks and bonds. These theories have worked well in the sense that they seem to provide fairly accurate explanations of the link between financial managers' decisions and changes in financial security prices. Let us now examine some of the key factors an investment manager considers before making any investment decisions.

Time and Uncertainty

The astute financial manager must factor in what effect uncertainty and time may have on the value generated by an investment decision. Firms often have the opportunity to invest in assets that generate little or no cash flow in the short run and expose the firm and its shareholders to considerable risk. Good examples of this type of investment are research and development expenses. The investment, if undertaken, may have to be financed by debt that cannot be fully repaid for many years. The firm cannot simply ignore that such choices involve difficult trade-offs—someone has to decide whether the opportunity is worth more than its costs and whether the additional debt burden can be safely borne. An improper assessment of the costs and benefits of such decisions can create financial hardship for the corporation, or even bankruptcy.

Understanding the Value of Information

Information is an unusual and valuable commodity throughout the world of business. In financial markets, the right information can be worth millions—but only if other investors do not have the same information at the same time. Suppose, for example, you learn that one company will imminently make a takeover offer to acquire another company at a price that significantly exceeds that company's current market price. Such information is potentially worth a tremendous amount of money. Unfortunately, fiduciary responsibilities and legal restrictions preclude the selective dissemination of valuable information prior to complete public disclosure. Because financial markets are efficient, as soon as important financial information is revealed, it travels instantly to New York, London, Tokyo, and all the other major financial centers.

Companies spend considerable time and money providing information to investors. If they did not do so, investors would be skeptical and unsure of a firm's future prospects. They would have to expend personal resources trying to collect information for themselves, and they would be unwilling to pay as much for the firm's shares. This would increase the company's cost of obtaining the financing it needs for its investment decisions. This would reduce a firm's ability to invest profitably, hurting society as a result.

As the saying goes, talk is cheap. Should investors trust the information given out by companies? The answer is: not always. But institutions have been created to reduce this credibility problem. Sometimes a firm of accountants or investment bankers, who put their reputations on the line when they certify a company's financial reports and statements, certifies the information. Sometimes managers send a message of confidence by "putting money where their mouth is." For example, it is easier to raise money for a new business if you have already invested a large fraction of your own net worth in the company.

Many financial decisions take on extra importance because they convey or signal information to investors. For example, the decision to reduce the cash dividends paid out to shareholders usually signals trouble for the firm. The stock price may fall sharply when the dividend cut is announced, not because of the dividend cut per se, but because the cut portends poor performance in the future. Given the complexities a financial manager must factor into any decision, how does one act to create value?

How Do Managers Maximize Share Price?

What types of decisions and actions should management take to maximize the stock price of their firm? First, consider the potential link between stock prices and profit. Does *profit maximization* result in stock price maximization? If so, then a manager can simply concentrate his or her effort on the tangible objective of profit maximization. Investors in the financial markets can then price the company's stock appropriately. To answer this question, we must consider the relationship and distinction between total corporate profits and *earnings per share* (EPS).

For example, suppose IBM had 50 million shares outstanding and earned $200 million, or $4 per share. If you owned 50 shares of the stock, your share of the total profits would be $200. Now suppose IBM sold another 50 million shares and invested the funds received in assets that produced $50 million of income. Total income would rise to $250 million, but earnings per share would decline from $4 to $250/100 = $2.50. Now your proportional share of the firm's earnings would be $250, far below the anticipated $400. You (and other current shareholders) would incur what is known as *earnings dilution,* even though total corporate profits had risen. Therefore, other things held constant, this example suggests that if management is interested in the welfare of its current shareholders, it should perhaps concentrate on maximizing earnings per share rather than total corporate profits. If we refer back to our "firm-as-a-pie" analogy, although the pie has grown larger in this example, the new shareholders receive a disproportionately large piece.

Next, we consider the question of whether maximization of expected earnings per share will always maximize stockholder welfare. Should management also consider other factors in its decision? Let's consider the *timing of the earnings.* Suppose IBM had one project that would increase earnings per share by $0.20 per year for 5 years, or $1 in total. Management would like to compare this project against an alternative project that would have no effect on earnings for 4 years but would increase earnings by $1.25 in the fifth year. Because management must choose between these two alternatives, such projects are referred to as mutually exclusive. Which project is more beneficial for shareholders? In other words, is $0.20 per year for 5 years better or worse than $1.25 in Year 5? The answer depends on which project adds the most to the value of the stock, which in turn depends on the time value of money to investors. Thus, timing is an important reason to concentrate on wealth as measured by the price of the stock rather than on earnings alone. Therefore, managers need an accurate, straightforward method for assessing the impact of time on the value of the firm's stock price.

Another issue relates to risk associated with investment projects. Suppose one project is expected to increase earnings per share by $1, while another is expected to raise earnings by $1.20 per share. Now let's suppose that the first project is not very risky. It is expected that if the project is undertaken, earnings will almost certainly rise by about $1 per share. However, the other project is considered quite risky by management and shareholders, so while our best estimate is that earnings will increase by $1.20 per share, we must realistically consider and weigh the possibility that there may be no earnings increase at all, or even a reduction in overall corporate earnings. Depending on how adverse shareholders are to risk, the first project might be preferable to the second. Therefore, managers need a methodology that allows them to assess the trade-off accurately between the expected returns and risks associated with alternative investment decisions.

The risk inherent in a firm's projected earnings per share (EPS) also depends on how the firm is financed. Many firms go bankrupt every year, and the greater the use of debt, the greater the threat of bankruptcy. Consequently, while the use of debt financing may increase projected EPS, debt also increases the riskiness of projected future earnings. There-fore, managers need to assess whether the additional finan-cial risk created for the firm's shareholders by the use of higher levels of debt creates a sufficient reward opportunity. The increase in EPS may be more than offset by the higher level of risk, or the risk may not be warranted given a small increase in EPS.

If a firm is profitable, management must decide whether it should retain earnings and reinvest them in the firm, or pay dividends to the firm's shareholders. Dividends return cash to shareholders, while retentions will increase future profits and thereby create the opportunity for higher dividends in the future. Shareholders like cash dividends, but they also like the future growth in EPS that results from reinvesting earnings profitably back into the business. A financial manager decides exactly how much of the current earnings to pay out as divi-dends as opposed to how much to retain and reinvest—that is called the *dividend policy decision*. The optimal dividend pol-icy is the one that maximizes the firm's stock price.

Our discussion thus far suggests that the firm's stock price depends on the following factors:

1. Projected earnings per share
2. Timing of the earnings stream
3. Riskiness of the projected earnings
4. Use of debt
5. Dividend policy

Every significant corporate decision by management should be evaluated in terms of its effect on these factors and hence on the price of the firm's stock. For example, suppose Gen-eral Mills' restaurant division is considering developing a new line of eateries. If management decides to implement this new policy, management first assesses whether it can be expected to increase EPS. Is there a chance that operating costs will exceed estimates, that prices and customer patronage will fall below projections, and that EPS will be reduced because the new restaurant line was introduced? How long will it take for the new restaurant division to show a profit? How should the capital required to finance construction and invest in equipment be raised? If debt is used, by how much will this increase General Mills' riskiness? Should General Mills reduce its current dividends and use the cash thus saved to finance the project, or should it maintain its dividends and finance the additional restaurants with external capital? The methods of corporate finance provide a framework that is designed to help managers answer questions like these, plus many more.

A BASIC METHODOLOGY FOR MEASURING VALUE

As we've covered, financial managers need to know how value is determined for both *financial assets* (such as stocks and bonds) and *real assets* (such as projects, business units, or even whole companies). In both cases, value depends directly on the cash flows the assets are expected to produce. The process of valuing streams of future cash flows is called *discounted cash flow (DCF) analysis.* The DCF methodology is a widely used framework with many applications in corporate finance. Some common applications include estimating a firm's cost of capital, assessing the valuation effects of issuing different types of securities, determining the value of new investment projects, and estimating the value of takeover targets.

The fundamental underlying rationale for discounted cash flow (DCF) analysis is the *time value of money.* A dollar in hand today is worth more than a dollar due some time in the future, because a dollar received today can be invested and thus be worth more than a dollar in the future. The DCF methodology tells a financial manager how much additional value would be gained or lost by changing the timing of cash flows from an investment.

The actual process of performing a discounted cash flow analysis can be broken down into four steps.

1. *Estimate the future cash flows.* Estimating future cash flows for some assets, such as bonds, is relatively easy. In

that case, since the asset's cash flows are contractually fixed, the promised flows will be realized unless the issuer defaults. Estimating cash flows for other classes of assets can be extremely difficult. This is because cash flows from other assets are more difficult to estimate accurately. For example, when Microsoft decides to develop new software, it has to estimate research and development costs, and the future revenue and operating cost cash flows, all over a multiple year project life. Cash flow estimation under such conditions is obviously challenging, and highly accurate forecasts are quite difficult to come by.

2. *Assess the riskiness of the flows.* One single scenario of the estimated cash flows is usually insufficient because of the inherent uncertainty in the cash flows. The financial manager therefore also needs to quantify the amount of risk in the estimated cash flows.

3. *Incorporate the risk assessment into the analysis.* The effect of risk on asset values can be included in the analysis in either of two ways: (1) by the *certainty equivalent (CE) approach* or (2) by the *risk-adjusted discount rate (RADR) approach.* In the CE approach, the expected cash flows are reduced or adjusted downward to account for risk. The higher the risk of the project's cash flows, the lower the risk-adjusted, or certainty equivalent, cash flow. In the RADR approach, the discount rate rather than the cash flow is adjusted for risk—the higher the risk of the project, the higher the discount rate. As a practical matter, the risk-adjusted discount rate will reflect risk from two sources: the riskiness of the project's cash flows (business risk) and the financial risk created by the way the project is funded (financial risk).

4. *Find the present value of the flows.* The final step is to find the present value of the cash flows. This step informs a financial manager about the expected value of a stream of future cash flows in today's dollars. Thus, the process of discounting eliminates the problem of comparing cash flows that occur at different times in the future.

The concept of opportunity cost plays an important role in DCF analysis. To illustrate, suppose a firm retains all of its earnings from the previous year, and is now evaluating several investment alternatives. Should a cost be assigned to these retained earnings, or should the funds be considered as "free" capital? One line of reasoning might suggest that the funds have a zero cost—after all, the retained earnings have no apparent cost, since the firm already has access to those funds. However, an opportunity cost must be assigned to each alternative. By investing the retained earnings in one alternative, the firm forgoes the opportunity to invest those funds in any other alternative. Moreover, the firm's shareholders have not been given the opportunity to invest those funds elsewhere in alternative investments, since the firm retained all its earnings rather than return them to shareholders as a cash dividend. Thus, there is a cost to the firm and its shareholders, and this cost should be incorporated into the investment analysis.

The discount rate applied in DCF investment analysis must reflect foregone opportunities, but how does the financial manager decide which alternatives should be considered? The appropriate discount rate should reflect the return that could be earned by investing the funds in the best alternative investment opportunity of *similar risk*. However, it may be very difficult to estimate the returns available on comparable alternative real asset investments. When Microsoft was setting the opportunity cost rate for its Windows 2000 investment, the most logical choice was the return expected on other new software investments. However, such information is rarely available, so the expected rates of return on financial assets are usually used to set the opportunity cost rate for all investment decisions. For most projects, a firm will determine its cost of capital, and use that rate as the opportunity cost for many of its investment decisions. The cost of capital is simply a weighted average of the returns that investors expect to receive on its existing set of financial securities. New projects that have risks very different from the firm's existing projects are often evaluated using more advanced techniques, such as the method of comparables.

We see, then, that in any DCF analysis it is necessary to assign an opportunity cost discount rate. In general, that rate must reflect the following three factors:

1. *The riskiness of the cash flows.* The discount rate must reflect the risk inherent in the cash flows–the higher the risk, the higher the discount rate. For example, the

discount rate used to evaluate corporate bonds will be higher than that used to evaluate Treasury bonds, and the rate applied to cash flows from a firm's common stock (dividends plus capital gains) will be higher than that applied to its bonds.

2. *The prevailing level of rates of return.* The discount rate must reflect the prevailing level of returns in the economy for the same period of time. Thus, in December 2001 the discount rate applied to cash flows having the same level of risk as a 3-month Treasury bill was 1.61 percent, but in July 1996 the rate was only 5.3 percent. Because of changes in expected inflation, in risk aversion, and in supply and demand conditions, the prevailing return on short-term Treasury securities rose by 180 basis points in four years.

3. *The timing of the cash flows.* The final consideration is the timing of the flows; that is, do the flows occur annually, quarterly, or over some other period? In general, most analyses are conducted in terms of annual discount rates, and in many situations the cash flows do occur annually. Under these circumstances, no adjustment to the annual discount rate is necessary. However, if the cash flows occur over some period other than annually, say, semiannually, then the discount rate must be adjusted to reflect this timing pattern.

RECENT INNOVATIONS IN APPLIED VALUE MEASUREMENT

In our previous discussion of the potential conflicts of interest between management and shareholders, we described how shareholders could encourage managers to maximize shareholder wealth through the use of incentive compensation systems. Several types of incentive-based compensation are commonly used in practice, including *executive stock options* and *performance bonuses* based on profitability goals. However, stock options can be designed to reward managers even when shareholder wealth is not materially enhanced, while performance bonuses based on accounting profitability may or may not be highly correlated with how well managers have done for their shareholders. For example, corporate managers may make decisions designed to increase accounting profits, but which may not improve the corporation's overall cash flow. Such decisions would not be expected to increase share prices. Two analytical approaches have been developed recently that focus attention directly on management's success or failure in maximizing shareholder wealth: market value added (MVA) and economic value added (EVA).

Market Value Added (MVA)

As we have discussed throughout this chapter, the primary goal of any corporate manager should be *shareholder wealth maximization*. This goal obviously benefits shareholders, and it also ensures that scarce economic resources are allocated as efficiently as possible. Although this fundamental concept is widely accepted, it is easy to confuse the objective of maximizing the firm's total market value with the objective of shareholder wealth maximization. Raising and investing as much capital as possible can increase a firm's total market value, but such decisions are not necessarily in the best interests of the firm's shareholders. For example, corporate managers may mistakenly invest in poor projects in an effort to increase the size of their firms. As we discussed previously, it is important to distinguish between profitable and unprofitable growth. Shareholder wealth is maximized by maximizing the *difference* between the firm's market value of the firm's equity and the amount of equity capital that investors have supplied to the firm. This difference is called *market value added (MVA)*:

MVA = market value of equity − equity capital supplied

Note that MVA can also be defined in terms of total capital supplied, including both debt and equity. Total capital supplied would be relevant in those cases where the objective is to measure changes in the total value of the firm, not just its equity value. However, since some forms of capital are not publicly traded (e.g., bank loans), it may not always be possible to obtain accurate values for all of the firm's capital. Therefore, MVA measures usually emphasize equity value.

To illustrate, consider General Electric. In 1995, its total market value was $121 billion, while its investors had supplied only $32 billion. Thus, General Electric's MVA was $121 – $32 = $89 billion. This $89 billion represents the difference between the cash that General Electric's investors have put into the corporation since its founding—including retained earnings—and the value the shareholders would receive by selling the business at its current market price. By maximizing this difference, management maximizes the wealth of its shareholders. Generally speaking, management has created incremental value for its shareholders whenever the difference is positive, and destroyed the value of some of its shareholders' investment whenever the difference is negative.

While the managers of General Electric did a remarkable job of increasing shareholder wealth, Kmart's managers did a poor one over the same period of time. In 1995, Kmart's total market value was $3 billion. However, investors have supplied Kmart with $5 billion of capital, so Kmart's MVA was a negative $2 billion. In effect, Kmart had only $0.60 of wealth for every dollar investors put up, whereas General Electric turned each $1 of investment into $3.78.

There is a direct link between MVA and the net present value (NPV) capital budgeting rule. The NPV capital budgeting rule is a widely used, DCF method that compares the discounted value of an investment's cash inflows and outflows. A positive value indicates that the present value of the inflows exceeds the present value of the outflows, and hence the project would be considered acceptable. To illustrate, consider a company that decides to retain $5 million in earnings for investment in a project, but the present value of future cash flows from the project is only $3 million. Even though the project will cause the total market value of the company to be $3 million greater than if the earnings had been paid out as dividends, shareholders would have $2 million less wealth. This net reduction in shareholder value occurs because shareholders have been denied the opportunity to receive the $5 million and reinvest those funds in alternative investments that would have a market value of at least $5 million. With $5 million added to the capital invested in the company but only $3 million added to the company's total market value, the firm's MVA would fall by $2 million. Note, also, that the project would have an NPV of negative $2 million. Since NPV measures the amount that a project can be expected to add (or subtract) from MVA, managers can follow the NPV rule and should, at a minimum avoid accepting negative NPV projects. This, in turn, would ensure the firm's MVA continues to increase. Of course, those companies with the highest MVAs, such as General Electric, have done a spectacular job of identifying and investing in positive NPV projects. These lucrative investments have, in turn, caused investors to bid up the firm's stock price, thereby increasing its MVA.

Economic Value Added (EVA)

While MVA measures the aggregate effect of managerial actions and decisions on shareholder wealth since the inception of the company, *economic value added (EVA)* focuses on managerial effectiveness in a given year. Hence MVA is a longer-term measure of a manager's historical performance, while EVA provides a timelier but short-term measure of value creation. The basic formula for EVA is:

$$\text{EVA} = \text{operating profit} - \text{cost of all capital}$$

$$= (\text{sales revenue} - \text{operating costs} - \text{taxes})$$

$$- (\text{total capital supplied} \times \text{cost of capital})$$

Operating profit is defined as sales revenues minus operating costs and taxes. Hence, it measures the total cash available from operations on an after-tax basis that is available to make payments to the corporation's providers of investment capital while the cost of the capital is estimated as total capital times the weighted average cost of that capital. To illustrate, suppose a firm had $200 million of sales, $160 million of operating costs, and $20 million of taxes, so its operating profits as defined were $20 million. We'll assume these results are for the firm's 2002 fiscal year. Suppose also that the firm had $100 million of debt and equity capital, and the weighted average cost of that capital was 10 percent. The firm's 2002 EVA would thus be $10 million:

$$\text{EVA} = \$20 - \$100(0.10) = \$20 - \$10 = \$10 \text{ million}$$

EVA is an estimate of a business's true economic profit for the year, and it is usually significantly different from that firm's accounting profits. EVA represents the residual income that remains after the opportunity cost of the firm's entire capital base has been deducted, whereas accounting profit is calculated without recognizing a cost for equity capital. EVA depends on both operating efficiency and balance sheet management: Without operating efficiency, operating profits will be low, and without efficient balance sheet management, there will be too many assets and too much capital. This results in higher-than-necessary capital costs, which would lower a firm's EVA.

Note that EVA (but not MVA) can be calculated for individual business divisions as well as for the entire company. The cost of capital should reflect the risk of the business unit, either for the whole company or for an operating division. Note also that the specific calculation of EVA for a company is much more complex than we have presented here because of the many accounting issues, such as inventory valuation, depreciation, amortization of research and development costs, and lease financing that must be adjusted properly when estimating a firm's true economic operating profit.

EVA is an intermediate measure of firm value that begins with the NPV of an individual project and ends with the firm's MVA. Each project's expected economic profitability, which is initially measured by its NPV, contributes to the firm's EVA for any given year. MVA is the present value of the EVAs that the firm is expected to produce in the future. Thus, the creation of good investment opportunities (positive NPV projects) creates the expectation of high EVAs, which investors recognize by bidding up the price of the firms stock. This, in turn, creates a large MVA.

Although EVA is a timely and important topic for corporate managers today, the underlying concept is not new. Managers have always known that they need to earn more than the cost of capital. However, this basic premise is often lost because of a mistaken focus on accounting measures of profitability. EVA provides managers with a relatively straightforward and accurate way to assess the likely impact of a firm's investment, financing, and dividend decisions on the wealth of the firm's shareholders. Thus, using it as a tool to evaluate a manager's performance can reinforce EVA.

Using EVA as a Managerial Incentive

In the past few years, many highly successful firms, including Coca-Cola and AT&T, have adopted incentive compensation systems based on EVA. The primary motivation is that EVA is linked both theoretically and empirically to shareholder wealth. For example, AT&T found an almost perfect positive correlation between its EVA and its stock price, whereas the correlation between accounting profits and stock prices was much lower. Thus, managers can focus on the tangible objective of accepting projects that have positive EVA. When executive compensation is tied to EVA, managers are given the proper incentive to adopt decisions and implement the set of actions that contributes the highest incremental value for the firm's shareholders. Moreover, what holds for AT&T holds for stocks in general—security analysts have found that stock prices track EVA far more closely than other measures such as earnings per share, operating margin, or return on equity. Had analysts and investors used EVA as an evaluation tool in the 1980s, they might have foreseen that IBM's EVA was negative during most of the decade. This was a clear signal that IBM's managers were committing capital to projects that were not good investments for the firm's shareholders. Not surprisingly, IBM's stock price performed very poorly throughout the decade.

SUMMARY

Finance has become one of the most complex, challenging, and interesting topics in business today. During the 1990s and into the 2000s, an increasing number of corporations have publicly and vocally advocated the merits of maximizing shareholder value. While this objective is praiseworthy, the modern financial manager needs to understand how to go about the process of actually achieving that goal. Rapid changes in competition, regulation, and the securities markets have made this objective seemingly more difficult. The material and methods outlined in this chapter provide the reader with important insights regarding how managers should think about how to succeed in maximizing shareholder value.

INTERNET RESOURCES

BradyNet Financial Information (www.bradynet.com). Updated continuously, the site features the latest financial news and research from around the world. Valuable for the international investor; however a membership fee is required for most of the research information.

CNNfn - CNN Financial Network (money.cnn.com). CNN's network compiles complete news coverage of U.S. and international markets, quotes, commodities, currencies, and events.

Finweb.com (www.finweb.com). Lists a selection of finance journals and research sources while also acting as a good gateway to other databases and finance/economics sites on the Web. Managed by Professor James R. Garven at the University of Texas at Austin.

Investor Words (www.investorwords.com/a1.htm). A remarkably handy resource for all acronyms or terms that suddenly slip your mind.

Yahoo (www.finance.yahoo.com). Provides basic financial information for capital markets and other fundamentals.

FINANCE CRITICAL REFERENCE MATERIALS

Books

Bartlett, Joseph W. *Equity Finance: Venture Capital, Buyouts, Restructuring and Reorganizations.* New York: John Wiley & Sons, 1995.

Equity Finance is a very in-depth, comprehensive, three-volume text that hopes to explain and discuss the important aspects of any investment activity that involves billions of dollars. Early stage investing, joint ventures, buyouts, restructurings, and pooled investment vehicles are thoroughly discussed.

Business International Corporation. *101 More Checklists for Global Financial Management: An Action Guide for Building a High-Performance Finance Function.* New York: The Corporation Publishers, 1992.

This book offers 101 pointers on financial strategy, organizations, and treasury management systems. The list of pointers was compiled from various Business International publications and represents the most current thought in treasury management.

Higgins, Robert, *Analysis for Financial Management.* New York: McGraw-Hill, 2000.

Intended for nonfinancial managers and business students, this book is one of the best introductions to the basics of financial management. Used at top business schools and in training programs around the country, it introduces financial concepts in nonacademic language and uses real-world examples to reinforce concepts. This paperback text presents standard techniques and modern developments in a practical and intuitive manner, with an emphasis on the managerial applications of financial analysis.

Livingstone, John Leslie. *The Portable MBA in Finance and Accounting.* New York: John Wiley & Sons, 1992.

This book covers an extensive range of the basic, key concepts in finance and accounting. The material is presented in an easy-to-read "how-to" fashion with clear and helpful examples. Each chapter was written by various academic and business experts in their given field who have gained national recognition. It is a basic and broad source of information for anyone hoping to touch up their finance and accounting skills.

Journals

CFO: The Magazine for Chief Financial Officers. Boston: CFO Publishing Corporation.

CFO is a monthly magazine that gives advice on financial tools, strategies, and risks for people in management positions. Its emphasis is on the actions and reactions of major corporations.

Corporate Finance. London: Euromoney Publications PLC.

Corporate Finance is a monthly journal with a magazine-type format that analyzes and discusses the financial maneuvering of some of the world's top companies and corporate executives. All aspects of finance are discussed, along with how these aspects are utilized in different global economies.

The Corporate Finance Sourcebook. New York: McGraw-Hill.

A complete guide to the financial services and capitol investment resources that are used by business communities worldwide. Provides the reader with sources for potential funds and sources for companies that can help manage their funds. There are nearly 4,000 entries in this comprehensive guide.

Financial Markets, Institutions and Instruments. Cambridge, MA: Blackwell Publishers.

Each journal consists of one paper written about a specific aspect of the financial market. The work is written by leading authorities on the subject who are from either the academic community, business community, or who have worked within both areas.

Moody's Bank & Financial Manual: Banks, Insurance and Finance Companies, Investment Trusts, Real Estate. New York: Moody's Investors Service, Moody's Banks and Finance News.

Moody's Bank & Finance Manual gives summaries of investment opportunities offered by banks, insurance companies, investment companies, unit investment trusts, and other financial opportunities. The manual is broken down by company with the investment opportunities of each specific company blocked together. It also offers ratings of these opportunities through Moody's rating system.

Entrepreneurship

The United States is one of the world's most "entrepreneurial" nations because, from its inception as a capitalist country, it has offered determined would-be business owners the opportunity to succeed—and fail—at starting and managing new ventures. In return for this support, the United States benefits economically from entrepreneurs' ability to innovate and capitalize on this innovation. The benefits of entrepreneurship are threefold;

1. Entrepreneurs' innovations improve the quality of life both at home and abroad.

2. Entrepreneurs create new jobs across the economy.

3. Entrepreneurs drive economic growth and create new wealth.

And indeed, some 95 percent of all radical innovations are attributable to small businesses. Among these innovations are the airplane, the heart valve, the helicopter, the high-capacity computer, soft contact lenses, and prefabricated housing.[1]

This chapter begins with a profile of the typical "entrepreneur." It then discusses the process for identifying business areas charged with entrepreneurial potential, as well as defining the different forms new businesses can take. Finally, this chapter provides an overview on how to write a business plan, and concludes with a discussion on financing for new ventures.

THE ENTREPRENEURIAL PROFILE

Let us begin with one critical assertion: *Entrepreneurial* is not a synonym for *unemployable.* Do not confuse the entrepreneur's drive with a personal reluctance to work for someone else. There is also an enormous difference between being an entrepreneur and being self-employed. Accordingly, every entrepreneur must give issues of motivation serious consideration to prevent precipitous decisions and possibly, grave mistakes.

What, then, is an entrepreneur? According to Joseph Schumpeter, a prominent economic theorist writing in the early 1900s, an entrepreneur is "a person who destroys the existing economic order by introducing new products and services, creating new forms of organization, or by exploiting new raw materials. This destruction can be done through forming a new business, or by working within an existing business."[2] For the purposes of this chapter, an alternate, simpler definition of the entrepreneur is "someone who perceives an opportunity and creates an organization to pursue it."[3]

Given this definition, are there personal characteristics that make one person more apt to be successful at entrepreneurship than another? Most entrepreneurs see a market inefficiency or unserved customer niche and create a business to exploit it. Surprisingly, the majority of entrepreneurs do not start out as experts in a particular field. Instead, research has shown that successful entrepreneurs do have certain character traits and skills largely in common. These include:

Vision.   The successful entrepreneur has a clear and communicable vision of the opportunity his or her business will create or exploit, and is completely dedicated to making this vision a reality, even when it means taking risks.

Determination.   The successful entrepreneur is completely determined to succeed, even in the face of doubts of close friends and associates. Jann Wenner started *Rolling Stone* when he was 21 years old. Steve Wozniak, who helped found Apple Computers, was not particularly distinguished as an engineer at Hewlett-Packard. Martha Stewart was a housewife. What made these entrepreneurs successful was not solely their education or their intellect, but their determination. Determination enables the entrepreneur to be decisive and fuels the entrepreneur's energy level to complete tasks, even when this means working tirelessly or incessantly.[4]

Motivation.   For the entrepreneur, making his or her vision a reality takes on a self-actualizing importance. As a result, very little takes priority over moving toward the goal of realization. "Very little" can include personal relationships, outside interests, or other projects that are financially rewarding in the short term.

Focus.   As the bearer of the vision, the entrepreneur ensures that the "big picture" strategy is complete while overseeing the low level, yet critical details. The entrepreneur must always be focused, never allowing precious time, energy, and other resources to be taken from the project.

Devotion.   To maintain the level of focus and vision just mentioned, entrepreneurs must enjoy working on the project and be deeply committed to the ideas and beliefs on which the project is founded. Having sole responsibility for the success or failure of a venture is often what motivates entrepreneurs. Accordingly, entrepreneurs are rarely driven by financial gain, as money alone does not provide the motivation needed for the work involved in starting a new venture. If the venture is successful in all other aspects, financial gain will follow.

As previously stated, there is no formula that yields the ideal entrepreneur. However, anyone even considering launching an entrepreneurial venture must realize that being an entrepreneur means always having the ultimate responsibility for making decisions, solving problems, resolving conflicts, and keeping morale high.

ENTREPRENEURIAL OPPORTUNITIES

Every entrepreneurial venture that succeeds is the culmination of several events. The first of these is the discovery or conceptualization of a marketable innovation. Second, the entrepreneur must have the expertise and desire to bring this innovation to market. Third, the entrepreneur must also have access to the resources needed to produce this innovation and can operate within an environment conducive to the project's success. Although the late 1990's "dot.com" boom made it appear as though anyone with a marketable idea could get rich, there is no guarantee an innovation will come to fruition or that any new venture will be a success. Let us further discuss these necessary steps.

The Idea

You don't need a unique idea: in fact, most entrepreneurial ventures take existing services or products and make some minor improvement to them. McDonald's dominated the fast-food market by guaranteeing (and marketing) a consistent dining experience and food taste to its customers. Google.com, one of the Internet's most reliable and popular search engines, succeeded by keeping its user-interface simple and uncluttered. So, it is neither likely nor required for a business idea to be "new"; in fact, odds are that someone, somewhere has had the idea before. Truthfully, what is far more relevant is an entrepreneur's ability to implement an idea. The reason that an idea may appear "new" to a would-be entrepreneur is that the last person with the idea did not have the implementation skills to make it a reality and as a result, the product or service never made it to the market.

An entrepreneurial idea can emerge within any industry, but several current industries, by their very nature, seem ripe for entrepreneurial innovation. A few of these include:

Wireless

- Instant Messaging
- Point of sale transactions (coke machines)
- Remote monitoring and control (e.g., your dishwasher)
- Peer-to-peer nurtured computing (completely decentralized)

Biotech/Medicine

- Protein discovery
- Gene therapy

Optical networks

- Immense data transfer speed
- Allows much more online content delivery

International Goods Distribution

Changes in the global political climate have opened new markets for U.S. entrepreneurs. The relaxation, and in some cases elimination, of trade barriers in many Eastern European and Asian countries creates significant opportunities for the exporting and distribution of products desired but previously unavailable in these markets.

While an entrepreneur must pay attention to protecting his or her ideas, don't waste time and energy obsessing over them. An idea is no more than a pleasant thought without the ability to implement it, and most people are without the interest and resources to really "steal" an idea.

The Product Concept and Market Need

An entrepreneur also must be able to describe a product or service in terms of its features and benefits, as well as describe the target markets for this product or service. An "idea," no matter how ingenious, is simply not enough. For a venture to be successful, the entrepreneur must have a clear and specific idea about what a product or service provides that is unique to the market. However, a product idea often goes through several iterations as the entrepreneur researches what the market and customer really wants and what is feasible. Entrepreneurs may have to weigh the trade-offs between a high-cost, perfectly engineered product and a lower cost, mass-market product.

Moreover, the entrepreneur must concretely establish that customers will be interested in the product or service once it exists. An entrepreneur must be able to identify the target population in terms of numbers, demographics, and potential sales. Often, entrepreneurs will conduct extensive market surveys and focus groups to establish a definition of their customer base. Ideally, entrepreneurs have customers who are committed to purchasing the product as soon as it is completed. A venture based on a product for which there is no demand will be unsuccessful and a waste of valuable time and resources.

Expertise, Resources, and Environment

Once an entrepreneur has a product concept, he or she must also have the expertise to translate the concept into a reality. This expertise may come from the entrepreneur's education or training, or by forming a partnership with others who have more specialized knowledge and skills. Physical resources are then needed to bring an idea to life; these include everything from access to the materials, production facilities, and the technology to produce the product, to the office space and communication tools needed to facilitate all of these activities. Of course, physical resources require capital, and a discussion of potential capital sources follows at the end of this chapter. The entrepreneur's roadmap and vehicle for requesting capital investments throughout this process is a well-developed business plan. If at all possible, the geographic area surrounding the new enterprise should be rich with other entrepreneurial enterprises, venture capital (VC) companies (80 percent of VC is invested within 60 miles of the VC office), and access to the appropriate human talent to fuel growth and innovation.

BUSINESS PLANS

A business plan is a document summarizing the key objectives and strategies of a venture idea. Business plans serve many purposes, and can be used for everything from helping an entrepreneur evaluate an idea to helping an entrepreneur obtain bank financing or investment funds. Business plans can vary in length, depending on the specific purpose for writing the plan or the audience to whom the plan is directed. In general, a summary business plan, of about 10 pages, is a good place to start. A summary business plan should include the following sections:

1. *Cover Page.*   A page including the company's name, address, and phone and fax numbers. The cover page may also include the name of the person to contact with questions and his or her direct phone number. The cover page is also a good place to include a message regarding the confidential nature of the document and to establish any rules for sharing or reproducing the information contained inside.

2. *Table of Contents.*   This page should be as detailed as possible, providing section titles and their accompanying page numbers.

3. *Executive Summary.*   This page should include a concise summary of information about the company, the product,

the target market, as well as the strategy for pursuing the market. A good summary will also include a timetable and the action you want whoever is reading the business plan to take. Executive summary pages should be broken down into subsections whenever possible and should be kept to 2 pages in length.

4. *The Company.*   This section should provide detailed information on the company's management team, including biographical information, prior business experience, and current role within the new company. Remember to include a concise, easy to follow account of the company's overall business strategy and philosophy. This can be accomplished by providing a history of the company, reporting on its current status, and describing the company's future goals and the process by which these goals will be reached. Incorporating a company mission statement in this section is also useful.

5. *The Product.*   This should include a discussion of what the product or service does, its main features and benefits, and how it will appeal to the target audience. Discussions of pricing can be included in this section, as well as any pictures, diagrams, or other visual aids.

6. *The Market.*   This section should define the specific market segments (see the Marketing chapter for more on segmentation) and the value of the product to each as specifically as possible, including a quantified breakdown of the market size and any identifiable areas of growth. Include a detailed discussion of the existing market need that the product or service satisfies, other products or services that can be viewed as competitors or substitutes, and how the new product is superior to these potential competitors or substitutes.

7. *Marketing Plan.*   This section should describe how the entrepreneur plans to introduce, promote, and sell the given product or service. Be as specific as possible, providing a detailed description of all elements in the marketing mix (again, see the Marketing chapter) and their expected degrees of efficacy.

8. *Challenges.*   This section should identify and address any challenges or problems the business may encounter, as well

as proposed solutions or strategies for dealing with these problems. Any potential problem an investor may recognize should be mentioned and explained in this section.

9. *Financials.* The financials section should include a balance sheet, income statement, and cash flow statement for any historical period of operation as well as for the period of projected operation. If the business plan is being directed at a specific investor, the entrepreneur should include any supplemental analyses that the investing party requests.

Typically, after completing a business plan an entrepreneur will discover weak spots in a business structure, or feel the need to revise parts of his or her business strategy. In fact, this is the direct benefit of completing a business plan. Better to fix problems before presenting an idea to an important third party than having the third party point them out to you. Further, in customizing a business plan to fit the needs of a particular third party, such as a venture capital firm specializing in biotechnology, the entrepreneur should first get a sense of precisely what criteria the third party uses to evaluate ventures, and then structure his or her presentation accordingly. Many resources are available to assist you in developing a business plan, including the Small Business Administration and several web sites with software designed to guide you through the creation of a business plan.

All entrepreneurial opportunities, no matter how well thought out, no matter how clearly defined in a business plan, require and depend on one crucial event—securing capital. The following section discusses sources of capital and what to consider when approaching these sources.

SOURCES OF FINANCING

A broad range of capital sources are available to the entrepreneur. While some sources of funding encourage specific kinds of proposals or ideas (such as technological innovations in the realm of healthcare), a determined entrepreneur can find the funds to get his or her business off the ground.

When deciding on what kind of capital to start your company, consider what the money is going to be used for. Some types of capital work best for certain stages of a venture. For example, if you run a company that specializes in lighting airplane interiors and you are looking for "seed" capital to start research and development on a new solar-driven interior lighting device, you will probably have trouble interesting banks and venture capital firms because R&D takes a lot of money and a lot of time to produce a return. In this case, raising money from private investors may be your only choice. However, if you are looking to expand this same lighting company overseas or into new domestic markets, you will probably have an easier time with banks and VC firms.

The following is a brief discussion of potential funding sources:

Grants and Loans

Private companies and the federal government make millions of dollars per year available to entrepreneurial ventures. A number of different grants exist; some encourage entrepreneurship among certain populations, such as ethnic minorities or women, and others are awarded to businesses planning to open within certain geographic areas known as *empowerment zones.* An example of this sort of grant is The New Markets Venture Capital (NMVC) program, which has the specific mission of aiding economic development in low-income areas. Through a combination of equity-type financing and intensive operational assistance to small businesses located in low-income areas, the program assists local entrepreneurs, creates quality employment opportunities for residents, and builds wealth within these communities.

Still other grants are awarded based on the nature of the venture being pursued, such as a business that focused on renewable energy and the environment. Government agencies, such as the Small Business Administration, provide low-interest loans to entrepreneurs who apply and meet certain professional requirements; for example, the entrepreneur cannot be involved in real estate or other speculative activities.

Bank Loans

Many private banking institutions grant low or competitive interest, noncollateralized loans for the purposes of starting a business. A *noncollateralized loan* is one in which the lending bank does not demand that an asset be pledged against the loan note as security.

Terms of loans vary from bank to bank, but there are two basic types of loans: short-term and long-term. *Short-term loans* (e.g., working-capital loans, accounts-receivable loans, or lines of credit) have a maturity of up to one year. *Long-term loans* (used for large business expenditures such as real estate, equipment, vehicles, and furniture) have maturities greater than one year but usually less than seven years. Remember, applications and conditions vary from institution to institution, which means that a loan rejection at one bank does not mean a rejection at every bank. To be successful in obtaining a bank loan, you must be prepared and organized. Know exactly how much money you need, why you need it, and how you will pay it back. The critical step is to convince your lender that you are a good credit risk. Requesting a loan when you are unprepared sends a message to your lender that you are a high-risk application.

Private Investors

Individual investors, often called *angels,* make capital investments in entrepreneurial ventures in return for equity (partial ownership) in the business. These arrangements are usually created on the basis of a privately negotiated agreement predicated on the fact that the investor hopes to earn a high return on his or her invested capital if the business succeeds, as compensation for the risks associated with investing in an unproven business. Finding private investors can be a difficult task and it often requires you or your partners to use already established networks. Alternatively, individual investors with a personal preference for specific industries or toward specific kinds of products can also be helpful. Some angel investors are motivated by a desire to support a particular industry (e.g., renewable energy), to see growth within a local community (e.g., rural communities in the Midwest), or simply to cultivate the entrepreneurial spirit. As previously stated, angel investors often have prior acquaintance with or knowledge of the founder or founding team.

Venture Capital

Venture capital firms pool and then manage the funds of multiple investors for larger capital investments. VCs agree to invest (as documented in the "term sheet") in exchange for an equity stake in the new company. They choose to assume risk of funding unproven ideas because they see the potential for significant financial gain. Every VC firm has its own philosophy and process for evaluating start-up businesses and the associated risks, so you must conduct careful research before you approach any firm for funding. Information about a venture capital firm's strategic focus as well as its current portfolio of investments is usually available on its web site. As with angel funding, a personal connection to a venture capital firm significantly increases your chances of receiving funding.

Beware of issues surrounding the division of equity and control, as some forms of capital are more attractive to the entrepreneur than others. For the die-hard entrepreneur, however, any form of capital is better than no capital at all. Many start-up ventures have been financed on personal savings and credit cards. Of course, this option is not ideal, and with organizations like the SBA you shouldn't have to finance a venture by yourself. The general rule of entrepreneurial financing, while something of a cliché, is never to invest one's own money in a venture. If the venture is really worth pursuing and you present the idea successfully, there should be enough external capital available to meet the venture's requirements.

Having created a business plan and secured start-up capital, the entrepreneur must at some point direct his or her attention to creating a formal, legally recognizable business entity. The choice of which form to take usually rests on considerations of the nature of the good or service a business provides, as well as the personal preferences of the entrepreneurs involved.

BUSINESS FORMS

The creation of any of these forms requires substantial legal documentation and should be carried out with an attention to detail as well as additional market research. Two key issues to consider are: (1) who has ultimate control over the business; and (2) your willingness to accept personal liability for the business.

The most common business forms are as follows:

1. *Sole Proprietorship.* This business form is the legal default form for any person who does business in the

United States but makes no effort to organize the business otherwise. This is a business owned and operated by one person, who assumes total control and liability for the business. No legal entity is formed. While the sole proprietor may have employees, he or she does not have co-owners.

2. *Partnership.* This is a form in which two or more parties go into business together and have a legally documented structure for sharing profits, losses, and liabilities.

3. *Corporation.* This is a business form created by state governments upon the filing of an application and payment of a fee. It creates a legal entity, separate from its owners (the shareholders). A corporation also eliminates any personal liability the owners have for the business.

4. *Subchapter S Corporation.* This is a subclassification of corporation that can be requested and granted after the applying organization passes a number of tests. The primary difference between an S-corp and a regular corporation is the ability of the owners to directly pay the corporation's taxes.

5. *Limited Partnership.* This business form combines a partnership and a corporation. It affords general partnership status to some parties, and all benefits and liabilities that go along with it. It also affords limited partnership status to some parties, where limited partners are entitled to rights and liabilities similar to those of shareholders.

6. *Not-For-Profit Entity.* A business form similar to that of a corporation, with the absence of a profit-making initiative and the exemption from government tax liabilities.

SUMMARY

The United States fosters an entrepreneurial spirit through its national culture as well as through public and private support. If someone can recognize an opportunity, has the right skills and resources available to capitalize on that opportunity, and is completely committed to turning a concept into a reality, then starting a new venture is a risk worth taking. Developing a strong business plan and securing capital are the critical starting points.

INTERNET RESOURCES

Entreworld.org (www.entreworld.org/). Contains more than 1,000 articles, audio clips, tools, databases, and even town-to-town small business event listings—to give you instant access to essential entrepreneurial resources.

The Idea Cafe (www.ideacafe.com/). Self-proclaimed as "A fun approach to serious business!", the Idea Cafe provides expert advice, a regular newsletter, links to more resources, and a feature called "CyberSchmooz" enabling you to network with fellow entrepreneurs.

Quick MBA (www.quickmba.com). An extensive section on entrepreneurship, including a model business plan, tips on attracting stakeholders to your venture, and tips for making a successful pitch to venture capitalists.

Startup Journal (startup.wsj.com). The publishers of *The Wall Street Journal* offer articles on starting and buying a business, running a business, and franchising, also including a database of venture capital firms.

Venture Wire (www.venturewire.com). A great resource for researching which start-ups received funding in which locations and sectors.

ENTREPRENEURSHIP CRITICAL REFERENCE MATERIALS

Bygrave, William. *The Portable MBA in Entrepreneurship.* New York, John H. Wiley & Sons, 1994.

Bygrave provides a comprehensive overview of relevant topics for those interested in the study or practice of entrepreneurship. Topics include start-up strategies, guidance on how to spot market opportunities, how to prepare a business plan, how to secure financing and manage debt, and legal and tax information.

Collins, Jim. *Good to Great: Why Some Companies Make the Leap . . . and Others Don't.* New York: HarperBusiness, 2001.

Collins, coauthor of *Built to Last,* wanted to know what corporate traits enabled a few companies (11 by his count) to make the transition from "good" to "great." To answer this question, Collins and his team of researchers sorted through a list of 1,435 companies, looking for those whose performance had improved dramatically over time.

Drucker, Peter. *Innovation and Entrepreneurship.* New York: Harperbusiness, 1993.

This book, first published in 1985, predicted the effects of the IT revolution, coined the concept of lifelong learning, and identified the need for sound managerial practices in entrepreneurship. The book presents innovation and entrepreneurship as purposeful and systematic discipline, and explains and analyzes the challenges and opportunities of America's entrepreneurial economy.

Gladstone, David. *Venture Capital Investing.* Englewood Cliffs, NJ: Prentice Hall, 1988.

This book is a detailed account of the process associated with investigating private business opportunities, complete with a checklist of questions to ask before investing in a small or private business. It also provides an in-depth analysis of the venture capital process, including locating and structuring suitable investments, legal closings, monitoring the investor, and realizing a gain on the investment. The author was the president of Allied Capital Corporation, the largest venture capital company in the United States.

Keen, Peter. *Every Manager's Guide to Information Technology.* Boston: Harvard Business School Press, 1991.

Since many new ventures stem either from a technological innovation or a product concept to fill a technological need, entrepreneurs and investors alike must be well versed in technology terms and concepts. This guide provides information on key terms as well as key concepts that dominate in the information technology industry.

Timmons, Jeffrey. *Venture Capital Creation.* Homewood, IL: Irwin Press, 1994.

This book provides insight into the traditional profile of the entrepreneur, in an effort to expand this conception to fit the entrepreneur of today. Further, it works to assist the entrepreneur in understanding him or herself, in an effort to facilitate the reader's better self-management as well as enhancing his/her managerial skills with relation to others. It focuses specifically on the topics of entrepreneurship defined, the entrepreneurial environment, the entrepreneurial task, the entrepreneurial personality, and the entrepreneurial career.

International Business

Over the past several decades, striking changes in the political structure of nations and the communication structure of people around the world have affected all aspects of society. The advent of the Internet and continued advancements in transportation and electronic technology has rendered geography less vital than ever before. Politically, the 1991 fall of the Soviet Union substituted a world of dual superpowers for one leaning increasingly toward a multipolar network of intensely interdependent nations.

Nowhere have these various changes had a more pronounced effect than in the business world. Mirroring the political realm, the current business landscape has changed from one where a few major players presided over the vast majority of all business transactions, to one that is truly global in its inclusion. In the past 25 years global trade has tripled.[1] As walls continue to fall and barriers lift—with milestones such as China's long-awaited entry into the World Trade Organization (WTO) in November 2001—endless opportunities emerge in new markets for businesses equipped to take advantage of them.

This chapter focuses primarily on four topics: (1) a discussion of the need for businesses to successfully compete in a global environment; (2) the skills and characteristics necessary for a business to be competitive in a global environment; (3) the new benefits and opportunities associated with assuming a global business perspective; and (4) the need for businesses to be aware of today's prevalent antiglobalization movement.

THE GLOBAL MARKETPLACE

In an earlier time, foreign markets were viewed by some U.S. companies as new markets only—a potential customer base that could be tapped or just as easily left untapped, without interrupting the normal flow of business. Today, this is a negligence businesses cannot afford. Instead, large companies now realize that their very survival relies on being competitive worldwide.

The elimination of many barriers to entry in world markets has put increasing pressure on companies to compete globally. Yet now companies must not only compete for a customer base, but also for the supply of raw materials, technology, and distribution networks on a global level—drawing many companies into transnational transactions merely to remain competitive. A company must seek out the most beneficial relationships with suppliers and distributors, even when they are outside the company's home nation, because its competitors are doing so. A company must also seek out the most profitable markets in which to conduct business, because its competitors are doing so. Many sources of sustainable competitive advantage exist solely on a global level. A company that is unwilling to compete on a global level, given the evolution of today's global marketplace, may very well lose its market share and its ability to compete in domestic markets as well.

With an impetus to remain competitive to stay alive, companies are realizing the need to expand operations and relationships on an international level. To do so, "managers must recognize the need for simultaneously achieving global efficiency, national responsiveness, and the ability to develop and exploit knowledge on a worldwide basis."[2] It is not enough, however, for companies to recognize this need and plunge blindly into global expansion. Companies must manage this expansion strategically to find success in international markets.

THE COMPETITIVE ADVANTAGES NEEDED FOR GLOBAL COMPETITION

What does it mean for organizations as small as a single company to those as large as a nation to be competitive on a global level? Michael Porter offers a comprehensive explanation to this question in his work *The Competitive Advantage of Nations*. Porter suggests that the only meaningful measure of a nation's competitiveness is one that measures that nation's level of productivity—not merely vast territory or natural resources as previous arguments have suggested. Instead Porter points to productivity being pivotal to success, where productivity "depends on both the quality and the features of products and the efficiency with which they are produced."[3] Porter backs his claim by pointing to examples around the globe; geographically significant countries such as India and Russia have struggled with poverty, while relatively tiny nations inhabited by small populations, such as Switzerland and Singapore, have achieved success and prominence by adapting quickly and avoiding complex political and economic problems.[4]

To maintain this type of productivity, companies must continually upgrade their methods through seeking out quality improving practices and more efficient means of production. This quest inevitably leads many national companies into the international arena.

Before we continue with the discussion of Porter, we must define what being a "global" company today actually means, and to distinguish companies with global operations from those with multidomestic operations.

In their work *Managing Across Borders: The Transnational Solution,* Christopher Bartlett and Sumantra Ghoshal stipulate that for firms to undertake an appropriate competitive strategy, they must distinguish their areas of operation as either a part of a *multidomestic industry* or a *global industry.*

In a multidomestic line of business, a large distinction exists between the characteristics of the services a company provides within a particular country versus the characteristics of those it provides in other countries. In any service-based industry, the service must be customized to fit the needs of the particular customer base. Since the needs of the customer can vary widely from country to country depending on the nature of the service being provided, the actual services a company provides must also vary accordingly.

Given these conditions, a company that provides these highly market customized services has little opportunity to recognize benefits from economies of scale, consolidation of tasks, or universal strategy application in multidomestic industries. Competitive advantages are then confined to the individual countries in which a company is competing, and strategy is restricted to measures of profitability related to individual market share.

Global industries, on the other hand, are affected in completely the opposite direction. Competition is truly global—meaning a firm's competitive position and reputation in one country directly affects its position in other countries. Further, a global industry firm is able to draw on competitive advantages that not only span more than one country, but also those stemming from a presence in more than one country. These competitive advantages include economies of scale, transfer of brand equity, and a more integrated, universal strategic approach. Equipped with this working definition of a global company, we will resume our discussion of Porter.

THE DETERMINANTS OF NATIONAL ADVANTAGE MODEL

Given these important distinctions, Porter developed The Determinants of National Advantage model to identify the key economic forces at work and to depict their relationships to each other. Figure 9.1 displays this "national diamond" model.

Porter defines the forces of firm strategy, industry structure, and competitive behavior—located in the top box in the diamond—as the prevailing conditions in a given nation that govern how a company is created, organized, and managed. This concept also refers to how other, national rival companies compete with the given national firm.

Factor Conditions—captured in the box on the extreme right of the model—refers to a nation's available factors of production. These include access to raw materials, skilled labor, infrastructure, and technology. Diametrically opposite in the box on the left side of the model is Porter's concept of demand conditions. This force refers to the nature of the demand, as expressed through customer identity and expectations, for the product or service a given industry provides.

Lastly, in the box located at the bottom of the model, are the forces of related and supporting industries. These refer to the significance of the presence, or absence, and role of

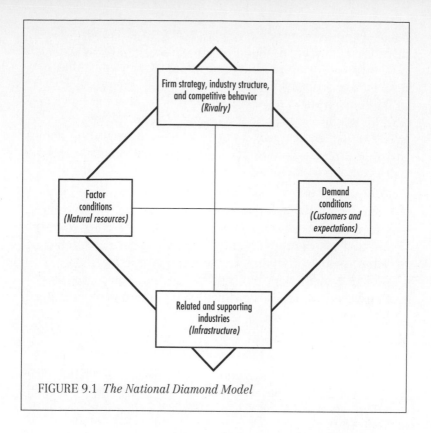

FIGURE 9.1 *The National Diamond Model*

supplier industries and related industries that are internationally competitive.

Porter uses the diamond shape to emphasize the interactive nature of these forces in creating a national competitive advantage within a given industry. If a nation can manage its industries domestically to foster an environment of continual improvement and evolution, the competitive advantages developed within a given industry will be sustainable beyond the borders of the country internationally.

OPPORTUNITIES ASSOCIATED WITH A GLOBAL APPROACH—JOINT VENTURES

Success in global business markets is attainable through more methods than just the sole expansion efforts of individual companies. Expansion into new markets and new industries can also be successfully accomplished through the process of a *joint venture*. What, exactly, constitutes a joint venture can and does vary from situation to situation. This flexibility is one of the primary reasons that joint ventures facilitate expansion in otherwise impossible situations.

All joint ventures have certain attributes in common. Simply put, a joint venture happens when two or more parties agree to undertake a project together where resources, liabilities, and profits will be shared. As legal agreements, joint ventures come in three forms:

1. *Contractual Joint Ventures.* Under this arrangement, the joint venture is not created as a separate legal corporate entity. Rather, it is an enterprise in the form of an unincorporated association, created to carry out clearly defined activities and to attain specific goals over a specific time period. A clear separation exists between the companies that agree to cooperate where each of them is responsible for its own liabilities.

2. *Equity Joint Ventures.* Under this arrangement, two partners agree to the formation of a legal corporation with limited liability and joint management. There is pooled equity in the corporation from which an equity ratio is determined, as well as the profits and losses associated with the venture.

3. *Hybrid Joint Ventures.* Under this arrangement, partners agree to maintain the corporate status of a separate legal entity, but may do without the limited liability option. Partners also agree to the specific responsibilities and time constraints described in the contractual joint venture.

In her work *Managing for Joint Venture Success,* Kathryn Rudie Harrigan explains the specific benefits of joint ventures in their various forms. She also highlights the potential benefits of joint ventures as strategic alliances and as methods of establishing sustainable core competencies for both corporate parties involved.

Essentially, the specific form a joint venture takes on should depend largely on the collective and personal objectives of the parties forming the joint venture, as well as external factors operating in the market the two partnering companies are entering. Collectively, firms generally consider a joint venture option to minimize the risk involved in pursuing a new line of business or industry by sharing the risk with another company. Further, a firm that maintains a desire to expand operations would probably do so on its own if it had all of the resources, both physical and human, required to do so. Joint ventures usually arise out of two firms recognizing that they have a mutual interest in a given business pursuit and that, collectively, they have complementary resources and capabilities needed to succeed in the specified pursuit.

Joint venture projects can provide both companies participating with numerous advantages. Yet, it should be recognized that, almost without exception, joint venture businesses are far harder to manage than their solely-owned subsidiary counterparts. The prevalence of joint venture projects, however, stands as an indication that the benefits of this kind of corporate cooperation outweigh the drawbacks, and that corporate executives will continue to choose joint venture options. This leaves managers with the challenge of adapting to these new situations through developing new ways to manage them more effectively.

Just how innovative and flexible a joint venture manager needs to be depends on internal as well as external factors. To start with, if the two venturing parties are having an especially long or difficult time learning to work together, any competitive advantage or synergistic benefits potentially gained from a joint venture can be squandered. Joint venture managers must be especially flexible, both in determining how each entity's corporate strategy must change to accommodate the other, as well as in the ability of the joint venture company to adapt its product or service to the changing needs of the marketplace.

This is especially true of new or emerging industries, where the demand for products and services is not mature and there is a high degree of uncertainty as to how a product or service will need to be modified to fit within the market. In cases like these, Harrigan advocates that the joint venture agreement be designed such that it is short in duration and as unbinding as possible. If an industry is developing so rapidly that the product idea around which a given venture is formed becomes obsolete before it can even be delivered to the market—like in the technology industry—short-term agreements protect each venturing party from being stuck in a relationship that drains resources and may prompt managers to manage losses rather than cut them. In many emerging markets, being an early entrant and acquiring dominant market share creates sustainable competitive advantage.

Cases also exist where the two venture parties experience a learning curve so steep when working together that its presence eliminates any hope of the new venture gaining early entrant status and dominant market share. Here again, a shorter term, less binding agreement enables each party to move on when it becomes obvious that the venture will either not work or has missed its window of entry opportunity.

Lastly, short term, loosely binding joint venture agreements offer companies much more flexibility and many more opportunities to learn and adapt. More specifically, they allow companies to work with and learn from other companies, and then move on to repeat the process with other companies. This type of strategy can be especially useful in developing markets or industries, where joint venturing with multiple partners can keep one company apprised of new industry trends and developments through intercompany information share.

Let's look at the opposite side of the coin now. In the same way that there are business contexts where short-term, non-equity joint venture agreements are optimal, certain contexts also exist in which longer term and more concretely binding agreements facilitate greater success. This phenomenon happens more frequently when the two venturing partners are planning on entering an industry that is just beginning to mature. This means that there is some standard for the product itself, consumer demand and quality levels already in place. In such cases, the two venturing partners are usually working together to attain sustainable competitive advantages.

For example, two partnering companies may be working together so that any inefficient production methods that either company may have can be replaced with efficient ones without either company running the risk of producing to excess. To accomplish this end requires rather significant capital investment on both parties, as well as the exchange of information on best-in-class production methods. When the level of investment in a joint venture is high, a long and involved commitment between partners adds a comfort level to the interaction. This is accomplished by providing an assurance that the joint entity will exist long enough for both parties to profit, and that it is in both parties' best interests to facilitate each other's profit making, rather than engage in competitive and undermining behaviors.

In yet another long-term application, maturing industries can use joint venture partnerships to invite industry giants from related industries to enter. It is better for these relationships to be conducted in a joint venture structured to be longer lasting and more legally binding for two primary reasons. First, partnerships between well-established and respected entities create interesting power alliances. The benefits these kinds of alliances reap in an industry are more fully harvested if the two entities in question are committed to a long-term relationship. Say an industry recognizes each corporate venture partner independently as a major industry player, and the industry believes that the partnership will be long-lived. The industry is more likely to accept the dominant power position of the joint venture partners in the industry, instead of trying to find ways to dominate or undermine the joint venture entity competitively.

Second, in cases like these, the two venturing entities have more of a mutual respect for each other. This level of respect manifests itself in a more intense loyalty and effort to work together, rather than for one partner to attempt to dominate the other. There are occasions when a budding corporation will join forces with a mature industry giant to bring a product or service to market. For the budding company, access to the larger company's production, distribution, and materials base, as well as its reputation is the clear benefit. Meanwhile, the larger company gains the opportunity to enter into a line of business or market that otherwise might have gone ignored. Yet, in these situations, the larger company knows that the smaller company's very existence depends largely on them. As a result, the larger companies have been known to use many methods to exploit this power imbalance. The imbalance manifests itself in ways ranging from the larger company's management style used to handle problems in the partnership to how the profits are divided. This kind of behavior happens far less frequently when both partnering entities are influential, powerful, and established independently.

Whatever the structure a joint venture takes on, these kinds of partnerships remain the most viable method for a great number of companies to expand globally. Joint ventures are especially beneficial for companies who wish to expand into international markets while having little or no international base on their own. Companies from different nations who engage in a joint venture simultaneously establish business channels, relationships, and resources in a foreign country. Further, joint venture partnerships have the potential to expand to other areas of operation, where two companies can share production capacity and distribution channels in their respective markets. This is an especially viable option when the partners in the original joint venture are not directly competing in the same markets.

As mentioned earlier, joint ventures also provide opportunities for entrepreneurial ventures, as one partner with resources can be matched with a partner with a viable product concept. Again, in these instances, the ability to cross international business borders is an extra benefit. Moreover, the introduction of a new innovation on an international level allows both partners to enjoy many competitive advantages—such as early entry, market share dominance, and economies of scale—that may prove to be sustainable over time and as markets expand.

Although the disequilibrium of power can create certain drawbacks for the entrepreneur or developing nation alike, many may feel that an imperfect opportunity is better than none at all, especially if entry into international markets is one of the benefits of the joint venture opportunity.

THE BACKLASH AGAINST GLOBALIZATION

Businesses must recognize that the disequilibrium of power produced within the global marketplace has become a point of extreme contention and hostility over the past decade. Those opposing globalization—such as the protestors during the December 2000 protests at the WTO summit in Seattle—argue that Porter's doctrine of competitive advantage does not accommodate those less advantageous, with a history of political oppression and inadequate education, for example. In contrast, supporters contend that by enabling smaller entrepreneurs to play in the league of large corporations, globalization breaks down inhibiting barriers of geography and nationality, thus bringing the world closer to the classic theoretical model of capitalism.[5] While advocates reiterate that globalization must be pursued to ensure viable economic interaction between developed and less-developed countries, critics continue to claim that the interaction is inevitably lopsided to unevenly benefit the former.

Whether or not one believes it has succeeded, the global economy—propelled further by the lightning speed of technological advances to eliminate isolation and provide real-time information—holds the potential to increase productivity, open previously inaccessible markets, spur entrepreneurship, stimulate economic innovations, and allow knowledge to permeate the globe.

SUMMARY

Regardless of an existing backlash, the fact remains—a global marketplace constitutes today's reality. Prevailing trends of globalization make it imperative that nations, as well as the businesses they foster, develop the skills to compete on an international level. While this may seem an intimidating proposition for some companies, the benefits and opportunities associated with international expansion are numerous. Not only are there opportunities to improve on best practices in the areas of quality and efficiency, but there also exists enormous potential to discover and implement new technologies and innovations.

Even in cases where firms are unwilling or unable to forge into new markets or industries on their own, the option of a joint venture can be used as a solution that minimizes risk and has the potential to aid companies in establishing a presence in new international markets while creating sustainable competitive advantages.

These factors, operating in conjunction—along with the opportunities they provide—will continue to foster a global business climate that encourages higher standards for business products and practices across all nations.

INTERNET RESOURCES

AILEENA World Media Index (www.aileena.ch). An exhaustive resource, indexing approximately 5,500 links to news media—including newspapers, radio, and television stations—in 174 countries. Links are categorized by region to make the index even more user-friendly.

Bloomberg (www.bloomberg.com). The online edition of *Bloomberg Business News* provides extremely detailed reports on international business happenings, especially with its internal links to international market info and the "FedWatch" link under "News." Includes news from world markets and headlines from many newspapers around the globe.

Business Week (www.businessweek). The Global Business section of *Business Week*'s online component features stories from international versions of the magazine and is separated into sections for Latin American, European, and Asian news. The site is continually updated with international news headlines.

Expansion Management Magazine (www.expansionmanagement.com). The online version of *Expansion Management* includes archives from 1998–2001 issues that provide useful information regarding the expansion or relocation of companies.

International Herald Tribune (www.iht.com/frontpage.htm). The *Herald Tribune*'s site offers special reports researching specific industries and countries, as well as featured news stories from around the globe.

INTERNATIONAL BUSINESS CRITICAL REFERENCE MATERIALS

Bartlett, Christopher, and Sumantra, Ghoshal. *Managing Across Borders: The Transnational Solution.* Boston: Harvard Business School Press, 1989.

This book begins with a reclassification of business organizations into categories of the multinational corporation, the global corporation, and the international corporation. It then defines the transnational corporation as a combination of these three, assigning to it specific characteristics from each business category. The rest of the book proceeds to explain how a corporation can manage its functions, strategies, and practices to integrate the characteristics of the multinational, global, and international organizations in such a way that the corporation gains all the benefits these different business forms provide, without experiencing the drawbacks. Less pragmatic than other sources on the subject, this work offers a highly theoretical approach to managing across borders.

Govindarajan, Vijay, Anil K. Gupta, and C. K. Prahalad. *The Quest for Global Dominance: Transforming Global Presence into Global Competitive Advantage.* New York: Jossey-Bass, 2001.

Quest for Global Dominance outlines the three chief reasons why increasing a company's global presence is so imperative in our day and age, to become well aware of the respective opportunities and threats existing worldwide. The authors instruct readers on how to identify market opportunities globally and, in the process, maximize corporate competitiveness. The book provides useful conceptual frameworks to help readers better understand the realities and risks defining our modern-day global economy.

Harrigan, Kathryn Rudie. *Managing for Joint Venture Success.* Lexington, MA: Lexington Books, 1991.

Based on the fundamental acceptance of Porter's theory of National Competitiveness, this book explains in detail the benefits of establishing a joint venture between firms from different nations, especially in terms of changing competitive conditions to create competitive advantages for both parties. The book identifies several common problems many joint venture partners face, and provides suggestions on how to structure a joint venture such that these potential problematic issues are addressed even before the venture itself is underway.

Porter, Michael. *The Competitive Advantage of Nations.* New York: The Free Press, 1990.

What makes a nation competitive in the international arena? This book summarizes Porter's four year study on the 10 "important trading nations," which include Denmark, Germany, Italy, Japan, Korea, Singapore, Sweden, Switzerland, the United Kingdom, and the United States. Porter puts forth a theory that no one factor makes a nation competitive; rather, it is a series of factors working in tandem that enable a nation to become and remain competitive in the global business world. Porter defines these forces, as well as captures the dynamic interaction between them, in his national competitiveness model. This model serves as a basis for the work of many other international business scholars, and is referred to frequently as a fundamental framework for understanding the international business scene.

Weiss, Kenneth D. *Building an Import/Export Business,* 2nd edition. New York: John Wiley & Sons, 1997.

This fundamental guide encompasses all aspects of building a successful import or export business—from initial start-up considerations to marketing recommendations and the intricacies of trade regulations. Weiss outlines critical steps when first setting up your business, searching for buyers, establishing a target market, and getting the most out of trade pacts such as GATT, WTO, and NAFTA.

The Job Search

I If you are reading this chapter, you are in one of two situations: either you are just out of college or graduate school, or you have reached what Andy Grove, the former CEO of Intel, calls a "strategic inflection point." A strategic inflection point is one of those "times in the life of a business or a person when fundamentals are about to change. That change can mean an opportunity to raise yourself to new heights. But it may just as likely signal the beginning of the end."[1] We all have coworkers and friends who always have an updated copy of their resume available. These individuals are not only savvy but also understand their industry, their company, and their own skills. This knowledge enables them to anticipate change and how it may affect them down the line. Consider the employee who never took the time to become skilled with any of the innovative software available at the office, and is working for a company that just purchased a multimillion-dollar computerized MRP system. Who has the advantage now, the young kid fresh out of college, or the older employee who's been at the job—doing it the old way and probably doing it well—for 20 years? Regardless of whether or not it's fair—it's often the young, trainable employee starting his or her career. Given the almost constant state of technological and economic change, the ability to innovate, and do so quickly, is imperative. So keep an updated version of your resume on hand to be prepared when an opportunity comes along.

On a larger scale, consider the owners of Blockbuster Video, who built a multibillion-dollar empire renting video cassettes. Blockbuster approached a strategic inflection point with the onset of digital satellites, telecommunications deregulation, and the prospect that consumers soon would be able to order any of thousands of movies via the Internet and emerging wireless technologies. How often will the suburban family run out to the video store to pick up the latest release when it's available for the same price simply by clicking on their satellite offerings?

Microsoft's 1995 response to the Internet—with the launch of its online service, MSN—is a good example of a positive response to a strategic inflection point. Late to the market, Microsoft understood the impact the Internet would have on its business and it rallied to capture quickly the attention of a significant portion of the consumable market. Such revolutionary changes in the markets are occurring daily, and what makes you marketable is your ability to recognize and respond to such changes before they occur. To take advantage of change, you must foresee it. Accordingly, you must have an extensive knowledge of the job market before attempting a job search.

Once you have a sense of the job market, the best time to look for a job is when you already have one. You are much more attractive to an employer if you are already working. It tells the potential employer that another firm—preferably a name with market equity—has already bought into your capabilities. If you are out on the street looking for a job you have to initially overcome whatever caused you to lose your job— both on paper with your resume and in person during an interview.

If you're just starting out on your career (having graduated from college or graduate school), you'll need to overcome the classic dilemma: How can I get a good job without experience and how can I get experience without a good job? We address these questions further in the chapter.

Finding a job requires you to know what sort of job you are looking for, and this can be harder than it appears. Second, during the course of your job search you will need to create a resume as well as a network of contacts whom you can ask for help and eventually send your resume. Finally, you will go through an intense period of interviewing for various positions.

While covering the problems of recruiting and the job search, this chapter also covers the often-overlooked process of thinking about your career strategically; this will help you identify and ultimately land the job of your choice. Throughout the process, remember that searching for a job is a skill, and one that improves each time you use it.

FIRST, A COHERENT CAREER PLAN

While finding a job that offers good pay, benefits, intellectual challenge, and opportunity is important, you need to be patient and perpetually aware of your own strategic inflection points. Much like the stock market, where a short-term perspective leads to irrational market behavior, your career is the same: think for the long term. Timing is important; you don't want to overplan your career because any number of events, from the economy to your personal life, can quickly render a 10-year career plan obsolete. A three-year plan is a good place to start—long enough for you to factor in patience and transcend business cycles, but short enough to force regular alteration to your plan. Developing your working career plan is not unlike writing a business plan. Now, your career is the entrepreneurial venture. Accordingly your career plan must live and respond to both cultural and economic changes. Refer to it on a regular basis. See your career plan as the document that, if blended with enough substance and inspiration would secure you funding, convince a client to buy a product (in this case, yourself), or scare away your competition. Your career plan is sacred and ideally you should use it as a professional mantra.

ESTABLISHING A CAREER PLAN

To determine your present and future career plan, create a list of requirements and expectations for your current job; do this by asking yourself several critical questions:

Why Do I Work?

If your answer is "to earn money," now ask yourself why you want the money? To be financially secure? To be financially independent? If you were to achieve those goals, what would you then use your earnings for? To travel? To give back to particular organizations in your community? Perhaps spend time doing what you "really love"? If so, why aren't you doing what you "really love" right now?

If your answer is "to achieve recognition" or "be successful," now ask yourself what you mean by recognition or success. Is recognition being quoted by reporters "as an expert" in your field? Is success having family members ask you for advice and guidance on important matters? Or do you ultimately desire the status and respect that accompanies earning a certain amount of money?

If your answer is "establish myself in my profession," now ask yourself how you will know when you are "established." Is it a certain number of clients you want to have? Or a particular journal you want to publish papers in?

Take the time right now to think about these questions— your answers may surprise you, and give you a deeper understanding of your real long-term goals.

How Much Money Do I Really Need?

The answer to this question varies from person to person and is directly tied to your long-term goals. At the least, you should sit down and figure out how much money you need to meet your minimum living expenses. Keep in mind that you should have at least three months of living expenses saved and available for withdrawal at any given time as a basic form of security. Knowing how much you need to live will help you make the sometimes hard decisions about what kind of job or industry you are looking for.

What Is Rewarding About the Work I Do?

Ask yourself this question. Jot a few notes. Is it the people you work with? The tangible product you produce? The places you get to travel on the job? Think about what it is that would make you feel successful and content in your work. Then think about what you are willing to sacrifice to achieve that feeling.

These questions are only meant to get you thinking—articulating what your long-term goals are and then creating a career plan that will achieve them is a time-consuming task. A number of good books have been written on the subject—go to your local bookstore and browse the career or financial planning section. Buy a few that interest you and take the time to read them. You'll be amazed at how the process of reading what other people have to say on the subject will help you clarify what you believe.

After you've spent some time thinking, make a short list of your goals and leave it in a place you see every day—in a day planner, on the mirror, or on the refrigerator. After living with them for a period of time, rework them until they express exactly what you mean.

You are now ready to seriously consider the job search. Once you have a sense of the market, the next steps are to build a strong resume and an equally strong network of contacts who can provide both guidance and access to available jobs.

THE ONLINE SEARCH

Most aspects of the job search—with the exception of in-person interviews—are occurring with increasing frequency online. As with many topics, the Internet is a fantastic source of information on industries, individual companies, executives, economic trends, and virtually any business-related topic. In addition, it's an invaluable place to search for current job opportunities. Corporate web pages have "career opportunity" links dedicated to listing available positions. Moreover, the Internet gives you real-time access to all of this information.

Employers like the Internet because it provides them with greater access to a wider candidacy pool. Job seekers like it because it's fast, inexpensive, and readily available 24 hours a day. A recent poll conducted by Lee Hecht Harrison revealed that 40 percent of job seekers who used the Internet to post their resume or retrieve job listings got interviews as a result. Even more telling, 96 percent used the Internet to find job openings, and 76 percent posted their resume on the Internet.[2]

RESUME WRITING FOR SUCCESS

Coming up with a strong resume is critical, and it is the first step in any job search. Doing it right the first time combined with knowing what type of resume to use will save you time and resources. Nothing is worse than hearing about a job you'd like to apply for and not having a resume ready to submit. Instead of frantically rushing to create one at the last minute, be poised and have a polished resume ready.

First, a few things you need to know about your resume and what it means to potential employers. A resume is a window into your working history. As an historical sales document, it should present your experiences in such a way as to generate the desire to meet and interview you. Keep in mind, a resume is not an autobiography; it cannot communicate everything about you. Most of your personal or biographical attributes are not relevant in a resume. Focus instead on your work experiences and just enough personal information to interest a potential employer.

Granted, it's hard to write about yourself, and the exercise of writing a resume is frustrating because nobody really enjoys touting his or her own successes. It helps to remember that a resume is one of the few places you have a chance to truly *sell* yourself. Seeing a resume as a marketing campaign of sorts can help distance you from your accomplishments. This in turn allows your resume to sound self-assured and confident without lying or bragging.

How can you express your skills and experience in a resume without losing a great deal in the translation? One way is to talk to people you have worked with. Ask them to describe you, the business you worked in, and your job responsibilities there. This will give you perspective and build your confidence in your professional abilities. Even if you know exactly what you did, it can be hard to articulate your activities in an appropriate way. Take notes to summarize what you learned from these interviews. This process allows you to develop a keen understanding of your work experiences and a familiarity with the best way to describe them.

BASIC RESUME ORGANIZATION
Education

Your resume should have an education section. If you have recently left school and are not currently working, the education section should be at the top of your resume. Otherwise, the education section should be at the bottom of your resume;

10 years out of college, your work experience speaks more to who you are than a college GPA. The only exception to this is if you have a degree from a well-known university or college; in that case, the education section (including where you attended high school) can go first. However, that decision is best left to individual preference and your assessment of just how critical where you went to school will be in influencing a potential employer. If you know (or suspect) a corporate recruiter attended the same small high school (or a comparable school), by all means, add the information. If you were all-American everything in high school or the class valedictorian, make mention of it on the resume even though the information is old. SATs and your high school GPA, unless they were in the top 5 percent, should not be included. There are times when these sorts of information are irrelevant or inappropriate, so have two versions of your resume prepared.

Regardless of where the education section is placed, it should include the name of the college (not abbreviated), its location, the month and year you received (or expect to receive) your degree, the number of years you were there, the degree conferred, specific honors, relative coursework, and any college related, extracurricular activities that are job related.

Work Experience

Your prior work experience tells a potential employer the most important information about your candidacy. These sections must be honest and relate to the job you are applying for. Of course, you cannot change your work experience, but you can alter the perception of that experience by constructing a resume that showcases the skills needed in the job you are currently seeking. Previous experience is only one part of your presentation. Part of your success on your resume as well as during an interview is your interest and enthusiasm for the job and the company. Most employers would rather hire an enthusiastic person who is willing to learn than an experienced person without enthusiasm. Of course, directly applicable work experience on your resume will help you. Similar experience needs to be augmented by enthusiasm and a pattern of increasing responsibility in your prior work.

Career Objective—To Add or Not to Add?

The only time to add a specific career objective to your resume is if you have a specific job in mind. For example, if you know you want to be an investment banker in New York City to the exclusion of anything else, then go ahead and say so. You will run into problems, however, when an informed recruiter sees your resume and wonders why you've limited your options. Jobs in many industries require similar skills, so being completely single-minded doesn't necessarily make sense, as stating a defined career objective can compromise your candidacy for other positions. Additionally, if you cannot define a specific goal don't add a vague goal simply to have a career objective on your resume. For example: *Career Goal: To secure an entry-level position within a growing and dynamic firm that provides a cross-functional experience ultimately leading to increasing responsibility and a senior management position.*

This is pretty much the same thing everybody wants, so why bother stating the obvious? Career goals or objectives are meaningless unless they are specific, short, and focused on the near-term. Even then, however, stating a career objective is risky because once you submit your resume for a position you no longer control where it goes. Therefore, you may be overlooked for a position you would have been eager to accept, simply because the career goal on your resume does not fit.

Personal Web Sites: A Cautionary Note

While including a personal web site URL on a resume can showcase your technical skills nicely, think carefully about what your web site reveals about you. Do you have links to inappropriate sites? Do you have pictures posted of you in potentially unprofessional clothing or situations? Sometimes a personal web site is simply that, personal and should be left as such.

RESUME TYPES

There are a variety of resume types, many of which you are no doubt familiar with. In the course of your search, you will use several types. The *functional* and *chronological resumes* are old standbys. Both work very well, largely because everybody uses them and they are easy to comprehend. Examples of both are included in Figures 10.1 and 10.2. The variety that

Shawn H. Smeallie

1 Topnotch Lane
Weeds, MA 03750

home telephone: (617) 555-5555
home fax: (617) 555-5555
e-mail: Shawn H. Smeallie dartmouth.edu

Demonstrated Skill in . . .

- Setting goals, determining objectives, and devising strategies toward the development of new business areas;

- Formulating and defining product concepts consistent with strategic marketing directives, developing business/marketing plans to develop and introduce same;

- Executing plans, mobilizing resources, and directing the development and marketing processes;

- Communicating and presenting concepts and plans to all interested stakeholders; building consensus, gaining agreement, and driving process.

Skills Developed with . . .

Leahy Clinic, Burlington, MA   2000–present

Development Director responsible for capital gift fund-raising for this academic medical center

- Managed all development activities of the Cancer Center and the Weiderecht Center for Clinical and Evaluative Studies.

- Developed marketing strategies to raise prospect/public awareness. Worked with physicians and individuals to increase private donations.

- Directed fund-raising efforts for new cancer center building ($20 million goal), fellowship programs, and research support.

St. Lawrence University, Canton, NY   1993–1998

As Associate Director, Major Gifts, managed the cultivation and solicitation of 250 major gift prospects in Midwest region, where $30 million was raised during the "Everybody Loves a Saint" campaign.

- Coordinated project activities related to targeted fund-raising.

- Traveled extensively with senior officers, deans and faculty, trustees.

- Enlisted, trained, and managed Chicago Volunteer Committee.

(Continued)

(Continued)

Education . . .

- Masters of Business Administration—The Tuck School of Business, Dartmouth College, 2000
- Bachelor of Arts, Economics—MIT, 1993, Honors Program, Dean's List

Personal

Single; avid fan of thoroughbred racing; four sons; attempting to be a decent downhill skier

FIGURE 10.1 *Functional resume*

is probably somewhat less familiar is the *electronic resume,* either in text or in multimedia form. However you run your job search, the Internet will play an important role in that search. Keep in mind that you have less control over who sees your resume if it is posted on the Web and that again, the tone of your resume should match the job you are applying for.

RESUME RED FLAGS
Check Your Spelling

It is easy to spend so much time working on your resume that you stop seeing the text actually on the page. Read your resume backwards, word for word, and have a good friend do the same if he or she is willing. There is nothing more unprofessional than a typo in a resume.

Check Your Grammar

Be sure to use complete sentences; watch for subject-verb agreement; try to avoid the passive voice; and avoid wordiness.

Check Your Data

Are the phone numbers on your resume current? Are the people listed as references still working at the company you list?

Jennifer Ruth Thomas

The Amos Tuck School · 514 Byrne Hall Hanover, NH 03755
(603)-555-7365 · E-mail:j.sotak@dartmouth.edu

Education

THE TUCK SCHOOL OF BUSINESS, DARTMOUTH COLLEGE   Hanover, NH

Candidate for Master of Business Administration degree, 2003. Prospective Student Host,
Marketing Club; Organized Marketing Career Panel.

UNIVERSITY OF MASSACHUSETTS   Amherst, MA

Bachelor of Business Administration in Marketing, Minor in Economics, 1995.
Graduated cum laude. Economics Honor Society (Omicron Delta Epsilon).

Experience

1995–2001 A. T. Kearney, Inc.   New York, NY

Associate

Performed broad range of consulting services for Fortune 500 companies, including
marketing-related consulting for leading consumer products companies.

Managed client relationships and worked in joint client and consultant teams in formulating
recommendations for change.

- *Category Management Strategy:* Developed category management strategies and
  enhanced category position of a leading bottled-water manufacturer through
  improved trade presentation media. Assessed New Age beverage category market
  and its impact on bottled water. Developed a micromarketing tool for optimizing
  shelf space in retail locations.

- *Market Assessment:* Conducted customer, competitor, channel, and market expert
  interviews to assess competitive position of a leading home security equipment
  manufacturer. Performed extensive market research to project market growth and
  potential share expansion. Provided synthesized results to a major diversified
  conglomerate considering acquisition of the manufacturer.

1994, 1995 JC Penney   Garden City, NY

Assistant Merchandise Manager

Executed full range of merchandise management activities during summer internships.
Selected as regional champion for District Intern Scholarship and qualified for nationwide
competition.

(Continued)

(Continued)

- Managed sales team of ten full-time and eight part-time sales associates.
- Executed seasonal assortment planning, visual merchandising, and in-department promotions.

Personal

- Enjoy volunteer work, YMCA Big Sister Program
- UMass Alumni Club Member (NY Metro Area)
- Conversational Italian and German, familiar with Russian

FIGURE 10.2 *Chronological resume*

Part of having an updated resume is keeping these numbers current.

Avoid Being Cute

Unique resumes are sometimes successful. Mostly, however, cute resumes fall flat. Potential employers, reading hundreds of resumes, like to look at certain parts of a resume for certain types of information. They are busy and sensitive to time; if your resume confuses them, they will not regard it or you any further. Give them the information where they expect it.

Avoid Buzzwords

Buzzwords in a resume sound nice to the uneducated or inexperienced, but indicate foolishness to the well-trained eye. A buzzword, writes *Webster's New Collegiate Dictionary,* is "an important sounding usually technical word or phrase often of little meaning used chiefly to impress laymen." Avoid the use of the buzzword.

Resume Length

How long should a resume be? At the early stage of one's career a single-page resume is enough to convey the most important experiences of your working history. At some point, when you are established in a field, you will switch to a longer resume with more detail.

NOW THAT IT'S DONE . . . POSTING A RESUME ON THE INTERNET

Posting your resume on the Internet is a simple process. A number of programs exist to translate your word-based resume to a searchable document so you don't waste time mastering the intricacies (though they are relatively simple for anybody who wants to try) of programming in HTML.

Tricks to Finding the Right Job on the Net

Key Word Searches

Many search programs scan your resume in search of words an employer selects; words they consider represent the type of person they are seeking for a specific job. What you should avoid are the classic action verbs like "facilitated," "strengthened," and "launched" in favor of nouns that have more meaning to an employer. A financial position might seek references to "CPA," "Accounting," "Arthur Andersen," "Series 7."

Resumes you post on the Internet can provide links to bodies of work you've created, writing samples, etc. Your resume can be built in a such a way as to make the information highlighting your skills easily available to the browser.

Cautions

Be Wary

Check your resume often. If you are paying to have your resume listed in a database, make certain access is secure and that there is a reimbursement procedure if your resume is lost or altered.

Lack of Information

Avoid any web site that does not list a street address, a phone number, or any other way to contact the "owners" of the site. If possible, try to call firms using the service and ask them directly if they have ever hired a person off the database you are considering joining. Screen them as you expect they will screen you. As much as you want a new job, don't compromise your integrity or your pocketbook to find one.

Avoid Scams

Be careful of sites that charge you to list your resume. While some of them do provide a premium service, there are plenty of sites available that won't cost you any more than your monthly fee to dial-up and connect to the Internet. For some job seekers, paying $50 to list their resume on a premium site is a small price to pay for the chance to land an $80,000 job. For others who need to watch every cent, however, especially if you're out of work, avoid the fees before the service is rendered—if at all.

NETWORKING

Networking is part of the job search process, and the rules for networking have not changed dramatically over time. Good networking comes down to preparation, attitude, and perseverance. Like a good pilot running through a preflight checklist, a job seeker should run through a checklist of events prior to networking. To successfully network, you must know exactly what you are attempting to achieve. Anybody worth talking to probably has little time for you. Therefore, be direct and focused. Let the right people know you're willing to take a chance or even willing to work for free or in a temporary position to get into the right industry.

Sources of Information

Who Do You Network With? Sometimes the best people to network with are midlevel employees, not the CEO. Start where you can within a firm, and go from there. Also consider unique sources like your neighbors. In an age where many of us barely even know our neighbors, let alone their career experiences, you might consider breaking down that barrier and finding out where your neighbor (or any acquaintance you might not think about speaking to in terms of your career) works or worked before.

Your neighbor may have relatives who are well-connected to your target industry or firm, or maybe a relative who has conducted his own successful job search and has an abundance of leads he can no longer use. One student found her job lead for a position in Chicago while riding the chair lift in Colorado. Brief encounters can lead to big results.

Get over the fear that not having a job (if this is your condition) means you are some sort of failure. Most successful people have been out of work during their careers and many, if not most, have also been fired as well. These people will tell you that being fired or let go in a "downsizing" was often one of the most positive career changes they've had. Sometimes it takes an unexpected change for a person to realize the job they had wasn't the one they really wanted. Whatever the circumstances, if you are out of work, you must not consider this a detriment to your success. Rather, see it as a chance to use the full workday to discover the job that's perfect for you.

Networking should not be a finite activity used only when you are seeking a job. A successful network is a part of your career and requires attention and maintenance—a systemic strategy of contacting people in your network on a regular basis. A successful network requires you to cultivate a knowledge base of people who, in a variety of ways, may help you along your career path or be a resource you can pass on to a person networking with you.

Remember generosity has significant payback value. Good deeds done today often result in the opportunity of a lifetime later. It's like buying stock in a start-up firm and just forgetting it's a part of your portfolio—until it turns into the next Microsoft or Netscape. Be patient throughout. Your timeline is your full career—probably close to forty years of working experiences. Networking requires a long-term view.

INTERVIEW

At some point, your job search will land you interviews. This is the single most important part of finding a job, because this is where you have a chance to sell personally yourself. Accordingly, the interview is the true test of your powers of persuasion. Nothing is as bad as bombing the early part of an interview and having to struggle through the remaining time knowing that there is no chance you will get the job. If this type of interview sounds horrendous, well . . . it is. Do everything possible to avoid this. Make a first and lasting good impression.

To do this you need to do your homework, and this includes researching the company you are interviewing with. Take advantage of the ample materials available online. Also take a look at your local paper, as there is a chance that events described in it have a bearing on the company you are courting. *The Wall Street Journal* is also important to read daily. Know enough about the business of the company to recognize what issues of the day might affect its success. This includes knowledge of the competitive marketplace; you should be able to name and speak confidently about at least two of the company's competitors.

Be careful not to sound like a know-it-all. The person interviewing you already has a job—and so, you need to display respect for them and their accomplishments. The intelligent employer will always hire the best person for the job, even if that means hiring someone smarter than he or she is. That doesn't change the fact that young, driven employees with greater intelligence or expertise can easily threaten older colleges. Be an emotionally intelligent job seeker and be sensitive to the insecurities, if any, around you.

Anticipate and have a response to every conceivable question. If you already understand the worst-case scenario ("Please describe a situation in which you failed at something important") and you have a well-rehearsed answer, then you have little to worry about. Write out the questions you anticipate and ask a family member or friend to run you through a series of mock interviews. Have these sessions videotaped; you'll be shocked by your body language. Any senior interviewer will be aware of your body language, so you should pay attention to controlling it.

Your interview starts with the clothes you wear and continues through to the thank-you letter you write the same day of the interview. Be polite to everyone you meet, including the support staff (often the receptionist is one of the savviest and most-liked members of any staff). Everybody already holding a job at the firm is judging you, so treat everyone at the firm with the respect you would want to see from a job seeker. Start strong and end strong.

Many job seekers express dismay about not getting a job after an interview they thought had gone well. But you need to know that if you bomb in the first five minutes, the strategies for moving forward typically follow one of two paths. Short of kicking you out of the interview room after the first five minutes, the next best way to make the following 25 minutes or so as painless as possible *for the interviewer,* is to keep interactions as friendly as possible. Some of the best interviews are the ones where you're pushed to the edge and forced to respond—not the ones where you engage in friendly conversation.

Don't let the first five minutes kill your candidacy. Most employers make a decision in the first minutes of meeting you and then spend the rest of the interview gathering information to support their gut feeling. Practice your opening salvo and anticipate a variety of questions. Make the right first impression and ride that success until the last few minutes— then end strong. Take the initiative and ask what the next steps are.

Don't ask stupid questions. Yes, there is such a thing as a stupid question. And the craziest questions are the ones you ask at the end of the interview that would require another 30 minutes for the recruiter to respond. Avoid questions that can be answered simply by reading the company marketing literature or annual report. Avoid questions that are best asked after an offer has been made. Do not talk about money until asked or the end of the interview cycle.

Don't Make Hasty Decisions

If offered the job, thank the employer and express your satisfaction. Ask how much time you have to consider the offer and, if they suggest anything less than 48 hours, ask for more time. Any firm attempting to force you to respond during the interview is probably not a firm you'd like to work with anyway, so don't worry too much about asking for more time. They have offered you a job and have indicated their interest in having you. The power has now switched to your side and you can dictate the terms . . . within reason. Consider the offer and go as far as to inform other employers interested in your candidacy you have already interviewed with about your offer. (They may match or better the offer.)

The following checklist may be helpful in making a decision about a company and an offer. Remember that each search will be unique to you and your long-term goals—no two checklists will be the same.

Following is an example checklist:

Company: _____

Position: _____

Why do I want to work in this industry? _____

for this firm? _____

How does this job fit into my long term goals? _____

Is this job one that I will find rewarding? _____

How so? _____

Do I like, respect or trust the people who work here? _____

Comments	Issues	My Criteria
_____	Salary	Bottom line $60,000
_____	Bonus Signing	Require $10,000
_____	Bonus Starting	Require ($5,000)
_____	Bonus Annual	(Based on personal performance, division or company as a whole?)
_____	Job Security	(High, Medium, Low) Question—Why is this job available?
_____	Advancement/firm	(High, Medium, Low) Question—Why is this job available?
_____	Advancement/ industry	(High, Medium, Low) Question—where is this business going?
_____	Weekday Hours	How long?
_____	Weekend Hours	(Yes or No) and how often Question: are weekends necessary for advancement?
_____	Overtime	(Yes or No) Question: My choice or theirs?
_____	Vacation	(how long) Question: Do people actually take their vacation?
_____	Intellectual Challenge	(High, Medium, Low) Question—will I be bored?
_____	Travel	(A lot, A bit, none) Question—Do I like to travel a and do I like where I'm going?

_____	Flexibility	(A lot, A bit, none)
		Question—Do I like to travel and do I like where I'm going?
_____	Variety	(High, Medium, Low)
		Question—will I be bored?
_____	Social Responsibility	(High, Medium, Low)
		Question—am I embarrassed to say I work here?
_____	Workforce Diversity	(High, Medium, Low)
		Question - Am I all alone?
_____	Environmentally Friendly	(High, Medium, Low)
		What will I sacrifice to know I'm not harming the environment or a specific group?
_____	Workplace	(Team work or Individual)
_____	Technology	(Do I know it or can I learn it?
_____	Commute time	(How Long?)
_____	Commute Style	(How done?)
_____	Socializing	(Do I like my co-workers?)
_____	Benefits	(Competitive?)
_____	Health Care	(How Much?)
_____	Dental Care	(How Much?)
_____	Retirement	(How Much, How important?)
_____	Educational Assistance	(How Much?)

Most Offers Are Negotiable

Negotiating is a fine art and much has been written explaining and teaching the process. Negotiating is all about providing solutions to conflict, which arises when there is a difference in opinion. That being said, we negotiate every day, whether we know it or not, and a basic understanding of how to negotiate will not only improve your daily life but will arm you with the skills necessary to optimize your job search. There are no guarantees when negotiating, but there is much to be gained from trying. Len Greenhalgh, Professor at the Tuck School of Business at Dartmouth, lists the eight rules of negotiating:

1. *Be ready to make a commitment.* You cannot negotiate from strength if there is not an offering level at which you would say "Yes, I will take that job." Know what your bottom and top lines are and when you would accept a position.

2. *Emphasize that you really want to work for the firm.* Your candidacy is going to be that much stronger if you express an interest. Some industries and firms are willing to pay more for a candidate who really wants to work for them as this reduces the risk and cost of turnover. But be honest—do not express the same sentiment to ALL firms.

3. *Empathize with the corporate side.* Know that the employer may really want you but the market for a person of your caliber is higher than the firm is offering. Firms are often constrained by the equity structure of the salaries that are already in place. When negotiating, you are accepting pay in the abstract, but the employer has to live in reality. It's not often the actual money; rather, it's the meaning of the money that causes problems for the employer.

4. *Depersonalize the "asking for money."* It's okay to ask for a lot of money. Do not make an economic sacrifice to work for the firm because you are afraid to ask for what you believe you are worth.

5. *Negotiate with the right person.* Often the HR person will make the offer and will toe the line on negotiations. However, the line manager may have more wiggle room or may have the power to influence change. Find allies within the firm and negotiate with people who understand your worth and can make decisions.

6. *Avoid ultimatums.* You don't like to get them, so don't give them. They are counterproductive.

7. *Sign-on bonus.* It's a cheap way for a firm to hire you. Consider the time value of money and the benefits of starting at a higher base. Granted, the lure of an extra 20k or more in your pocket is appealing, but taxes will have to be paid on that money and, if the job has a performance bonus (or any kind of increase) based on base salary, wouldn't you rather start from a higher point?

8. *Take the job for the right reasons.* Money alone is usually a bad reason to take a job. Make sure the people, the location, the responsibility, the career path, the product, the industry, and the lifestyle are all right for you. Don't take the job for the wrong reasons.

WHAT IF YOU DON'T GET THE JOB—WHAT NEXT?

Do it all again! But before doing so look back and try to figure out what went wrong. Don't expect the employer to tell you—although you might get lucky—for it no longer has any vested interest in you. This is where mock interviews can be extremely useful and where the comforting wisdom of people you trust is valuable. Often you will be your own best critic, and you simply have to be strong enough to recognize your own faults.

Unprofessional Resume Preparation

There are a lot of bad resumes floating around out there, and oftentimes they are responsible for getting an unsuccessful job pursuit off on the wrong foot. A professional resume is more than just a well-formatted document. It demands a highly specialized style of writing and incorporates years of knowledge about the finer points of resume do's and don'ts. Computer programs that help you prepare resumes can do a good job of formatting and help a little with wording. However, such programs simply can't supply the years of acquired knowledge a professional resume writer has. Consider having a professional prepare your resume. The advantage you gain over your competition is worth the investment, but make certain you are fully aware of what is on your resume in case you are asked specific questions.

Lack of Skills and Experience for the Position

You must possess the skills, qualifications, and experience for the position you are applying for. If you don't, be honest about it. You will eventually get caught if you misrepresent your qualifications.

Poor Personal Appearance

Would you hire a poorly-dressed applicant? Or one who was poorly groomed or dirty? A March 2001 CareerBuilder Inc. workplace survey revealed that almost three-quarters of U.S. workers agree that clothes and personal appearance influence employers' attitudes about their professionalism. Be sure to shape up and be appearance-conscious prior to your interview.[3] If you are unsure what appropriate interview apparel is, buy a book on corporate dress, or go to a large, upscale department store (in the city you are interviewing) and explain you are interviewing for a job. Have them suggest something appropriate. Even if you don't agree or buy their suggestion, you'll have an idea of what to wear.

Inability to Speak Clearly or Express Yourself; Inarticulate; Bad Grammar

Would you hire a person to meet and greet your customers who abused or defiled the English language? Communication skills are important in the interview as well as on the job.

Expects Too Much Too Soon

"You have to work your way to the top" is a proven, time-honored philosophy that seems to have disappeared . . . at least in the expectations of a few. If you target a position you are not qualified for, you won't get it.

SUMMARY

We are measured not by how we respond to good news but by how we react to bad news. Character establishes how you are perceived and how you view yourself. If you got the job, the trick is to keep it until you find yourself at another strategic inflection point. If you did not get the job, you just have to revisit the process and keep on trying. Looking for a job is a full-time job itself and so requires the same commitment of time and resources. Realize that life is imperfect; jobs can be unpleasant, people get laid off. The only aspect of life you have control over is your actions. So, arm yourself with a core set of skills, the right attitude, and go out there and sell yourself.

INTERNET RESOURCES

America's Job Bank (www.ajb.dni.us/seeker/). Enabling you to search by occupation or key word, America's Job Bank is the biggest and busiest job market in cyberspace. The site posts clock of available jobs nationwide (November 2001 cited 1,050,813 currently available jobs).

Brassring.com (www.brassring.com). A job search site specializing in finding IT jobs, tech jobs, Internet jobs, and job fair information. Post your resume to high-tech employers here.

High Technology Career Magazine (www.hightechcareers.com).

Joboptions.com (www.joboptions.com). Job Options' database has information on over 6,000 employers and is searchable by keyword, industry, and location with one-click resume forwarding to the employer.

Jobweb.com (www.jobweb.com). Provides online career counselors to answer specific questions, links to other useful job search sites, and job market updates/articles. Compiled by the National Association of Colleges and Employers, the site includes employer profiles, resumes/interviewing, and career planning.

Kiersey Temperament Sorter (www.keirsey.com/). A self-assessment tool to help you gauge your personality temperament (artisan, guardian, rational, or idealist) through a Myers-Briggs personality type questionnaire.

Monster.com (www.monster.com). A reliable stand-by; Monster's user-friendly searchable database contains career opportunities in all fields, nationwide and internationally.

Nationjob Network (www.nationjob.com). Job listings focusing specifically on the Midwest.

Recruiter on-line (www.recruitersonline.com). Over 2,000 executive search firms, recruiters.

Salary.com (www.salary.com). Provides extensive salary range information for every possible field of work.

The 2000–01 Occupational Outlook Handbook (www.bls.gov/oco/). Revised every two years, this site provides a job search function with resulting information such as nature of the work, working conditions, employment training, advancement opportunities, job outlooks, and earnings in a wide range of occupations.

(Continued)

(Continued)

Vault.com (www.vault.com). The workplace network offers much information on career fields but is harder to navigate because of the amount of information on the page. Offers job descriptions, career profiles, message boards, and a range of career fairs.

Wetfeet.com (www.wetfeet.com). Features WetFeet's "Industry Quick" with pages of industry overviews, industry tables, "love-hates" about the job, job tips, and profiles of people in the field.

JOB SEARCH CRITICAL REFERENCE MATERIALS

Beatty, Richard H., and Nicholas C. Burkholder. *The Executive Career Guide for MBAs: Inside Advice on Getting to the Top From Today's Business Leaders.* New York: John Wiley & Sons, 1996.

The Executive Career Guide is written exclusively for MBAs. Its 12 chapters are meant to provide all of the necessary tools for finding and getting a successful executive job. Information for the first half of the book is based on extensive surveys and interviews with top business executives.

Bolles, Richard. *What Color Is Your Parachute?* Berkeley, CA: Ten Speed Press, 2002.

This is the updated edition of Richard Bolles' popular book on job hunting. Often referred to as the "gold standard of career guides" this best-seller helps job hunters define their interests, experiences, goals, and attitudes by asking two questions: What do you want to do? and Where do you want to do it? *What Color Is Your Parachute* offers good career advice for those looking for their first job as well as those who want to change careers.

Buckingham, Marcus, and Donald O., Clifton. *Now, Discover Your Strengths.* New York: Free Press, 2001.

Using a web-based interactive questionnaire by the Gallup Organization, *Now, Discover Your Strengths* enables readers to determine their own top-five inherent strengths. The book reveals that not only can the discovery of your strengths aid in a job search, but it can also facilitate finding a successful management strategy and philosophy.

Holton, Ed. *The New Professional: Everything You Need to Know For a Great First Year on the Job.* Princeton, NJ: Peterson's Guides, 1991.

The New Professional is for people who are starting their first full-time professional job. It focuses mainly on those people making the transition from student to professional. 100 newly hired workers and their managers were interviewed to give the reader an accurate account of what to expect during his or her first year on the job.

Krannich, Caryl Rae, and Ronald L. Krannich. *Interview For Success: A Practical Guide to Increasing Job Interviews, Offers, and Salaries,* 5th edition. Manassas Park, VA: Impact Publications, 1995.

Interview For Success thoroughly covers all aspects of the interview process. It also includes quizzes and questionnaires that determine what you know, and what you have yet to learn, about the interview process.

Leape, Martha P., and Susan M. Vacca. *The Harvard Guide to Careers,* 5th edition. Cambridge, MA: Harvard University, 1995.

The Harvard Guide is intended to teach students the skills that are necessary for career exploration and decision making. It also discusses how today's global marketplace affects certain issues of career development. The book's broader topics include: the changing nature of careers, career exploration, career decision making, job search, transition, and career development skills.

Michaels, Ed, Helen Handfield-Jones, and Beth Axelrod. *The War for Talent.* Cambridge, MA: Harvard Business School Press, 2001.

In our age of competitive recruiting, many companies have come to realize that superior corporate performance is directly correlated with superior employee performance. With this truism in mind, the authors of *The War for Talent* studied 13,000 executives in 27 companies to help establish which programs and behaviors were most successful in attracting and retaining top-notch employees.

Sturman, Gerald M. *If You Knew Who You Were, You Could Be Who You Are: Your Personal Career Profile.* Bedford, NY: Bierman House, 1992.

If You Knew is a workbook-style text that is meant to

help individuals figure out what type of occupation is best for them. There are quizzes, charts, and questionnaires that, when filled out, are meant to assist the reader with the self-discovery process. By analyzing the reader's style, career type, motivation, skills, and internal barriers, the book helps to create, and apply, a personal career profile.

—A—

Activity-Based Costing (ABC)

An accounting method that assigns identifiable costs and allocates common costs to specific product lines or business segments; also known as *product-line costing.* By using this method, a company can determine the profitability or profit contribution that each activity, segment, and product line brings to the company as a whole.

Activity Cost Drivers

A unit of measurement for the level (or quantity) of an activity that is performed within a business organization. Hence, an activity cost driver represents specific units of work or activities performed to satisfy customer needs but that consume costly corporate resources.

Advertising

Advertising includes any printed or broadcast message sent and paid for by an identified organization to a target market via television, radio, newspapers, magazines, direct mail, billboards, transit cards and online bankers.

Advertising Frequency

This refers to the number of times an average customer is exposed to an advertisement within a specific time period.

Aggregate Demand

When referred to in the context of GNP or GDP, aggregate demand measures the sum of what is spent by different parties in the United States for goods and services. These parties include:

1. *Households.* This value measures what households spend on personal consumption items as well as what investments they make in residential housing.

2. *Businesses.* This value measures what businesses spend on nonresidential property, plant, and equipment as well as inventory.

3. *Foreign Entities.* This spending measures the value of all goods exported by the United States, less the value of all goods imported by the United States, or net exports.

4. *Government.* This value measures what American government entities spend on goods and services.

Aggregate Supply

When referred to in the context of GNP or GDP, aggregate supply refers to the labor and capital required to produce the level of goods and services required to meet aggregate demand.

Allocation Function

The shifting or reallocation of production resources into or out of markets based on shifts in prices for the goods or services produced in that market. If price moves in a way that indicates an increase in demand, more firms may try to enter that market and provide a supply to meet that demand. Conversely, if price shifts in such a way that demand seems to be diminishing, some firms may choose to leave the market and direct their resources elsewhere.

Allocative Efficiency

The production of goods and services such that levels of production are closely tied to levels of consumer demand.

Anchoring

Anchoring occurs when a previous piece of information influences later decisions.

Angel

Individual investors, often called angels, make capital investments in entrepreneurial ventures in return for equity (partial ownership) in the business. These arrangements are usually created on the basis of a privately negotiated agreement predicated on the fact that the investor hopes to earn a high return on his or her invested capital if the business succeeds, as compensation for the risks associated with investing in an unproven business.

Antidilution of Ownership

The right of an investor to maintain the same percentage ownership of a company's common stock in the event that the company issues more stock.

Arbitrage Pricing Theory

Arbitrage describes the process of simultaneously buying a security, currency, or commodity on one market and selling it in another. Price differences between the two markets give the arbitrageur his or her profit. The arbitrage pricing theory is based upon the concept of arbitrage, and describes how assets should be valued if there were no riskless arbitrage opportunities. When security markets are competitive and efficient, then opportunities to profit from arbitrage should be nonexistent.

Arbitration

The use of a third party to decide between two sides deadlocked in a negotiation. The arbitrator's decision can be binding or nonbinding, as previously agreed upon by the negotiating parties.

Area of Dominant Influence (ADI)

The ADI is a geographic area made up of all counties that receive signals from radio and television stations in a particular market.

Asch Experiments

In these classic studies by Solomon Asch, groups of seven or eight people were put in a classroom and shown two cards by the experimenter. The first card had a single line on it; the second card had three lines, each of a different length. Ostensibly, the task was for each person in the group to say which of the three lines was the same length as the single line on the first card. The right answer was quite obvious and, under normal conditions, people choose the right answer more than 99 percent of the time. In these experiments, however, all but one in the group were confederates of the experimenter, and only one person was the true, unsuspecting subject of the experiment. In each case, the subject was the last person to say which line matched. One by one, the other group members gave the same, incorrect answer. In about 35 percent of the cases, the subject agreed with the rest of the group, even though the answer was wrong. The Asch experiments showed that conformity pressures could lead individuals to make incorrect choices in the interest of conforming and remaining a member of a group.

Asking Price

The price level at which sellers offer securities to borrowers.

Asset Acquisition

An alternate means of conducting a buyout by purchasing certain assets a company may have instead of purchasing that company's stock.

Attribution

When individuals observe behavior they attempt to determine if it is internally or externally caused. "Internally caused" means one believes that an event was under the personal control of the individual involved. For example, someone who missed a deadline did so because he is lazy. "Externally caused" means one believes an event was the result of outside causes. For example, someone missed a deadline because her boss had given her a heavy workload. This links to the *fundamental attribution error,* which is the tendency to underestimate the influence of internal factors concerning one's own behavior and overestimate the influence of internal factors when making judgments about other people's behaviors. For example, if Paul did well on a project Paul will attribute it to his own abilities. If Paul sees someone else doing well on a project Paul will attribute it to external factors such as luck, timing, etc. Conversely, if Paul did poorly on a project Paul will attribute it to external factors. If Paul sees someone else doing poorly Paul will likely attribute it to internal factors. This is commonly known as *self-serving bias.*

Audience Analysis

To enhance communication with your audience, you must first analyze it carefully to formulate a message in a way they will understand and find meaningful. Audience analysis can be accomplished in a variety of ways. Sometimes market research or demographic data is available, but frequently audience analysis is based on thinking about your impressions, empathizing, and imagining that you are a member of your audience, or by asking the advice of someone you trust. The audience can be analyzed individually or trends can be considered collectively for a group.

Augmented Product

An augmented product is one with attributes in addition to those needed to serve its core function that differentiate it from other products available in its class.

Available Market

This refers to the collection of those consumers who have an interest in a particular product or service, access to it, and the funds to pay for it.

—B—

Backward Integration

A strategy in which a company creates a competitive advantage by controlling the supply of the raw materials needed to make its products.

Balance of Payments

A summary of the statement of international transactions between U.S. residents and residents of foreign nations. This serves as a measure of the United States' international trade and capital positions.

Balance of Trade

The net difference between the dollar value of a country's imports and exports over a period of time. A country's current account reflects a currency drain when exports exceed imports. Although the balance of trade plays an important role in establishing national trade policies, it has little effect on a company's fortunes, other than as a long-term indicator of current stability.

Balance Sheet

A balance sheet is a statement representing a company's financial position at a specific date, usually at the end of an accounting period; also called a *statement of financial position*. The balance sheet, which presents a picture at one point in time of a company's financial standing, shows a company's resources the amount it owes creditors, and ownership value. Balance sheets categorize a company's assets, liabilities, and stockholders' equity according to the following formula:

$$\text{Assets} = \text{liabilities} + \text{shareholders' equity}$$

Bank for International Settlements (BIS)

A consortium bank founded to coordinate the collection and rescheduling of German reparations after World War I, the BIS has survived as an international central bank for 10 member countries. With consensus approval from its member central banks, the BIS sets standards for the global banking system.

Bear Market

A market in which stock prices are expected to fall.

Benchmarking

A process by which an organization reassesses its traditional business practices by comparing them with the best practices of other organizations. This process is designed to provide a manager with an understanding of how the best-performing organizations perform similar activities and processes. By studying the best practices of other organizations, the goal is to identify actions that improve a firm's performance.

Benefits
A benefit is the perceived use or value of a product characteristic to a consumer.

Best Efforts Offering
Unlike a firm commitment offering where a price is set and a fixed monetary amount is expected, the underwriter makes its best efforts to sell as many shares as possible at the initial offering price, and then adjusts the price as necessary to sell the rest.

Beta
A measure of the systematic risk, or market risk, of a particular security or portfolio. Systematic risk describes any risk that influences the value of a large number of assets. Beta measures a security's return over time relative to the overall market. (Note that market return is usually measured by Standard & Poor's 500 Composite Stock Index or the Dow Jones 30 Industrials.) The higher the beta, the riskier, or the more volatile, is the stock or portfolio. Beta is frequently used to analyze the risk of equity mutual funds by showing the volatility of a fund relative to the market as a whole (as measured by the Standard & Poor's 500 Index of the most widely held stocks). A mutual fund with a beta of 1.0 would have returns that match those of the S&P 500. A mutual fund with a beta greater than 1.0 is more volatile, or riskier, than the market. A mutual fund with a beta less than 1.0 is not as volatile, or risky, as the market.

Bid
The price buyers offer to acquire securities from sellers.

Blue Sky
Refers to laws that safeguard investors from being misled by investment people who misrepresent the value of investments to get the money of the financially naive.

Bond Indenture
An indenture establishes the formal terms of a lending relationship between a borrower and a lender. It is a written agreement, and it outlines important terms such as the principal, the rate of interest, the maturity rate, and other restrictions that the borrower agrees to abide by.

Brainstorming

An idea generation process that specifically encourages any and all alternatives while withholding any criticism of those alternatives.

Brand

A brand is a name, term, symbol, or design that is intended to clearly identify and differentiate a seller's product from the products of his or her competitors.

Brand Awareness

This is a measure of consumer knowledge that a particular brand exists.

Brand Extension

This is a marketing strategy that takes the brand name of one product category and extends it to another for purposes of acquired credibility and recognition for the new product category. An example of this would be Nike, an athletic shoe manufacturer, entering the clothing business.

Break-Even Point

The quantity of goods or services a company must sell for its revenue from sales to equal its cost of production for the same number of units. Thus, setting a firm's revenue equation equal to its total cost equation and solving will yield the production quantity at which revenue equals cost.

Bridge Financing

A type of short-term financing used to cover a company's short-term need; a loan that is expected to be repaid relatively quickly.

Budget Deficit and Debt

A budget deficit occurs when the costs of running a country exceed the revenues that country generates. This applies specifically to federal revenue and federal spending. The outcome of a budget deficit is usually the incurment of debt. The federal budget deficit represents a shortfall in savings in the federal government sector. When the federal government runs a deficit, households, businesses, state and local governments, and foreign entities must make up the difference. Economic forces, like recession or recovery, dictate which of these supplemental sources will have the actual resources to make up a federal shortfall.

Bull Market
A market in which stock prices are expected to rise.

Bureaucracy
First used by Max Weber to describe a type of organization characterized by division of labor, clearly defined hierarchy, detailed rules and regulations, and impersonal relationships. Originally described as an ideal type of organization, this theory was used as the design prototype for many of today's large organizations. Today, however, the word *bureaucracy* is often used to represent only the negative characteristics of this type of organization.

Burn Rate
The negative real time cash flow from a company's operations, usually computed monthly.

Business Communication
A term used to describe both a field of study (at the undergraduate level) as well as the process of communicating in business, business communication focuses primarily on skills, with a strong emphasis on writing. It also focuses on the micro level (sentence level) instead of the macro level (document level) of communication. Where corporate communication is narrow in its focus on function, business communication is broader.

Business Cycle
Graphic representation of the recurring pattern of macroeconomic activity and industry trends that affects the expansion or contraction of markets, a company's sales, inflation, employment, interest rates, and financial market share prices. One business cycle can be measured from peak to peak or expansion to expansion, or from trough to trough or recession to recession.

Business Plan
A document that details a business concept, its present and future strategy for development, and its financial position.

Business Strategy

The set of policies used to manage individual processes within a business, including decisions regarding individual products, services, suppliers, markets, and competitors.

—C—

Call Option

A call option is a security giving the owner the right, but not the obligation, to buy a prespecified amount of an asset at a fixed price during some specified time period. Call options on many common stocks are actively traded in the United States.

Cannibalism

This refers to the reduction of sales in one product caused by the introduction of another product, where both products are made by the same company.

Case Interview

A case interview is a structured situational problem presented to the candidate with the expectation that the problem will be solved during the course of the interview. A case interview is designed to test paradigms of thought, the ability to structure problems and solutions, and the ability to convey solutions in a convincing manner. All of this is done while interacting with the recruiter to disseminate important issues from nonimportant issues. Often, a case interview requires that the interviewee document his or her thinking patterns, including explanatory graphs or supplementary analytical frameworks.

Capital Asset Pricing Model (CAPM)

Part of the larger capital market theory that attempts to quantify investment risk. Under CAPM, systematic risk is measured by a statistical factor labeled *beta,* which is the mathematical expression of the relationship between the return on an individual security and the return on the market as a whole. The market return is measured by a market index, such as the Dow Jones Industrial Average or the Standard & Poor's 500 Composite Stock Price Index. In other words, beta measures the volatility of a given security against market averages. The CAPM states that the value of a financial security depends only on the statistical relationship between the security and the value of all securities that trade in the financial markets. Investors that purchase risky assets obtain an expected return that is higher than an investment in risk-free assets.

Capital Budgeting

Capital budgeting is the planning for the purchase and management of long-term assets in a corporation. A capital budget is usually prepared each year, and contains a complete list of the firm's planned investment projects. Major corporations often prepare longer-term capital budgets, which detail the firm's expenditure plans several years into the future.

Capital Expenditures

An expenditure of corporate funds to acquire long-term assets. The investments are typically designed to develop or introduce new products or services, to expand existing production or service capacity, or to alter the mix of current production or service facilities.

Capital Flight

A term used to describe the movement of capital out of or into a given market. Capital, by definition, is very mobile, and has become even more mobile in the age of instantaneous electronic transfers.

Capital Gain

The amount by which the selling price of an asset exceeds the seller's initial purchase price.

Capital Stock

The physical, nonhuman, reusable inputs used to make a product. Capital stock is measured by investment in things like property, plant, and equipment less replacement investment for items that have worn out or become obsolete.

Capital Structure

The common stock, preferred stock, long-term debt, and retained earnings a company maintains to finance its assets. Thus, it can be considered as the mix of the different securities a firm issues to finance its various investment projects. A firm's capital structure is often described in percentage (rather than dollar) terms, with each percentage reflecting the fraction of the firm's total financial obligations represented by each type of security.

Capitalization Rate

The internal interest rate a company uses to discount future income to arrive at their present value.

Cash Budget

A schedule of expected cash receipts and disbursements. Hence, it provides a summary of all cash inflows and outflows for a corporation during the budget period.

Cash Flow Statement

A financial statement that summarizes a company's sources and uses of cash over a specific period of time. Cash flow statements are generally broken down to include detail on operations, financing activity, and investment activity of a firm. Free cash flow is also calculated from these statements.

Carried Interest

A venture capital firm's share of the profit earned by a fund. In the United States, the venture capital firm usually earns 20 percent of the profit after all investors have been repaid any principal investments.

Cartel

A group of sellers in a particular market that has banded together to influence the price of a good or service by controlling the market supply. Although illegal in the United States as a violation of the Sherman Antitrust Act, cartels are not illegal in other parts of the world and enjoy the economic benefits of exerting such power. One very famous example of a cartel is the Organization of Petroleum Exporting Countries (OPEC).

Causality and Correlation

Often there may be a correlation between two events: That is, when event A happens, event B tends to happen. However, this does not mean that A causes B; causality is not the same as correlation. An example is that statistics show a correlation between the growth rate of grass and the consumption of gasoline. Does this mean that increased use of gasoline makes the grass grow? Unlikely. In fact, there is a separate, common, causal factor: Grass grows most in the spring and summer, when the weather is better. The amount of travel by families in the United States increases in the summer, hence, the greater gasoline consumption. The season is the causal factor. The message here is to make sure you are not mistaking correlation for causality: Be systematic.

Central Bank

The national bank at the apex of a national banking system. In the United States, it is the Federal Reserve Bank, in Great Britain it is the Bank of England, and in Japan it is the Bank of Japan. In the United States the Fed acts independently of federal fiscal policy. Like many other central banks, however, the Fed determines the nation's monetary policy by setting interest rates and determining the money supply for the country.

Centralization

Concentrating decision making at a single point in the organization makes the organization more centralized.

Challenge Interview

Aggressive interview behavior designed to test the resolve of the candidate and his or her ability to maintain composure when faced with hostile tactics (insults, demeaning behavior) that are common in certain industries.

Chronological Resume

Most common type of resume. Jobs are listed in reverse chronological order with the candidate's last job listed at the top of the resume. Descriptions of job experiences can be written in linear or narrative form.

Cognitive Dissonance

In the late 1950s, Leon Festinger proposed the theory of cognitive dissonance, which is the inconsistency that someone might see between two attitudes or between a behavior and an attitude. For example, if a person believes that honesty is important but lies to a boss about time spent on a project, that person is likely to experience dissonance. Festinger proposed that people would seek out a state in which there is the lowest possible dissonance. To achieve this a person can do one of four things: He can change his behavior to match his attitudes

(Stop lying), he can reduce the importance of the behavior (rationalize the small lie as not being that bad), he can change his attitude (honesty is overrated), or he can seek offsetting elements (I worked last weekend, so exaggerating my hours isn't that bad). If a person is rewarded for dissonant behavior (lying while believing honesty is important), the dissonant behavior will be attributed to the reward (a higher paycheck) rather than to any internal process.

Cohesiveness/Cohesion

The technical definition of cohesiveness is a "measure of the degree to which group members are attracted to each other and are motivated to stay in the group." There is some discussion as to whether the two elements of cohesiveness would be better addressed separately—that people can be motivated to stay in a group regardless of their attraction to the other members. Attraction does not necessarily mean liking. Group members can be cohesive and still not actively like each other in a social sense.

Cold Call

This refers to a selling technique in which a salesperson approaches a customer with little or no warning.

Collateral

An asset identified as forfeitable to secure a loan.

Collectivism

Collectivism is the degree to which a national culture or, in more recent usage, an individual believes that society should be based on a tight social framework in which people are responsible to and for other people for care and support. Someone with a great commitment to collectivism believes groups are the natural way that people work and live, and that group needs have priority over individual desires—that group comes first.

Command Process

The use of central authority, usually in the form of government, to decide policy regarding central issues faced by every economy. Usually, these questions stem from basics like, "What will we produce? How much of it will we produce? To whom will we sell it?" and involve government intervention in the allocation of resources to meet these ends.

Commodity

A commodity is a highly standardized product, such as gold or corn.

Common Stock

Certificates that represent ownership to a corporation. Usually, common stock shareholders have the right to vote for the election of corporate directors. In privately held companies they may also elect the corporate officers. Corporations may issue various classes of common stock; some with voting rights, some without. Holders of common stock normally do not have any right to receive dividends, although if a company's earnings permit, the board of directors may elect to declare a common stock dividend, either in cash or in additional shares. Common stock may be issued with a par value or with no par value. In either case, it is recorded in the stockholder's equity section of the balance sheet.

Communication Channels

Communication channels are the physical methods through which you communicate your message to your intended audience (e.g., memos, telephones, speeches, one-on-one meetings, etc.). You should select the best channel for your particular message (annual report, press release, television or radio advertisement, option piece in print media). Along with channel choice, the structure and content of the message itself are critical for successful delivery. With modern technology, the possibilities for channel-choice have widened to include e-mail, voicemail, electronic meetings, videoteleconferencing, corporate web pages, as well as multicasts over the Internet of important events such as shareholder meetings.

Communication Strategy

Communication strategy, developed as a concept in the 1980s by communication expert Mary Munter, serves as the basis for all management communication. It includes five components: (1) communicator strategy; (2) audience strategy; (3) message strategy; (4) channel choice strategy; and (5) culture strategy. In developing a communicator strategy you would set objectives, select a communication style, and seek to establish credibility. When thinking about audience strategy you would find out who is in your audience and then analyze how best to direct a message to them based on their level of knowledge and their probable biases. Message strategy involves organizing the structure of your message; this includes deciding if the message will be direct or indirect. Channel choice is a consideration of the how your communication will be physically conveyed to the audience (e-mail, voicemail, telephone call). Culture strategy recognizes that business operates in multicultural settings, and for your message to be most effective, it needs to be sensitive and flexible to cultural differences.

Communication Style

The act of communicating a message can be divided into four separate styles, as adapted from the organizational theorists Tannenbaum and Schmidt (see Figure 2.2). The two dimensions consider how much you want to maintain control over your content and how much you want to involve your audience. The more you control content, the less you involve your audience and conversely, the more you involve your audience in a presentation, the less control you have over the content of that presentation. The four communication styles include tell, sell, consult, and join. The *tell* style provides information with the objective of teaching the audience. In the *sell* style, you are persuading with the goal of convincing the audience to perform an action ("selling" them on an objective of your choosing). In the *consult* style you are interacting with your audience with some control (as in a question-and-answer session). The objective of the "consult" style is to learn from the audience. For a *join* style you and your audience are in collaboration to derive the content of the presentation (as in a brainstorming session).

Community Relations

This is a subfunction of corporate communication that focuses on the relationship between an organization and its community. The community surrounding an organization is made up in part by the company's employees, their families, and the local and regional government. Given the complexity and importance of this constituency, community relations are vital in managing an organization's image.

Comparison Advertising

This is an advertising strategy in which a company presents its product as significantly better than a competitor's product. An example of this strategy would be Listerine comparing its plaque removal powers to that of Scope.

Competitive Advantage

Any series of company practices or procedures which result in that company creating products or services that consistently surpass the products or services of its competitors. Any business practice that gives a company an edge in the marketplace.

Competitive Strategy (Formation of)

A framework developed by Michael Porter that provides a spatial representation of the five major factors governing the development of a competitive strategy. These factors include:

1. *Competitive Strategy.*   The plan a firm adopts to compete for market share within a given industry.

2. *Company Strengths and Weaknesses.*   An internal force. This concept refers to a firm's financial, technological, product, and human resources.

3. *Personal Values of Key Implements.*   Also an internal force, this concept refers to the management style and belief system used by a firm's managers.

4. *Industry Opportunities and Threats.*   Considered an external force, this concept refers to the position and behavior of a firm's competitors, and how competitors' behavior can give rise to risks and opportunities within an industry.

5. *Broader Societal Expectations.*   Also considered an external force, this concept refers to the societal norms, including legislation and popular opinion, that shape a company's behavior in the marketplace.

Components of a Competitor Analysis

A framework developed by Michael Porter to assist managers in completing a successful and informative assessment of their industry competitors. The following forces are identified in the model:

1. *Competitor's Response Profile.*   A list of questions that assist managers in considering what moves a competitor

might make on his or her own as well as what moves a competitor might make in response to the manager's own moves.

2. *Future Goals.*   Under the heading of "What Drives the Competitors," this is a reference to the firm's goals as they have been communicated to all persons within the company.

3. *Assumptions.*   Also under the heading of "What Drives the Competitor," assumptions refer to facts or beliefs a competitor holds about itself and its position within an industry.

4. *Current Strategy.*   Under the heading of "What the Competitor is Doing and Can Do," this refers to the status of how a business is competing and how it is performing within an industry.

5. *Capabilities.*   Also under the heading of "What the Competitor is Doing and Can Do," fall capabilities, or assessments of the competition's core competencies and weaknesses.

Conditioning

Classical conditioning is about learning a conditioned response. This response is built by associating a conditioned stimulus (e.g., the ring of a bell) with an unconditioned stimulus (e.g., offering a plate of meat in Pavlov's famous example). Classical conditioning is essentially passive, an automatic response to stimuli. *Operant conditioning* involves cognitive processes. In operant conditioning, behavior is seen as a function of its consequences: People learn to behave a certain way to get something they want or avoid something they don't want. If Pavlov is the father of classical conditioning, than the father of operant condition is B. F. Skinner. A simple example of operant conditioning is a reward system: A person works because he gets paid—a pleasant consequence, and so he will continue to work as long as he gets the reward (payment).

Confidentiality Agreement

A legal contract protecting the rights of a business in cases where company or trade secrets or other confidential information must be revealed in the course of doing business. Entrepreneurs who are presenting ideas to potential investors use confidentiality agreements to prevent potential investors from replicating the proposed business concept on their own after a detailed investment presentation.

Consumer Price Index

A measure of the prices consumers pay for a representative "basket of goods and services." This measure is compiled monthly by the Bureau of Economic Analysis and expressed on an index basis.

Consumption Function

A function capturing the dependent relationship between consumer spending and income, where changes in consumer spending are directly proportional to changes in income, but these changes do not occur in a one-to-one fashion. This means that if a person were to get a raise, he or she would not spend the entire increase on goods and services available in the economy, but would spend some of it.

Constituency Analysis

This involves identifying specific groups and subgroups within a community at large. These groups are characterized by certain qualities that will influence how they receive and interpret an external communication message about a company. The objective with constituency analysis is to first identify who the constituency really is, then determine what their attitude is toward the organization, and then determine what they already know about the communication in question. It is not always obvious who the main constituency is, and subgroups with different qualities will also likely exist. Thus, the analysis of relevant constituents is important because it ultimately determines the nature of your message. With the introduction of e-mail and the Internet, constituencies are becoming increasingly global, making constituency analysis that much more complicated and relevant to your organization.

Contingency Approach

Organizational behavior relies on a contingency approach to management in both theory and practice. Two people can act differently in the same situation, and a person's behavior is different in different situations. For example, not everyone is motivated by money, although some people are. This complexity means that organizational behavior must reflect situational behavior or "contingency conditions." We can say that behavior *X* leads to outcome *Y* but only under conditions *Z* (where *X, Y, Z* are the contingency variables). An example would be that an employee's effort leads to high productivity if the equipment is working at 100 percent efficiency. Hence, the state of the equipment becomes the contingency variable.

Contribution Margin
A measure of a firm's profitability and performance, this is a measure of how much a firm's revenues exceed its variable costs of production, and thereby contribute to covering the fixed costs associated with all levels of production.

Conversion Ratio
The number of shares of a company's common stock associated with one share of that company's convertible security.

Convertible Security
Preferred stock for a company that is convertible into common stock for that company at a previously specified ratio. It is the security holder's choice, or option, to make this conversion.

Coproduction
A type of buyback countertrade generally used for the transfer of management experience or technology. In cases where equity interests are a part of a coproduction arrangement, both companies profit from the sale of the products. Aside from the gains made from the direct sale of the product, each partner sees several other benefits. The host partner gains new technology and management expertise, and the outside partner acquires a direct investment in a foreign country without the risk of starting a new business from scratch.

Copyright
A legal proviso indicating ownership of written material such that the material cannot be reproduced without the expressed consent of the author.

Core Competency
A specialty or area of expertise in a given company that exceeds or eludes its competitors and serves as the foundation for the company to grow or diversify into new product lines.

Honda, for example, has a core competence in building high-performance engines.

Core Product

The primary and essential function that a good or service provides to a consumer.

Corporate Advertising

A subfunction of corporate communication that differs from product advertising or marketing communication. Instead of trying to sell a company's products or services, corporate advertising tries to sell the company itself—usually to a completely different constituency than customers. Image and identity are reflected in corporate advertising. In fact, these sorts of advertisements are often called *image ads* because they seek to establish or change the "image" of your organization. For example, companies might run advertisements that show potential shareholders not products, but the values of the corporation.

Corporate Communication

An emerging field that has been increasingly recognized as a critical functional area within business organizations, corporate communication focuses on an entire function of management. In most business organizations the corporate communication department is responsible for public relations, corporate advertising, media relations, community relations, financial communication, employee relations, corporate philanthropy, and public affairs.

Corporate Culture

A system of shared rules, beliefs, and values among members of a given company. Corporate cultures differ widely across companies. The corporate culture at IBM, for example, is far more formal in terms of dress, interoffice relationships, and office conduct than that of Microsoft.

Corporate Identity

This comprises the visual manifestation of the company's image as seen in the corporate logo, stationery, uniforms, buildings, brochures, and advertising. Identity consulting firms and graphic designers work with organizations to create logos and other manifestations of identity.

Corporate Philanthropy

This term refers to corporate donations to communities and other nonprofit organizations. To address the growing concerns of constituents in communities about the role of the company and to foster a unified corporate image and identity, organizations now house this function in the corporate communication department. Examples of corporate philanthropy include donations to cultural organizations such as museums or to community-based organizations such as First Book (which gives funds to communities in need to purchase books for school children).

Corporate Strategy

A method for managing a company's resources such that the company's strengths are maximized and its weaknesses minimized in relation to its competitors within the same market. A corporate strategy affects a company's goals and objectives and the policies the company will form and follow to meet these goals and objectives.

Corporate Vision

The concept of what a business can be, beyond how it actually exists in the present, and the method for realizing the concept. At the time they entered the American market, executives at Honda had a corporate vision that Honda would be the number-one selling midsize car in America within 20 years of entering the market.

Corporation

A business form created by state governments upon the filing of an application and payment of a fee. It creates a legal entity, separate from its owners (the shareholders). A corporation also eliminates any personal liability the owners have for the business.

Cost-Benefit Analysis

A method of determining whether the results or outcome of a business undertaking outweigh the costs associated with pursuing the undertaking. Generally, cost-benefit analyses start with the extrinsic considerations of the cost of a product versus the revenue it will generate. Intrinsic considerations, which are harder to quantify, are then evaluated and the overall "go" or "no go" decision is made.

Cost Center

A unit, whether a department, piece of equipment, process, or individual, within a company to which direct costs can be attributed. In addition to direct costs, many cost centers are also assigned a portion of the company's fixed costs, or overhead. A factory, for example, is usually considered a cost center. Managers of cost centers are usually responsible for optimizing the difference between standard costs (that is, the direct costs and overhead assigned to the cost center by management) and actual costs. Because of this, cost centers are sometimes called *responsibility centers.* The key to the effective use of cost centers is an accurate assessment and assignment of direct costs and overhead. In many cases, cost allocation is a matter of tradition rather than careful analysis. This can lead to a distorted perception of the profitability of various cost centers.

Cost of Capital

The rate of return available in the marketplace on investments comparable both in terms of risk and other investment characteristics, such as marketability and other qualitative factors. A more practical definition is the following: the expected rate of return an investor would require to be induced to purchase the rights to future streams of income as reflected in the business interest under consideration. Cost of capital is an integral part of the business valuation process. However, it is determined by the market and is totally out of management's control. Cost of capital represents the degree of perceived risk by potential investors: the lower the perceived risk, the lower the cost of capital.

Cost of Debt

The interest rate or rates charged to a company by its lenders for use of the capital.

Cost of Equity

The rate of return required by a company's shareholders as compensation for the investment of capital.

Cost-Plus Pricing

A technique for pricing goods and services where managers evaluate the cost of producing a good or service and then determine their corresponding prices by multiplying by a desired profit factor. Cost-Plus pricing requires that a manager have a good sense of what the market demand is for a particular good or service, such that the manager can negotiate between a desired profit factor and what a consumer will actually pay for a good or service.

Cost Structure

The relationship of a firm's fixed costs to its variable costs. Firms with high fixed costs and low variable costs have a cost structure where a high volume of production is more desirable, whereas firms with low fixed costs and high variable costs benefit from lower levels of production.

Countertrade

The exchange of goods, services, and currency for other goods, services, and currency. An export financing tool, countertrade enables companies to sell to customers in countries that could not otherwise buy goods and services because of the absence of hard currency.

Covariance

A measure of influence of one dependent variable to another, covariance represents the weighted correlation between two dependent variables.

Covenant

A set of restrictions imposed by a lender on a borrower regarding how the borrower must operate the business for which the capital is being borrowed. Violation of debt covenants is grounds for recalling a loan.

Cover Letter

Letter to accompany a resume, providing a recruiter with an introduction to a candidate. Should only be one page long and should briefly indicate how a candidate learned of the position, two to three reasons why the candidate should be considered for the job, and follow-up steps the candidate will pursue.

Crisis Communication

Most managers and all communications experts agree that crises need to be planned for and coordinated by the corporate communication function (or its equivalent). Typically, a broad group of managers from various parts of the organization are included in this process, but the actual execution of a crisis communication plan is the purview of the corporate communication department. Responsibilities for planning include risk assessment, setting communication objectives for potential crises, assigning teams to each crisis, planning for centralization, and deciding what to include in a formal plan. For the actual execution of a crisis communication plan, communicators are responsible for taking control, gathering information, creating a centralized crisis management center, doing the actual communication, and making plans to avoid future crises.

Crisis Management

An unplanned effort and dedication of resources to solve an unanticipated problem or set of problems that threaten a company's status as a going concern.

Cross-Cultural Communication

This term refers to the communication of the same message to different geographical regions that do not share the same cultural background, ideas, and practices. The impetus behind cross-cultural communication is the recognition that in the modern global economy business success frequently necessitates the ability to function or communicate with multicultural suppliers, employees, and clients. Before attempting to communicate cross-culturally it is important to develop first a basic understanding of another culture. The better your understanding of another culture the more successful you will be in developing an effective communication strategy.

Cross-Price Elasticity

The numerical value that represents the relationship between the quantity demanded for a good or service and the price of a substitute or complementary product. Generally, firms try to minimize cross-price elasticity through efforts to eliminate substitute products as viable options in the minds of consumers. Firms may also choose to minimize cross-price elasticity by packaging complementary products together.

Customer
Any individual, household, or company representative that acts as the buyer of goods and services offered to the mass market.

Current Account
The main measure of the international exchange of goods and services in the United States, measured by the net purchase of all goods, services, and investments made by foreign parties of U.S. product less those purchases of goods, services, and investments made by the United States in other countries.

—D—

Debenture
A document containing an acknowledgment of indebtedness on the part of a company, usually secured by a charge on the company's assets.

Debt/Equity Swaps
The exchange of debt securities for equity interests.

Decentralization
An organization power structure in which authority and decision-making responsibility are diffused throughout different levels of a company. Decentralization differs widely from the traditional functional organizational design where power rests with top management.

Degree of Operating Leverage
A measure of the firm's operating leverage, which is calculated as the contribution margin divided by income before taxes. A firm with a high degree of operating leverage will have a large proportion of fixed costs in its total costs. This type of firm will experience a larger percentage increase in income from a given percentage increase in unit sales.

Demand Function
The function capturing the dependent relationship between the price people are willing to pay for a good or service and other factors related to that good or service. These other factors include the cost associated with making the product, the

technology employed in making the product, the number of vendors operating in a market, the price at which competing vendors are offering similar products, and the supply of the product available to consumers.

Depreciation Tax Shield

The reduction in corporate income taxes due to the deductibility of depreciation from the firm's taxable earnings. Although depreciation is a noncash expense, the reduction in taxes represents the cash flow effect of a firm's depreciation expense.

Development Banks

Banks that function as coordinating and intermediary organizations to raise capital, attract investment, and provide technical assistance for the economic development for nonindustrialized countries.

Devil's Advocate

Explicit role undertaken by a group member who actively questions and challenges the group's ideas, process, and decisions. Such active questioning helps reduce the risk of groupthink.

Dialectic Inquiry

A method for group decision making in which members are forced to "debate" both sides of an issue. Dialectic inquiry forces consideration of factors that might otherwise not be considered and then examined. It has been shown to reduce the potential of groupthink and enhance the quality of decision making.

Direct Marketing

This is a marketing tool designed to elicit immediate action from the consumer through direct customer contact.

Discount Rate

The term *discount rate* relates to business valuations. It is the rate applied to a future stream of earnings or cash flow to calculate its present value. Discount rate and *capitalization rate* are used interchangeably to designate the premium charged by investors as compensation for the perceived risk, or uncertainty, in receiving forecasted future benefits. It can be thought of as the minimum rate of return required for an investment project to be considered acceptable.

Discounted Cash Flow

A method used to express a forecasted stream of future cash flows in terms of its present value, or its value in today's dollars. Discounted cash flow is the fundamental principle underlying business valuations and is used for various purposes:

- To calculate the expected future benefits to investors in either debt obligations or equity interests
- To determine the price of a partnership interest in a buyout agreement
- To value debt obligations for debt/equity swaps
- To value minority interests
- To designate the value of partial interests in an entrepreneurial business for divorce settlements
- To assess estate taxes

Many valuation methods are used by analysts, investors, appraisers, the IRS, and others, most of which employ discounted cash flow as the primary tool. For certain types of companies, such as hotels and other real-estate based businesses, the internal rate of return method can effectively calculate the discount rate to be used in discounted cash flow analyses.

Diseconomies of Scale

An increase in a firm's cost of producing an additional unit as all other factors of production increase. Diseconomies of scale can be caused by poor and inefficient management or disproportionate increases in indirect costs of production.

Disposable Personal Income

The amount of money remaining after taxes are removed that an individual has the opportunity to spend.

Distributive Bargaining

An approach to negotiation that seeks to divide up a fixed amount of resources.

Dividend

The distribution of a company's earnings to its owners—the stockholders. Cash dividends are most common, although dividends can be issued in other forms, such as stock or property.

Division of Labor
The specialization or breaking down of jobs into simple and repetitive tasks.

Divisional Structure
Some companies run as a number of separate, autonomous business units, coordinated by a central headquarters. This is a divisional structure.

Document Design
Refers to the overall "look" and design rather than the content of a document. Specific elements such as white space, limited paragraph length, lists, indentations, and effective margins enhance the readability of a document's design. Additionally, using headings and subheadings for organizational factors and having an easily readable type create a more powerful form of written communication.

Double Jeopardy
A situation where an entrepreneur's main source of income and net worth depend on the entrepreneur's business.

Due Diligence
The investigative process an investor should conduct into the operations and business plan assumptions of a company soliciting investors.

Dumping
In international marketing, when a company charges less for a product than it originally cost or less than the company charges in its home market. This technique is used to eliminate a surplus or quickly gain market share in a new country or market, and it is usually considered an unfair practice.

—E—

Economic Cycle
The economic cycle is the long-term pattern of alternating periods of economic growth (expansion) and decline (recession), characterized by changing economic indicators.

Economic Efficiency
The effort to produce goods and services in the least costly way without sacrificing quality.

Economic Profit
A firm's total revenue less its average total costs of production.

Economies of Scale
The decrease in the cost of each additional unit produced as all factors of production increase. Factors contributing to economies of scale include discounts on bulk purchases of raw materials, the ability to use fixed assets to full capacity, the ability to use specialized labor to its fullest capacity, and the ability to use management to govern the greatest number of people as effectively as possible.

Economies of Scope
The ability of a company to reduce its unit costs by producing two or more goods or services that involve compementary skills, experience and production facilities.

Economic Value to Customer
Economic Value to Customer = EVCx = [LifeCycle costs of a competitor's product in relation to a home firm] – [Start-up Costs for the home firm's product] – [Post Purchase Costs for the home firm's product] + [Incremental Value of the home firm's product].

Edge Act
A federal law passed in 1919 that enables national banks to conduct foreign lending operations through federal or state-chartered subsidiaries called Edge Act corporations.

Elasticity of Demand
This is a measure of how sensitive the sales volume of a product is to changes in that product's price, equal to the marginal change in sales, divided by the marginal change in price.

Employee Communication
More broadly called *internal communications,* employee communication is important in retaining a happy and productive workforce. Internal communications to employees cover a

broad range of topics; from the explanation of complicated health and benefit packages to changes in the marketplace that affect the company's future. Additionally, these communications must also serve to boost the morale of employees. As a result of these diverse demands, employee communication requires a deep understanding of your business as a whole. Although many of these activities can be handled through human resources departments, the communication itself and the strategy for communicating these ideas must come from communications experts in the corporate communication function. Most Fortune 500 companies now use corporate communication departments, instead of human resources departments, to address these issues.

Employee Ownership Stock Plan (ESOP)
A trust established to acquire shares in a company for subsequent allocation to employees over a period of time.

Employment
The measure of human input to the production process. In the United States, there are two major measures of employment, as determined by the Bureau of Labor Statistics. The first is the Household Survey of Employment, which measures the employment status of the population by counting the number of employed persons, regardless of how many jobs one person may hold. The second is the Establishment Survey of Employment, which measures the number of payroll jobs in the non-farm economy, and not the number of persons who hold them.

Employment Agreement
A contract between senior managers of a company and the company guaranteeing that the managers will live out a specific tenure with the company before even considering moving on to another company.

Empowerment
Empowerment is the outcome of processes, decisions, and procedures that increase employees' intrinsic motivation. Empowered employees perceive their work as meaningful, themselves as having responsibility and as being able to influence their own and other people's activities. Empowerment

is a popular buzzword, but achieving true empowerment requires a large investment in system and employee development.

Equity Theory

This theory proposes that individuals calculate their outcomes/input ratio. Equity theory recognizes that motivation is not the outcome of an absolute calculation but is a relative calculation. If they calculate that others are getting more outcome (salary, success) for the same input (effort) they perceive inequity. When people perceive an imbalance in their outcome/input ratio, tension is created which provides a basis for motivation as people strive for perceived equity and fairness. Based on equity theory in a situation of perceived inequity employees can be predicted to make one of several choices. They can change their inputs (decrease effort), they can change their outcomes (increase productivity), or reframe the situation (distorting perceptions by changing referent other). Equity theory is not limited to finance. It has been shown that job titles as well as office space and selection for project groups may also function as outcomes for some employees in their equity equation.

Eurobond

A corporate bond denominated in U.S. dollars or other hard currencies and sold to investors outside the country whose currency is used. Eurobonds have become an important source of debt capital for both large and small companies throughout the world. Normally, a Eurobond is syndicated by a consortium of international investment banks, providing wide exposure to investors in different countries.

Eurocurrency

A currency on deposit outside its country of origin. Such deposits are also known as *external currencies, international currencies* or *xenocurrencies.*

Eurodollar

U.S. currency held on deposit in banks located outside the United States, mainly in Europe. Eurodollars are commonly used for settling international transactions outside of the United States. Certain securities, debt as well as equity, are denominated in Eurodollars. This means that interest, principal repayments, or dividends are paid out of U.S. dollars deposited in foreign bank accounts.

European Community (EC)
An economic alliance, formed in 1957, designed to encourage trade and economic cooperation among its members. The EC is also called the *European Economic Community* and the *Common Market.*

Exchange Rates
The prices at which one country's currency can be converted into that of another country. Although perceptions in the currency markets of the security of a country's economic base certainly affect exchange rate movement, fluctuations are less a function of specific currency market manipulations than the outcome of a whole conglomerate of economic forces experienced on a worldwide level, such as inflation rates, interest rates, political unrest, financial market aberrations, and commodity prices. Furthermore, currency rates respond wildly to major economic shocks: local wars, oil cartel maneuvers, natural disasters, and anticipated political and economic actions of the world powers. Within a globalized economy such as the United States, exchange rates play a critical role in virtually every aspect of financial management. Companies that import or export or that compete against companies that import or export should watch exchange rates closely and if necessary enter into futures currency contracts or trade in financial futures to maximize profit potential.

Exit Strategy
The means by which investors in a company realize all or part of their investment, regardless of the company's success.

Expansion Financing
The securing of the working capital required for the support of an increase in accounts receivable and inventory associated with a company's initial expansion period.

Executive Recruiter
Individual hired by a firm who, acting alone as an agent or on the behalf of a candidate, is responsible for facilitating the

review, meeting, and selection of candidates seeking employment opportunities. Also known as *headhunters.*

Experience Law

This is a law of marketing stating that the unit cost of value added to a standard product, measured in constant currency, declines by a constant percentage each time the accumulated product doubles. This is one of the underlying precepts of economies of scale, in that quality becomes less expensive when the product is made in volume.

Export/Import Bank (Eximbank)

Federal Import-Export Bank, whose primary function originally was to compensate U.S. exporters for subsidies granted competitors by foreign governments. Eximbank has reached far beyond this goal to become the primary source of export credit and guarantees for American companies. Except in very unusual circumstances, Eximbank will not support exports to communist countries nor finance the sale of military products or services. Moreover, to qualify for Eximbank assistance, companies must provide evidence that exported goods or services have at least 50 percent U.S. content.

—F—

Factoring

A means of enhancing a business's cash flow whereby an outside company pays a firm a certain portion of its trade debts and then receives the full amount of cash from the debtor companies directly.

Federal Reserve Board

The Federal Reserve Board controls the nation's monetary policy, regulates banks, and seeks to maintain the financial stability of the United States. Its goal is to control the growth of the U.S. economy, known as *economic expansion,* and minimize shrinkage of the economy known as *recession.*

Federal Reserve System

The central banking institution in the United States responsible for determining United States monetary policy, including the setting of interest rates. The Federal Reserve System consists of a board of governors in Washington and twelve regional district banks.

Feedback

Feedback involves giving individuals direct and clear information to someone about their behavior or performance. Effective feedback is timely, specific, and constructive.

Federal Funds Rate

The interest rate that American banks that have funds in excess of the requirements dictated by the Federal Reserve use to make overnight loans to banks whose funds do not meet the levels dictated by the Federal Reserve.

Federal Open Market Committee

The principle policy making body of the Federal Reserve, the FOMC consists of 7 governors of the Federal Reserve System and 12 Federal Reserve District Bank presidents, where only 5 of the 12 members are voting members and the right to vote is rotated.

Fiedler Contingency Model

The first comprehensive contingency model for leadership proposing that effective groups depend upon a proper match between a leader style and situational context.

Firm Commitment Offering

An underwriter guarantees to raise a fixed amount of capital through an initial public offering (IPO).

First-in First-out Method (FIFO)

A method of inventory valuation based on the concept that merchandise is sold in the order of its receipt. In other words, if an electronics store buys 100 stereos in January and 50 in February, FIFO assumes that the units purchases in January will be sold before the units purchased in February. When inventory is valued with FIFO, cost of goods sold is based on the cost of older inventory.

First-Round Financing

The first investment made by internal investors.

First-Stage Financing

Securing the capital required to initiate full manufacturing and sales efforts.

Fiscal Policy

The government's use of spending and taxation to affect the level of macroeconomic activity. In theory, weak economic activity requires stimulative fiscal policy, which is delivered in the form of tax cuts or spending increases or both. Restrictive fiscal policy, used to suppress robust economic activity, can come in the form of tax increases, spending cuts, or both.

Fiscal Year

A period of 12 consecutive months used by a company to account for and report the results of its operations.

Five Cs of Obtaining Credit

The five crucial elements lenders examine before issuing credit include:

1. *Character.* This is a measure of the borrower's integrity as related to seeing the loan as an obligation that must be repaid.
2. *Capacity.* This is a measure of a business's ability to generate the cash flows required to service the debt on hand.
3. *Capital.* This is a measure of the borrowing firm's net worth.
4. *Collateral.* This is a measure of the firm's assets available to secure the debt requested.
5. *Conditions.* This is a measure of the conditions of the loan, as well as prevailing industry and general economic conditions that might affect the loan repayment.

Five Forces Model

A framework developed by Michael Porter that captures the dynamics of the prevailing environmental forces in which a company operates. These factors include:

1. *Rivalry Among Existing Firms.* At the center of Porter's model is the current state of affairs within a market, before any external forces are considered. Porter contends that firms are always jockeying for position within a market,

and that the rivalry among firms takes on the form of a constant battle for market share.

2. *Threat of New Entrants.* The first external driver, this force refers to the potential for new firms to enter an industry. Any time a new firm enters an industry, the competitive balance must be adjusted to account for changes in market share, new capacity and new resources.

3. *Threat of Substitutes.* Similar to the first external force, this second force represents the potential changes in market equilibrium caused by the introduction of products that represent a viable alternative choice to the products currently available in the market, and could reduce the size of the potential market by drawing sales away.

4. *Bargaining Power of Suppliers.* This force refers to the effect suppliers can have on determining the availability of materials, and consequently on the supply and demand dynamics operating within a market.

5. *Bargaining Power of Buyers.* This force refers to the effect buyers can have on determining the demand for goods or services, and thereby affecting the corresponding price for these goods and services.

Fixed Costs

The costs a firm incurs doing business that do not change in relation to production. Rent, for example, is a fixed cost because it remains constant whether goods and services are sold or not.

Financial Accounting

An accounting method that records, interprets, and reports the historical cost transaction of a company. A company records these transactions in bookkeeping journals and ledgers. To interpret the transactions, it uses, among other analytic tools, a series of ratios, such as acid test ratio, current ratio, inventory turnover, debt-to-equality ratio, and so on. Financial reports include financial statements (balance sheet, income statement, statement of cash flows), as well as special internal monetary reports that are unique to each company.

Financial Communications

Also called *investor* or *shareholder relations,* this corporate communication subfunction moves away from the traditional handling of the finance or treasury department presentation of numbers toward greater care in how the numbers are actually communicated to various constituencies. Financial communications involve direct communications with both large and small investors. Public firms have financial communications professionals who produce financial statements and annual reports. This subfunction also deals with securities analysts on both the "buy" and "sell" side. These analysts are often also a direct information source for the financial media, which this subfunction cultivates in conjunction with experts from the media relations area. Financial communicators must have a broad understanding of business and particular knowledge of finance and accounting.

Financial Leverage

In accounting and finance, the amount of long-term debt that a company has in relation to its equity. The higher the ratio, the greater the leverage. Leverage is generally measured by a variation of the debt-to-equity ratio, which is calculated as follows:

$$\text{Leverage} = \frac{\text{long-term liabilities}}{\text{total stockholders' equity}}$$

A company's optimal leverage depends on the stability of its earnings. A company with consistently high earnings can be more leveraged than a company with variable earnings, because it will consistently be more likely to make the required interest and principal payments.

Financial Reporting

The process of preparing the corporation's financial statements in accordance with generally accepted accounting principles. The statements prepared include an income statement, a balance sheet, and the statement of cash flows.

Flat Organizations

An organization with the minimum number of management layers between policy makers and front-line workers.

Flexible Benefits

Programs where employees tailor their benefit package to meet their individual needs by picking and choosing among a menu of benefit options.

Focus Group Interview

An interview conducted with 8 to 12 people who represent a target market for a product, where the group is asked specific questions related to a product and its use.

Follow-Up

The process of writing letters, calling, and providing deliverables to determine the success of an interview as well as the steps necessary to promote further action.

Foreign Credit Insurance Association (FCIA)

An agent of the Export/Import Bank, FCIA provides exporters with insurance coverage against both commercial and political risk. The main goals of the FCIA are as follows: (1) Protecting exporters against failure of foreign buyers to pay their credit obligations for commercial or political reasons; (2) encouraging exporters to offer foreign buyers competitive terms of payment; (3) supporting an exporter's prudent penetration of higher-risk foreign markets; and (4) giving exporters and their banks greater financial flexibility in handling overseas accounts receivable.

Foreign Exchange Rates

The proportional value of one currency to another, used to change currency from one denomination to another. For example, one British pound is worth approximately 1.6 American dollars or $1.60.

Forward Integration

A strategy in which a business expands its activities to include distribution or lines of business related to the selling of its core products.

Franchising

A form of organization in which a firm sells the rights to produce its product or service to other service providers who must then operate under the selling firm's name and pay fees to the original firm.

Free Cash Flow

Free cash flow represents the amount of cash generated by the existing operations of a corporation and that is not required for reinvestment in new projects in the firm. Free cash flow can be positive or negative for any corporation in a particular year. Ultimately, however, since this represents the amount that can be returned to stockholders, it must eventually be positive in order for the firm to sustain and increase its dividend payments.

Full Costs

Full costs include all variable and fixed costs and costs at all activity levels in a corporation. It is the total cost of producing and selling goods.

Functional Resume

Second-most-common type of resume. Skills based resumes identify specific skill sets that the candidate has knowledge of. Functionally based resumes identify a candidate's capabilities as they relate to specific business functions. The emphasis is *not* on chronological experiences.

Functional Silo

A phrase referring to the tendency of departments to become isolated from one another in a functionally structured organization.

Futures Contract

An obligation to purchase or sell an asset at an agreed-upon price on a specific future date. The buyer commits himself or herself to purchase the asset, and the seller commits himself or herself to sell the asset. Futures contracts are generally traded on organized exchanges, and changes in the value of the agreement are settled in cash each day. Futures contracts exist for currencies, stock indexes, commodities, and debt instruments.

Future Value

The value of an investment, based on the rate of interest paid at set time periods, at some point in the future. Future values incorporate both the earned rate of interest and the amount of interest compounded on interest already earned. Interest may be compounded annually, monthly, weekly, even daily. The more frequently interest is compounded, the higher the future value of the investment.

—G—

GAP Model of Service, Quality and Satisfaction
This model is designed to identify misperceptions or short-comings in the relationship between the consumer and the service provider in such a way that these gaps can be corrected and customer satisfaction can be improved.

General Agreement of Tariffs and Trade (GATT)
A multilateral treaty, the basic aims of which are: (1) to liberalize and promote world trade via multilateral trade negotiations; (2) to place world trade on a secure basis; and thereby (3) to contribute to global economic growth and development.

Generic Product
A generic product is an unbranded, inexpensive, plainly packaged version of a common consumer product, usually of standard or slightly substandard quality compared to its branded counterparts.

Ghost Shopper
A ghost shopper is a marketing specialist, posing as a regular consumer, who is hired to monitor and evaluate the presentation skills and salesmanship of the store's salespersons.

Global Marketing
The activity of a global corporation that seeks to achieve long-run, large-scale production efficiencies by producing standardized products of good value and long-term reliability for all consumers (or industrial users) in all segments of all markets; the marketing of a standardized product worldwide, with little allowance for, or acceptance of, regional or local differentiation of the marketing-mix strategies.

Globalization
The process of interlinking financial markets in different countries into a common, worldwide pool of funds to be

accessed by both borrowers and lenders. Came about as a result of the growth in international trade.

Goal-Setting Theory

Edwin Locke proposed that intentions to work toward a goal are major sources of work motivation. The theory states that specific and difficult goals lead to higher performance. Research has shown that the key to the effectiveness of goal-setting is not necessarily whether employees participate in setting the goals or not but rather that the goals are accepted and agreed upon by employees.

Golden Handcuffs

The combination of rewards and penalties given to managers to dissuade them from leaving a company.

Government Relations

This is a subfunction of corporate communication more frequently called *public affairs*. Depending on your industry, the importance of government relations varies. In heavily regulated industries such as utilities, government relations are particularly important.

Gross Domestic Product

A measure of national economic activity, GDP is measured from two different approaches. GDP can be viewed as the total value of all goods and services produced in the United States, or as the total value of all payments made to produce all American goods and services. Other measures of GDP exist that take into account inflation factors, so that the adjusted GDP is a more accurate representation of economic activity in the United States in real dollars.

Groupthink

A condition where group pressures for conformity prevent the group from critically evaluating alternative viewpoints. The classic example of groupthink, the United States' unsuccessful 1962 invasion of Cuba called the Bay of Pigs attack, shows how a narrow focus and lack of analysis can lead to potentially disastrous decisions made by a group.

—H—

Hacker

A person who delights in having an intimate understanding of the Internet workings of a system, computers and computer networks in particular.

Halo Effect

Drawing a general impression of an individual based on a single characteristic. For example, if someone is well-dressed, you might assume that he or she is intelligent even if there is no evidence for this characteristic.

Hard Currency

Currency in which there is wide confidence in the world markets, as opposed to soft currency, which is not widely accepted as legal tender outside the country of origin. Hard currencies can be exchanged for other hard currencies at a designated exchange rate.

Heuristics

Heuristic means by trial and error. In organizational behavior the phrase *heuristics* refers to the set of implicit biases and decision-making roles that individuals hold in their minds as a result of previous experience, misunderstanding of probability, and selective perception. These "rules of thumb" often lead to less than optimal decisions.

Hierarchy of Needs

Probably the most well-known theory of motivation, Maslow's hierarchy of needs suggests that every human being has a hierarchy of five needs. An individual moves progressively through this hierarchy, and the steps, from lowest to highest, are physiological, safety, social, esteem, and self-actualization. According to Maslow, if you want to motivate someone you need to first understand what level of the hierarchy that person is currently on and focus on meeting the needs at that level. The theory's intuitive logic and ease of understanding makes it appealing to managers. However, research does not generally validate the theory.

High Potential Venture

A company started with the intent of growing quickly to annual sales of at least $30 to 50 million in five years. It also has the potential to have a firm commitment IPO.

Housing Start

The start of the construction of a new housing unit. Housing starts are used as an indicator of economic development, since if there is increased demand for new homes, that means that families are prospering and are to make long-term investments.

Hygiene Factors

Hertzberg suggested that there are some factors that motivate people leading to performance and job satisfaction and that there are other, separate factors, which prevent dissatisfaction. These "hygiene factors" such as company policy, relationship with supervisor, work conditions and salary will, when adequate, prevent dissatisfaction. However, they alone are not sufficient for leading to job satisfaction. Hertzberg's theory of separate motivation and hygiene factors has been criticized for his methodology and for ignoring situational factors. Nevertheless, it is widely read and is valuable in demonstrating that satisfaction and dissatisfaction are not necessarily two ends of the same continuum.

Hypertext Markup Language (HTML)

Formatting language most common for web documents.

Hypertext transfer protocol (HTTP)

Common protocol or "language" computers use to "speak" to each other over the Web.

—I—

Income Elasticity

The functional relationship between the change in the quantity demanded for a good or service and the change in income of those persons demanding the good or service. If the demand for a good increases as a person's income increases, that good is said to be "normal." If the demand for a good decreases as a person's income rises, that good is said to be "inferior."

Income Statement

A formal statement of the elements used in determining a company's net income; also called *profit and loss statement*. The categories reported in an income statement are as follows: sales, gross margin, income from operations, income before tax, income from continuing operations, income before extraordinary items, or cumulative effect and net income.

Incremental Cost

The measured change in a firm's cost of production due to an additional activity pursued by the firm. Incremental costs can be measured as the cost difference between two business alternatives, or as the added cost a firm must incur to expand its operations. In the first case, the incremental costs would equal the difference between the production costs of two like products that differ on the basis of features only. In the second case, the incremental cost would be a measure of the cost of buying a new piece of equipment relative to the revenue that new piece of equipment enabled the firm to generate.

Industrial Goods

All goods and services that are used in the production of other goods and services subsequently supplied to consumers. Industrial goods fall into one of three categories: raw materials and components, capital goods and services, and suppliers.

Industrial Market

All individuals or companies that produce or acquire goods or services that are incorporated into the production of other finished goods or services subsequently sold to customers. The industrial market is also referred to as the *business* or *producer market*.

Industrial Policy

The course of action set by the government to influence the development of domestic industrial sectors in particular and the direction of the national industrial growth in general. A government's industrial policy may comprise such instruments as subsidies, tax incentives, regional development programs, training programs for workers, and R&D assistance.

Industrial Production

The output of U.S. factories, mines, and utilities. This output constitutes the production of things—the goods, portion of goods, and services. The Federal Reserve Board has measured industrial production since the 1920s. Industrial production is a coincident indicator of economic activity: It traces the behavior of the business cycle nearly exactly.

Industrial Production Index

The measure of the combined output of all mining, manufacturing, and electric and natural gas utilities companies in the United States as compiled by the Federal Reserve. The industrial production index, when divided by an index of productive capacity, yields the capacity utilization rate, which is a measure of capital use identical to the way the unemployment rate measures labor use.

Initial Public Offering (IPO)

Process by which a company raises money by issuing equity and gets listed on a public stock exchange.

Inflation

An overall and general increase in price level for goods and services in a particular economy. Inflation can be viewed as either an increase in the general cost of living or as an erosion of purchasing power. Inflation is a state of macroeconomic disequilibrium, usually associated with strong demand pressures on the economy.

Innovation

Any modernizing modification in a process or procedure that increases the efficiency of that process or procedure. Information technology has been the catalyst for much of the innovation in American companies in the last 15 years.

Interest Rates

The payment borrowers make for the use of the funds that they borrow and the payment that lenders demand for the use of the funds they lend (termed *interest*), expressed as a percentage of the principal (loan amount). This percentage is the interest rate. Interest rates typically are expressed in whole percentages and basis points. A basis point is one-hundredth of a percentage point. There are four main components to market interest rates:

- The risk (or default) premium
- The maturity premium
- An inflation premium
- The "real" rate

The risk premium is a recognition that different classes of borrowers have greater or lesser risk of default. Interest rates are higher for riskier borrowers; they are lowest for the U.S. Treasury, which is considered a "risk-free" borrower. The difference in interest rate between any other borrower and the U.S. Treasury for the same maturity is called a quality spread. The maturity premium reflects the fact that, in general, a longer loan will have a higher interest rate than a shorter loan of the same quality. The yield curve shows the change in interest rates as maturities are extended for a given class of loans. The inflation premium is a recognition that inflation may erode the purchasing power of the funds lent. Thus, interest includes compensation for the inflation expected over the length of the loan. The remaining portion of interest rates reflects the real rate of interest that must be paid to induce the lender to forego the use of the funds. (Note that this is not simply the interest rate less current inflation, but rather interest rates less the average expected inflation over the length of the loan. Subtracting the current inflation rate provides an inflation-adjusted interest rate. Often, since the future interest rates are assumed to conform to an average of past rates, lenders use some such average as a proxy for expected inflation.)

Internal Rate of Return

The discount rate at which the net present value (the value of all future cash flows, in excess of the original investment, expressed in today's dollars) of an investment equals zero. Internal rate of return is frequently used by financial managers to decide whether to commit to an investment. In most cases, an investment opportunity is accepted when the internal rate of return is greater than the opportunity cost (the projected return on an investment of similar risk) of the capital required for the investment. The profit percentage earned on a proposed investment once all costs are considered for a specific period of time.

Inventory Turnover

In accounting, a measure of the number of times that the average amount of inventory on hand is sold within a given period of time. In other words, the inventory turnover ratio shows how many times a company "emptied its warehouse" over a particular period of time. This ratio is calculated by dividing the cost of goods sold for a specified period of time by the average amount of inventory on hand for that same time period (average inventory is calculated by adding beginning inventory and ending inventory for a given time period and dividing the sum by two), or

$$\text{Inventory turnover ratio} = \frac{\text{cost of goods sold}}{\text{average inventory on hand}}$$

Investment Bank

A lending entity engaged in all phases of security offerings, including managing, underwriting, trading, and distributing new security issues.

Investment Tax Credit

A reduction in corporate income taxes equal to a percent of the cost of a new asset in the year the new asset is placed into service. The credit is periodically allowed by the federal tax authorities, but is not always available. The actual rules and rates change over the years. Currently, there is no investment credit available to firms that purchase new equipment.

Job Analysis

Developing a detailed description of the tasks involved in a job and ascertaining the knowledge, skills, and abilities necessary for an employee to perform the job successfully.

Job Banks

Bulletin boards receiving listing from employers—many of whom pay a fee to have jobs listed—or sourced from newspapers, etc.

Job Characteristics Model

Hackman and Oldman's model identifies five job characteristics and their relationships to personal and work outcomes.

Using the model, work can be redesigned to increase the level of motivation.

There are five core job dimensions:

1. *Skill Variety.* Can the worker use a number of different skills and talents?

2. *Task Identity.* Does the worker complete a whole and identifiable piece of work?

3. *Task Significance.* Does the work have substantial consequences for the lives and work of other people?

4. *Autonomy.* Does the worker have freedom, independence, and discretion in carrying out the work?

5. *Feedback.* Does the individual receive direct and clear information about his or her effectiveness?

The first three characteristics increase the perceived meaningfulness of the work. Autonomy leads to increases in perceived personal responsibility. Feedback gives the individual knowledge of the actual results of the activities. These three "critical psychological states" (meaningfulness, responsibility, and knowledge) lead to the following personal and work outcomes: high internal work motivation, high-quality work performance, high satisfaction, and low absenteeism and turnover.

Job Design

The way the tasks are combined to form a complete job. Job redesign focuses on changing the task combination or the way the task is done to enhance motivation and/or productivity.

Job Rotation

The periodic shifting of a worker from one task to another with similar skill requirements. While providing variety (which can increase motivation for some employees), job rotation does little to change the nature of the work itself.

Just-in-Time Inventory Management

An approach to dealing with materials inventories that emphasizes the elimination of all waste and the continual improvement of the production process. The process focuses on policies, procedures, and attitudes by managers and other employees designed to result in the efficient production of high-quality goods while simultaneously allowing the firm to maintain the minimum level of inventories.

—K—

Keiretsu

Corporate conglomerates whose members cooperate with each other for strategic purposes within the international business environment; a Japanese term.

—L—

Leader-Participation Model

Victor Vroom and Phillip Yetton developed this model that provides a set of rules to determine the form and amount of participative decision making in different situations.

Leadership

The exercise of responsibility, influence, and authority over a group of people.

There are theories that sort personality, social, physical, or intellectual qualities that differentiate leaders from nonleaders. Six traits identified are ambition and energy, the desire to lead, honesty and integrity, self-confidence, intelligence, and job-relevant knowledge. Research shows only modest correlation between these traits and effective leadership. The trait approach also overlooks the needs of followers and doesn't separate cause from effect (e.g., are leaders self-confident to start with or does leadership experience build self-confidence?).

Leading Economic Indicators

The 11 key economic indicators that have been found to lead business cycle turning points. Of the 11, 4 are commonly used in business; gross domestic product (GDP), employment statistics, personal income, and industrial production. The Fed and company managers alike use economic indicators to predict the movement to the economy.

Lease

A lease is a contractual arrangement allowing one party the use of some specific assets for a specific time period in exchange for a payment, similar to a rental arrangement. The leasee is the party that receives the use of assets under a lease, and the leasor is the party that conveys the use of the assets. An operating lease is usually a short-term cancelable arrangement, whereas a financial (or capital) lease is a long-term noncancelable arrangement.

Letter of Credit (LOC)
A popular bank instrument stating that a bank has granted the holder an amount of credit equal to the face amount of the L/C. A bank guarantees payment of its customer's draft up to a stated amount for a given period of time.

Leveraged Buyout (LBO)
Acquisition of a company through the accumulation of 70 percent or more of the company's total capitalized debt.

Lien
A legal claim on specific assets that were used to secure a loan.

Liquidity
The ability of an asset to be converted into cash as quickly as possible and without any discount to its value.

Listening Skills
To be an effective communicator you should not only know how to express your ideas but should also be a good listener. By listening well to others you will increase your understanding, receive more detailed information, and increase cooperation. One component of listening skills is nonverbal and includes maintaining good eye contact and looking and acting interested in what other people are saying. Show your interest by nodding your head and using brief encouragers such as "I see," or "Yes." Avoid obvious signs of impatience such as looking at your watch, reading, or looking out the window. The quality of your listening skills is directly related to your ability to be objective and empathetic.

Listing
Acceptance of a security for trading on an organized stock exchange.

Locus of Control
Some people see themselves as very much in control of their lives. Others see themselves as not being in control of the events around them. If a person believes she is in control, she

is said to have an internal locus of control; someone who does not see himself as in control has an external locus of control.

London Interbank Offered Rate (LIBOR)

The base lending rate that banks charge each other in the London Eurocurrency market. LIBOR is the European equivalent of the U.S. prime rate.

Long-Term Debt

Long-term debt is a debt obligation that has a maturity of more than one year from the date the obligation was incurred. The debt obligation commits the company to repay the amount borrowed and to make regular interest payments through the life of the loan. Failure by the borrower to make the required payments can result in bankruptcy.

—M—

Macroeconomics

This is the study of business forces on a national or global level.

Macrowriting

This term refers to issues in written documents that have to do with the document as a whole. Important macrowriting components include the overall organization, logic, flow, and layout. These issues apply to all types of written communication. The goals of macrowriting are to increase readability and appeal by using white space, headings, and typography to produce a document with a clear and coherent organizational structure and design. Another objective is to place ideas together in a way that promotes a logical flow by means of linking transitions and clear openings and closings. Strategies for editing at a macrowriting level include making the writing comprehensible if a reader were to skim the document and using introductions and conclusions in paragraphs as links to convey the intended message.

Management

The administration of a process or those conducting a process to ensure that the process meets completion in the most efficient way possible.

Management Accounting

An accounting discipline concerned with the use of financial information and the use of other relevant information by managers and other decision makers inside a specific organization. The information is designed to facilitate strategic, organizational, and operational decisions. The objective is to enhance the ability of management to perform its job of decision making, planning, and control.

Management Buyout (MBO)

The transfer of ownership of an entity to new owners where the old management and employee base are significant elements.

Management by Objectives (MBO)

Management technique based on *goal-setting theory* in which employees are given specific measurable objectives to achieve. MBO has been shown to be successful when the goals are realistic, when there is top management commitment, and when feedback and rewards are contingent on goal accomplishment.

Management Communication

The process of communicating in management itself. Effective managerial communication, either written or spoken, is based on a cohesive strategy combining communicator strategy, audience strategy, message strategy, channel choice strategy, and culture strategy.

Managerial Grid

Blake and Mouton proposed a managerial grid extending the two-dimensional view of leadership style into a 9×9 matrix. Along one axis is concern for people. Along the other is concern for production. Blake and Mouton's finding suggested that managers perform best under a 9,9 style that is high in both concern for people and concern for production. This model does not take into account situational factors.

Managerial Writing

This refers to a channel for management communication. Writing, as a means of communication, has specific advantages and disadvantages. Advantages include saving your audience time since reading is three to four times faster than listening. Writing also offers you the ability to convey larger volumes of detailed information and provides a permanent and legal record. Writing is a good channel when you do not need a response immediately or at all, as it enables you to clearly clarify, confirm, announce, or report. Writing is also more consistent than speaking as exact wording will remain consistent, and people can assimilate a greater volume of written details than through audio messages. The disadvantages to writing include the inability to control when, whether, and how thoroughly your message will be read. Additionally, writing can be misinterpreted in tone or meaning because of the lack of nonverbal interaction. E-mail and faxes provide written forms of communication that are spontaneous and interactive, but they have the potential disadvantage of limited privacy.

Market Efficiency

An efficient market is a market in which the prices of the assets or securities fully reflect all available information. When new information arrives, whether favorable or unfavorable, prices adjust instantaneously. Investors who purchase assets or securities in an efficient market can expect to receive fair value for their investment.

Market Growth

The measured potential for a product category to attract more consumer spending.

Marketing Mix

This comprises the marketing tools and techniques a company uses to achieve its goals relative to a specific target market audience.

Marketing Myopia

This is a phenomenon experienced when a company becomes so involved in the actual process of selling its product that it loses sight of the true nature and purpose of the product itself. When a company focuses more on selling a product than on the product itself, an outstanding opportunity for competitors to steal market share is created.

Marketing Orientation

If a company has a marketing orientation, its strategy rests in its marketing effort. Marketing becomes the business's philosophy, not just a functional area. Companies focus goals around managing customer retention and satisfaction through product definition, characteristics, and interfunctional integration throughout the company. Having a market orientation necessitates "the organization-wide generation, dissemination and responsiveness to market intelligence" (Kohli and Joworski, 1990). Alternative orientations a corporation can have include sales, finance, R&D, or manufacturing.

Market Segmentation

This refers to the process of breaking the mass market up into discernible subgroups, where each subgroup has obvious demographic and other identifiable differences.

Market Share

The percent of sales one product earns in relation to total market sales for all products in that category.

Marginal Analysis

Marginal analysis seeks to balance the cost of producing one more item (marginal costs) with the revenue gained from selling one more item (marginal revenue).

Marginal Cost

Marginal cost is the change in a firm's cost of production relative to a unit change in its output, or the added cost of producing the next unit. The marginal cost function can be found by taking the first derivative of the total cost function, and the marginal cost for a unit of production can be found by substituting that quantity into the marginal cost function.

Marginal Revenue

Marginal revenue is the additional revenue a company receives resulting from the sale of one more item of output. Marginal revenue is calculated by taking the difference between the total revenue both before and after the production of the extra unit. As long as the price of a product or service remains constant, marginal revenue equals price.

Mass Marketing

This includes the mass production, distribution, and promotion of one product for all buyers.

Matrix Structure

An organizational structure creating dual lines of authority (e.g., combining functional and departmental lines of organization).

McKinsey 7S Model

A framework developed by the consulting firm of McKinsey and Co. to chart the strategic relationships between forces existing in a company, where these forces determine a company's success or failure. The forces include: (1) strategy; (2) structure; (3) staff; (4) superordinate goals; (5) skills; (6) style; and (7) systems.

Mean

A numerical average, equal to the sum of terms in a given series divided by the number of terms in that series is the mean; also called the *expected value*.

Mergers and Acquisitions

Processes of business combination. There are three forms of business combination:

1. *M1*. This is the narrowest category, consisting of only currency, checks, demand deposits and traveler's checks. Of all the categories, M1 has the highest liquidity.

2. *M2*. This category includes all M1 money, but also includes savings, deposits under $10,000, money market deposit accounts, money market mutual account balances, overnight repurchase agreements and overnight Eurodollar deposits.

3. *M3*. This category contains all M2 but also includes term deposits for repurchase agreements and Eurodollar deposits, as well as dealer-only money market funds.

Monetary Policy

The Federal Reserve's aim to regulate the growth of the monetary aggregates to ensure sufficient credit expansion to foster economic growth, without inflation, while maintaining orderly financial markets.

Motivation

Motivation is the willingness to exert high levels of effort toward organizational goals. Usually conditioned by the efforts and ability to satisfy some individual need.

Mutually Exclusive Investments

Investment alternatives that are substitutes, so that the acceptance of one of the projects eliminates the possibility of undertaking the remaining projects.

—N—

Net Income

What remains of a company's revenue after all expenses and taxes have been paid.

Net Present Value (NPV)

In corporate finance, the present value (the value of cash to be received in the future expressed in today's dollars) of an investment in excess of the initial amount invested. When an investment or project has a positive NPV, it should be pursued. When an investment has a negative NPV, it should not be accepted.

Networking

The process of alerting the market that a candidate is seeking an employment opportunity, through a series of letters and informational interviews that are designed to exponentially broaden a candidate's knowledge of the marketplace. Similar to a pyramid scheme or a chain letter, the candidate expects to learn about positions from contacts within the industry, but the candidate also hopes that his availability will be made known to opportunities that are not listed, or are not apparent, to the candidate.

Nominal Group Technique

A group decision-making method in which individual members meet face to face, first, to generate ideas individually, and then to poll their judgments. Their decision is determined by the aggregate ranking of their ideas.

Nonverbal Communications
Message conveyed to and from a person without speaking (crossing arms, looking at one's watch).

North American Free Trade Agreement (NAFTA)
A multilateral accord between the United States, Canada, and Mexico. Also referred to as the *North American Free Trade Zone* (NAFTZ).

—O—

Offshore Financial Center
A location with banking facilities to accept deposits and make loans in currencies different from the currency's country of origin. Banks located in offshore financial centers are exempt from the bank's home country banking regulations. All off-shore financial centers, including those in the United States, offer tax preferences—usually, but not always, in the form of tax-free remittances of earnings to an offshore parent company.

Ohio State Studies
Studies undertaken at Ohio State University in the 1920s that identified two categories accounting for most leadership behavior as described by subordinates. The first behavior was *initiating structure:* the extent to which a leader defines and structures the roles of the group. The second behavior was *consideration:* the extent to which a leader develops job relationships based on mutual trust, respect for ideas, and regard for feelings. This model does not take into account situational factors.

Operating Budget
A collection or set of formal financial documents that details expected revenues and expenses, as well as all other expected operating and financial transactions over some particular period of time. Thus, it outlines the firm's operating plans over that time period. The operating cycle usually covers one year.

Operating Leverage

Operating leverage describes the degree to which a company's cost of operation is fixed as opposed to variable. Thus, it is a measure of how much a firm's profits can be expected to change when sales increase. Firms with a high degree of operating leverage will experience greater changes in profitability when sales change. Usually, companies with high operating leverage will maintain low levels of debt, or financial leverage.

Opportunity Cost

The amount that is sacrificed when choosing one activity over the next-best alternative. In industry, an example of opportunity cost is seen in the concept of the "hurdle rate" used by financial analysts in deciding whether to pursue a particular investment project. In financial analysis, the hurdle rate is the minimum acceptable rate of return needed to justify the investment in a capital project. If a company's managers can demonstrate that a particular project would have a rate of return that is higher than this, they are in effect saying that the benefits of this project exceed the opportunity cost of using the company's funds in this project.

Optimization

This is the practice of maximizing revenues and profits and minimizing costs, using marginal analysis.

Oral Presentation

Refers to spoken, rather than written, communication where information is presented to a group. Frequently used in business to reveal research and analysis results, oral presentations can also be used to foster internal and external promotions of image and identity. The spoken word is frequently augmented by visual aids such as graphs, charts, graphics or multimedia presentations.

Organization for Economic Development (OECD)

An international organization established in 1961 in Paris, France, to act as a global forum to stimulate world trade and economic development. The OECD's membership consists of the world's developed countries: Australia, Austria, Belgium, Canada, Denmark, Finland, France, Greece, Iceland, Ireland, Italy, Japan, Luxembourg, the Netherlands, New Zealand,

Norway, Portugal, Spain, Sweden, Switzerland, Turkey, the United Kingdom, and the United States.

Organization of Petroleum Exporting Countries (OPEC)

The most important international commodity group (ICG) in the world. It has a significant impact on the world price of oil and, subsequently, on the balance of payments of every country; and it is the model of a successful international cartel.

Organizational Communication

This is the study of communication within organizations, which fits well as a subset of corporate communication because it enables organizations to approach employees as one of numerous constituencies rather than the narrower perspective of human resource management. Hence, corporate communication's ability to unify internal and external communications under one business unit enables greater consistency in the corporate image and identity. Therefore, corporate communication can be used as a tool to facilitate more effective organizational communication.

Organizational Cost Drivers

The cost consequences that result from managerial choices concerning the organization of activities as well as the involvement of persons inside and outside the organization in the decision-making process.

Organizational Culture

A common perception held by the organization's members; a system of shared meaning. For most people, organizational culture is something they cannot define but they know it when they see it. It can perhaps be best understood as the set of informal rules, relationships, and norms that determine what is acceptable and unacceptable behavior within the organization. Organizational culture can often have a more powerful influence on behavior than the formal structures and systems.

Out of Cash

Calculated by taking a company's cash on hand divided by its burn rate, yielding the time period that the company will have enough cash to cover its needs.

Outsourcing
The purchase of parts from outside suppliers. It is the external acquisition of services or components used in the production of goods or services in an organization.

Over the Counter (OTC)
Refers to financial securities whose sale and purchase are not conducted over a stock exchange.

—P—

Panel Interview
Situation in which the candidate is interviewed by more than one recruiter at the same time.

Parallel Trade
A form of countertrade that involves the execution of two distinct and individually enforceable contracts: the first for the sale of goods by an exporter, the second for the purchase of the goods. Both contracts are requirements for insurance, and sometimes credit, for each shipment. Parallel trade agreements that involve cash transfers are also known as *counterpurchases*.

Parity Conditions
A parity condition describes the relative value of one country's currency to another country's currency. The condition states how, for example, differences in inflation or interest rates between countries should affect the relative values of their currencies.

Participative Management
Umbrella term encompassing management techniques where employees share a significant degree of decision-making power with managers. These include MBO, consultation committees, employee representation of policy-making bodies, group decision making, self-managed teams, and many other activities.

Partnership
A legally recognized business form in which two or more partners are co-owners, sharing profits, losses, and liabilities associated with the business they own.

Patent

A legal document ensuring exclusive rights to a process or product using a unique technological or structural innovation.

Payback Period

The amount of time, usually measured in years, it takes before the undiscounted cash inflows from a project equal the cash outflow. It indicates the length of time necessary for the firm to recover its initial investment in a project.

Penetration Pricing

This refers to a pricing strategy that dictates that the price of an item being introduced into a market should be set as low as possible to generate the greatest possible sales volume for that product.

Perceived Value Pricing

This refers to a pricing strategy that dictates that the price of a given item should be set based on the customer's perception of the value of that item, not on the seller's costs.

Perfect Competition

A market where conditions prevail such that buyers and suppliers are without the ability to manipulate price in any significant way; the market dynamics are determined almost completely by the forces of supply and demand.

Preferred Stock

A type of capital stock that gives its holders preference over common stockholders in the distribution of earnings or rights to the assets of a company in the event of liquidation. Preferred stock usually pays an established dividend. For example, a 5 percent preferred stock pays a dividend that equals 5 percent of the total par value of outstanding shares. Preferred stocks generally do not have any voting rights. Preferred stock may also carry a variety of features. It may be callable by the company, dividends may be cumulative, common stock warrants may be attached or it may be convertible to common stock under specific conditions, to mention only a few variations.

Performance Appraisal

A procedure used in most organizations to evaluate employ-ees' performance and decide on pay awards each year. In the-ory, performance appraisal is a valuable system for receiving information on obstacles to high-quality performance and for providing feedback to the employee on his or her work, processes, and outcomes. In practice many performance appraisal systems become politicized due the linkage of appraisal results and pay awards. More recently, in an effort to increase the value of the feedback element of the process, some organizations have moved to 360-degree feedback pro-grams and peer appraisal systems.

Performance-Based Compensation

Paying employees on the basis of performance measure. Instead of paying a person for time on the job, pay reflects productivity, quality, or some other aspect of the job that can be effectively measured. Effectiveness of performance-based compensation depends, as theorists suggest, on two main fac-tors: (1) Is the compensation valued? (2) Is the performance within the employee's control?

Persuasion

When communicating, your objective often is to persuade the audience to accept the message that you are conveying to them. Persuasion is connected to the feasibility of the message that you are promoting, but there are other factors that can also enhance the persuasiveness of your argument. Establishing credibility based both on initial impressions of the audience as well as the credibility acquired while speaking are integral ele-ments that enhance persuasiveness. Using an appropriate audi-ence strategy increases the chance your audience will evaluate your message in a way that appeals to them.

Phone Interview

Interview that occurs over the telephone.

Point-of-Purchase Advertising

This is a method of advertising designed to trigger impulse purchases through the use of eye-catching, attractive displays at the locations where customers actually pay for a product.

Portfolio

A portfolio is a combination of different securities or assets. A portfolio may consist of combinations of stocks, bonds, real estate, or any other asset held by an investor. By holding a collection of different assets, an investor's wealth will be less affected by adverse events that affect any one particular asset in the portfolio.

Positional Bargaining

An approach to negotiation in which each side takes a position, argues for it, and makes concessions to reach a compromise.

Power

The capacity to influence the behavior of other people so they do things that they would not otherwise do. The most important component of power is dependency. The greater a person's dependency on you, the more power you have in that relationship. For example, machine operators might seem to have low power but the organization is dependent on them to make the product they sell. Therefore, machine operators have power within the organization. The most commonly referred to sources of power are:

1. *Coercive Power.*   Power based on fear.

2. *Reward Power.*   Power to give positive benefits to people.

3. *Position Power.*   Power arising from a position in an organizational hierarchy or group.

4. *Expert Power.*   Influence based on special skills or knowledge.

5. *Referent Power.*   Influence held based on a person's admiration and desire to model themselves after you.

Like many things, power itself is neither good nor bad. It is how it is used by managers that makes the difference.

Present Value

The current value of a future payment or stream of payments. Present value is calculated by applying a discount (capitalization) rate to the future payment(s). The present value method forms the cornerstone of business or equity interest valuations and is also referred to as the *discounted cash flow method* or the *discounted earnings method*. It is widely used by companies and investors to determine the fair market value of a potential investment. Although it is extremely time-consuming to calculate present value manually, annuity tables, programmable calculators, and computer programs make the calculations easy and fast.

Price Discrimination
A practice where one firm sells the same product at different prices in different markets.

Price/Earnings (P/E) Ratio
A measure of a company's investment potential. Literally, a P/E ratio is how much a share is worth per dollar of earnings. The price-earnings ratio is calculated as follows:

$$\text{P/E ratio} = \frac{\text{market price per common share}}{\text{primary earnings per common share}}$$

A company's P/E ratio depends on investors' perceptions of a company's potential. Factors such as risk, quality of management, growth potential, earnings history, and industry conditions all come into play.

Price Elasticity
A measure of the change in demand for a product relative to unit changes in the price of the product. If the percentage change in quantity demanded is greater than the percentage change in price, the response to a change in price is said to be *elastic*.

Private Placement
The direct sale of securities to a small number of investors.

Producer Price Index
This is a measure of the prices of all goods produced in the United States. Unlike the CPI, the PPI is comprehensive and includes all goods produced excluding imports. The PPI is organized into three subgroups, including crude goods, intermediate goods, and finished goods.

Product
A good or service a company makes in quantity to sell on the open market is a product.

Productivity

A measure of a firm's efficiency, productivity is measured by dividing the company's output by the number of hours people worked to produce the output. Productivity can be increased by increasing outputs, decreasing worker hours, or both.

Product Lifecycle

Key terms include:

1. *Product Class.*   At the most generic level, this term refers to all products from all competing producers that serve the same functional purposes in roughly the same manner, despite smaller differences in appearance and performance; for example, all passenger cars manufactured in the world today are a product class.

2. *Product Form.*   A lesser generic level, this term refers to all products within a group that are more similar in customer perception and use than all items in a product class. Using the passenger car example, a product from within this product class would be luxury passenger cars.

3. *Brand.*   This term refers to several items in a product form produced by the same organization or company. Mercedes Benz is a brand within the product form of luxury automobiles.

4. *Model.*   The least generic classification, this term refers to a specific and individual item produced by an organization or company. A 300 E Class Sedan is a specific model produced under the brand of Mercedes Benz within the product form of luxury automobiles within the product class of passenger cars.

Product Margin

This is calculated as product sales minus the direct costs of selling the product.

Product Mix

The portfolio of products that a given company produces for market consumption is the product mix.

Profit Center

A separate unit or department within a company that is responsible for its own costs, revenues, and thus profit. Profit center managers are generally free to make their own decisions regarding key issues such as price, marketing, and product positioning.

Profit Margin
A measure of company performance, profit margins measure the percentage return a company is earning over the cost of production of the items sold.

Pro forma Financial Statements
In accounting, a financial statement in which the amounts stated are fully or partially estimates; from the Latin for "as a matter of form." For example, a company making a change in accounting principle must prepare pro forma financial statements estimating what the previous year's earnings would have been if the new principle had been in use. Usually, companies also disclose the underlying assumptions of any pro forma statement.

Prospectus
A document containing all relevant investor information regarding the operations of a company issuing securities.

Pull Strategy
This refers to a marketing approach in which a manufacturer promotes a product directly to consumers in the hopes that the consumers will then request the product from distribution channel members.

Punctuated Equilibrium Model
Connie Gersick's model of group development challenges the traditional forming/norming/storming/performing view of group development. Gersick's research showed that groups tend to follow a trajectory up to the midpoint of their project. At this midpoint there is a concentrated set of changes in norms, processes, and behaviors within the group. After this midpoint the group settles on a new trajectory. This model suggests (and subsequent research has indicated) that interventions aimed at improving group effectiveness are most effectively made at the midpoint of a group's life. Managers can create midpoints through the setting of milestones and intermediate deadlines.

Push Strategy

This refers to a marketing approach in which a manufacturer uses its sales force and trade promotions to sell a product actively to wholesalers and retailers, who in turn aggressively sell the product to consumers.

Put

An agreement allowing a holder of securities to sell them back to the issuer at a specified amount during a specified time interval. This method protects the downside risk for the holder of a security.

Put Option

A right that is granted in exchange for an agreed-upon sum to sell property. If the right is not exercised within the specified time period, it expires and the holder forfeits the money. Options are used most frequently in securities transactions, although stock options are also used as incentive compensation for key managers. Instead of exercising options, most investors prefer to buy and sell them in the open market before expiration, cashing in on increases in trading value. One of the interesting features of trading in options is the amount of leverage option buyers enjoy. Buyers put up relatively small amount of money to control a large amount of common shares, potentially leveraging sizable profits.

—R—

Recession

If the GDP decreases two quarters of the year in a row, the economy is in recession. A recession indicates that there may be an accompanying decrease in demand for goods and services within an economy.

Red Herring

Preliminary prospectus circulated by underwriters to gauge investor interest in a planned offering, which has yet to gain final approval from the SEC.

Reengineering

Reconceptualizing and restructuring business processes and practices with the intention of increasing efficiency, quality, and employee and customer satisfaction while reducing the costs associated with the procedure or practice.

Regional Banks

Large banks such as Mellon, First Chicago, Norwest, and Crocker function regionally in a fashion similar to money center banks at the national level. Regional banks serve as correspondents for smaller local banks in the same way that money center banks act as correspondent for regional banks.

Regression Analysis

This is a statistical tool used to discern the relationship between a dependent variable, such as sales, to one or more independent variables, like marketing spending, advertising spending, and promotional spending.

Relationship Marketing

This approach to marketing emphasizes the importance of personal relationship building between consumers, suppliers, and distributors inclusively, and marketing professionals with all parties.

Repeat Purchase Rate

This is the number of times a consumer purchases the same product within a specific time interval.

Reputation

This is a critical component in establishing credibility and an underlying component in successful corporate communication. Reputation is intricately related to shaping corporate image. A company with a good reputation strives to perpetuate that image successfully through its corporate identity. Reputation is the factor that precedes a company's product or services, and a good reputation can be a factor that causes clients to select one company over another. Just as reputation can enhance business it is also the component that can be harmed through poor crisis management or that can sustain a company in a time of corporate disaster.

Residual Income

For external reporting purposes, this term refers to the net income available for distribution to the firm's common stockholders. In managerial accounting, it refers to the excess divisional or segment income over the product of the cost of capital for the company multiplied by the average amount of capital invested in the division during the period over which the income was earned.

Response Rate

This is the percentage of responses generated by a direct marketing campaign.

Resume Banks

Posting opportunities to enter your resume into a database that is reviewed by employers. Costs range from free to as high as $100 for a limited run of your resume (anywhere from two weeks to one year).

Retrenchment

The refocusing of organizational forces and effort on core businesses and divestment of peripheral interests.

Return on Investment (ROI)

In accounting, a measure of the earning power of a company's assets. A high return on investments is desirable. ROI is broadly defined as net income divided by investments. However, the term *investments* has three distinct interpretations in financial analysis, each of which leads to a different calculation of return on investment: return on assets, return on owners' equity, and return on invested capital.

Revenues

This is the gross income received before any deductions for expenses, discounts, returns, and so on. Revenue is also called *sales* in most companies. A much less common usage refers to interest income, dividends, royalties, refunds, and claim settlements as *revenue*. Generally, however, each type of income carries its own designation—sales, income, fees, claims, and so on.

Risk Premium

A risk premium is the extra, or excess, return on a risky asset relative to the return on risk-free assets. Thus, it describes the additional return that an investor can expect to obtain by accepting a greater amount of risk. Since there are many types of risky assets, each asset commands a different risk premium. As a general rule, the riskier a particular asset is, the greater the risk premium that investors will require to be an investor in that security.

Risk Management

Many corporations and investors engage in activities designed to manage the risks they face. In the corporate world, managers seek to control business risks as well as financial and commodity price risks. As a result, managers often seek to use financial securities such as options, futures, and swaps to alter their risk exposure.

—S—

Sales Budget

A forecast of unit sales volume and sales dollars. Oftentimes, the budget will also contain a forecast of sales collections if the firm sells a significant portion of its products on credit terms.

Savings

The part of after-tax personal income that is not spent.

Second-Round Financing

The introduction of further funding by original investors or new investors to enable a new company to deal with unexpected problems or finance growth.

Securities and Exchange Commission (SEC)

Regulatory body for investor protection in the United States, created by the Securities Exchange Act of 1934.

Seed Financing

A small amount of money used for initial market research or product development for a new venture.

Segment Margin
The amount that a business segment in an organization contributes toward the common or indirect cost of the organization. Hence, it represents that segment's contribution to the overall profitability of the organization. It is usually measured as segment sales minus direct segment costs.

Self-Managed Teams
In these teams the members themselves not only perform the work but also measure, monitor, and manage their performance.

Self-Monitoring
A personality trait reflecting an individual's ability to adjust behavior to match situational factors. Individuals high in self-monitoring are very adaptable and responsive to internal cues.

Sequential Interview
Situation in which a candidate is progressed from one interviewer to another during the interview cycle. A common approach is for recruiters to try extracting different types of information from the candidate. Information from previous interview sessions is then conveyed to subsequent recruiters.

Sensitivity Analysis
A test of a company's performance projections based on varying the key assumptions used for forecast performance.

Shortage
A condition under which the quantity demanded for a good or service exceeds the available supply for that good or service. Shortages usually cause an increase in price to restore market equilibrium in the short term.

Situational Leadership Theory
A widely practiced leadership model developed by Paul Hersey and Ken Blanchard. This contingency theory focuses on followers and defines leadership effectiveness in terms of whether the leader is accepted or rejected. Situational leadership uses the same task and relationship dimensions. Depending on the maturity of the followers, and the ability and

willingness of people to take responsibility for their own behavior, leaders should use one of four specific styles: telling (high task, low relationship), selling (high task, high relationship), participating (low task, high relationship), or delegating (low task, low relationship).

Skimming Pricing

This pricing strategy dictates that the price of an item introduced into a market must be as high as possible, thereby identifying the segment of the consumers who are not price sensitive. Once that segment has been saturated, the price can be manipulated to appeal to other segments who are price sensitive.

Social Information Processing Model

Employees adopt attitudes and behaviors in response to the social cues of others with whom they have contact. This means that an employee's perception of the job or work environment often has more influence on their behavior than the manager's perceived reality.

Sole Proprietorship

This business form is the legal default form for any person who does business in the United States but makes no effort to organize the business otherwise. This is a business owned and operated by one person who assumes total control and liability for the business. No legal entity is formed. While the sole proprietor may have employees, he or she does not have co-owners.

Span of Control

The number of subordinates that a manager can efficiently and effectively direct.

Standard Cost

A predetermined cost representing the ideal or norm achievable by a company. Standard costs form the basis of a standard cost system used extensively in manufacturing companies. At the beginning of each year, companies normally review standards for material price and usage, labor efficiency, and wage rate, and overhead rates based on budgets.

Start-Up Financing

Capital provided to companies that have been in operation for less than one year, to facilitate all phases of bringing their product to market.

Statement of Cash Flows

A formal statement of the cash received and disbursed by a company. The statement of cash flows is divided into three sections: operating activities (usually a source of cash), investing activities (usually both a source and a use of cash), and financing activities (usually a source and use of cash). When cash is received or paid for more than one activity, it is allocated to that activity that is the prime motivation for the cash flow. For example, many companies consider cash spent on new equipment to be an investment activity rather than an operating activity.

Stereotype

The tendency to judge someone based on the perception of the group to which that person belongs. For example, if I know a person is athletic I might stereotype him as a "jock." This would then influence how I approach, interact with and manage that person. Stereotypes are one of several shortcuts we use when evaluating other people and may or may not be accurate.

Strategic Cost Management

A management philosophy pioneered by John Shank, in which decisions concerning specific cost drivers are made within the context of an organization's business strategy, its internal value chain, and its position in a larger value chain encompassing the initiation of a project and the delivery of the final product to its customers.

Strategic Inflection Points

The times in the life of a business or a person when fundamentals are about to change.

Subchapter S Corporation

A small business corporation form where the owners pay the corporation's income taxes personally.

Sunk Cost
A cost that has already been incurred and cannot be affected by present or future decisions.

Surplus
A condition under which the supply for a good or service is in excess of the demand for that good or service. When this happens, there is usually a reduction in price to restore market equilibrium in the short term.

Syndicate
A group of investors who act together when forming a company.

Synergy
The concept that two or more different businesses, activities, or processes will, when working together, create an overall value greater than that of the sum of the parts were they working separately.

Systematic Risk
Systematic risk is any risk that affects the value of a large number of assets, although each asset will have a different degree of sensitivity to the underlying risk. In financial markets, if investors maintain large, well-diversified portfolios, then asset prices will be affected only by this type of risk. Higher systematic risk will increase an investor's expected returns. Thus, systematic risk cannot be diversified away.

—T—

Tangible Product
The physical attributes of a product constitute a tangible product.

Target Market
This is the collection or population of customers or consumers that a company has in mind as the primary audience for its goods or services and to whom the company gears its marketing efforts to sell the good or service.

Target Return Pricing

This pricing strategy dictates that the price of an item being introduced into a market be determined based on a calculation of return on investment, or that sales for the product reflect some predetermined return on the capital required to bring the product to the market.

Task Interdependence

The extent to which a task requires people to work interdependently for successful completion. For example, making a car can be designed as a series of independent tasks (i.e., an assembly line). Alternatively, it can be designed as a highly interdependent task where a group of people work together to produce a car (e.g., Volvo, Sweden). Research has shown that for self-managed teams to be effective, their work needs to be designed as a highly interdependent task.

Where task interdependence is high, reward interdependence should also be high.

Tax Shields

A tax shield describes any reduction in a corporation's tax bill that can be brought about by management. Depreciation, for example, creates a tax shield because depreciation is a non-cash expense that is deductible for income tax purposes. Similarly, managers can reduce their taxable income through the use of debt because interest expense is deductible for income tax purposes (dividends, however, are not). Other types of tax shields are periodically available, such as investment tax credits.

Tax Haven

A country with tax-preference laws for foreign companies and individuals. Three classes of jurisdictions are referred to as tax havens: those that (1) have no relevant taxes; (2) levy taxes only on internal taxable transactions, but none at all or very low taxes on foreign source income; and (3) grant special tax privileges to certain types of companies or operations. The principal functions of tax havens are to avoid or postpone taxes, avoid exchange controls, and act as a shield against confiscation, nationalization, and other forms of expropriation.

Theory of Needs

David McClelland proposed that three needs are important in organizational settings for understanding motivation:

1. The need for achievement, which is the drive to excel and desire to do things better.
2. The need for power, which is the desire to be influential.
3. The need for affiliation, which is the desire to be liked and accepted by others.

McClelland proposed that individuals differ in which need is most important to them. Therefore, to effectively motivate employees it is important to understand each individual's primary need and match the work and management style appropriately.

Theory X and Theory Y

Douglas McGregor suggested that managers hold two distinctive views of their employees and that these views have implications for how managers motivate their workers. Theory X assumes that employees dislike work, are lazy, dislike responsibility, and must be coerced to perform. Theory Y assumes that employees like work, are creative, seek responsibility, and can exercise self-direction. McGregor proposed that Theory Y assumptions were more valid than Theory X. Therefore, participation, responsibility, and good group relations would maximize employee motivation.

Time Value of Money

The time value of money is the price or value placed on time. It is generally thought of as the opportunity cost associated with a particular investment. Money has positive time value associated with it, in the sense that a given amount of money is worth more than the certainty of having the exact same sum available at a later time. The reason is that any money received today can be reinvested to earn additional profits during the intervening time period.

Total Quality Management (TQM)

Developed by W. Edwards Demming, TQM is a series of business practices designed to monitor the quality of production throughout all phases of production. TQM has its foundation in the concept that there is systematic and asystematic error inherent in every process, and that each process should be controlled such that systematic error is minimized or eliminated while asystematic error remains.

Trademark
This is the legally recognized right of a seller to the exclusive use of an identifying symbol or brand.

Trade Credit
The credit granted to buyers of exported goods and services.

Trade Deficit
An imbalance in merchandise trade that results in an excess of imports over exports.

Trade Finance
The financing of imports and exports.

Transactional Leader
One who guides or motivates followers toward goals by clarifying role and task requirements.

Transformational Leader
One who excites and inspires followers through intellectual stimulation and charisma.

Transfer Price
The price charged when one segment of a company provides goods or services to another segment of the company.

—U—

Underwrite
An arrangement under which investment banks agree to buy a certain amount of securities of a new issue (typically an IPO) at a given date for a given price, thereby ensuring that the issuer gets the full proceeds of the issue.

Unemployment Rate
A measure of labor force utilization, the unemployment rate is equal to the number of people unemployed as a percentage of the total labor force.

Unity of Command
The principle that each subordinate should be responsible to only one manager.

—V—

Valuation Models
A valuation model describes the exercise of applying economic and financial principles to estimate the value of an asset. Discounted cash flow valuation models attempt to determine the value of an asset by estimating its stream of future cash flows, and then discounting those future cash flows at a particular discount rate. Valuation models are used extensively in the field of finance by analysts, investment bankers, and corporate finance specialists.

Values
Basic convictions or beliefs that specific behaviors and outcomes are more desirable than others. Values are judgmental in that they include our ideas as to what is "right," "good," or "moral." Values are important in organizational behavior because they influence attitudes, motivations, and perceptions. An individual's belief as to what "ought" and "ought not" to be will influence his/her behavior in the workplace and what he/she sees as acceptable and unacceptable management styles. For example, if you have a meritocratic value, (i.e., people should be paid on the basis of performance and not on the basis of time served), you are likely to evaluate a pay system based on seniority as "wrong," "bad," and "unfair."

Value Additivity
In an efficient market, the value of any two assets can be estimated as the sum of the values of the two individual assets. This is a variation on the theme that the whole must be equal to nothing more than the sum of the separate parts.

Value Chain
The collection of activities within a company that allows it to compete within an industry. The activities in a value chain can be grouped into two categories. The first is primary activities, which include inbound logistics, such as materials handling;

operations; outbound logistics, such as distribution; marketing and sales; and after-sales service. The second is support activities, which include human resources management, company infrastructure, procurement, and technology development. Note that each of the primary activities involves its own support activities. By considering each activity within a company in terms of the value chain, it is possible to isolate a potential source of competitive advantage.

Variable Costs
Expenses that vary directly with changes in business activities. For example, the cost of raw materials increases and decreases as the volume of production units changes. Total variable cost rises with the number of units produced. Per unit variable cost remains constant.

Variance
A measure of dispersion, the variance represents the average distance from any given observation in a series to the mean of that series, in units squared.

Venture Capitalist
A company in the practice of providing capital to fledgling companies with high growth potential in exchange for equity stakes and/or management control.

Visible Venture Capital
The organized, established firms that constitute the venture capital industry.

Visual Aids
These are tools for gaining and sustaining audience attention when presenting oral presentations. Visual aids provide concrete support for your ideas and keep the audience's concentration on your presentation. Visual aids increase audience comprehension and retention by making them actively analyze the visual information presented. By adding interest, variety, and impact, visual aids enhance the presentation, and may provide a visual memory that stays with the audience longer than words do.

—W—

Warrant

A long-term call option to purchase common stock at a specified price.

White Knight

A friendly potential acquirer sought by a target company threatened by a less welcome suitor.

Working Capital

Working capital is measured as the difference between a company's current assets and its current liabilities. Thus, it is interpreted by some as a measure of a firm's liquidity, or its ability to pay its bills on a short-term basis. However, excess investment in working capital can be costly for a firm as the rate of return on a company's working capital is likely to be lower than alternative long-term investment project returns. Thus, the maintenance of excessively high working capital creates too much liquidity and hence lowers overall returns.

CHAPTER 1

1. Thomas Peters and Robert H. Waterman, *In Search of Excellence* (New York: Warner Books, 1982).

2. Gary Hamel and C. K. Prahalad, "Strategic Intent," in *Harvard Business Review,* May/June 1989, Vol. 67, p. 63.

CHAPTER 2

1. Mary Munter, *Guide to Managerial Communication* (Upper Saddle River, NJ: Prentice-Hall, 2000).

2. Barbara Minto, *The Minto Pyramid Principle* (London: Minto International, 1996).

3. Mary Munter, Priscilla Rogers, and Jone Rymer, *Guidelines for Writing E-Mail* (forthcoming publication).

4. Edward Tufte, *The Visual Display of Quantitative Information* (Cheshire, CT: Graphics Press, 1992).

5. F. Kluckhohn and F. Strodtbeck, *Variations in Value Orientations* (Evanston, IL: Row, Peterson, 1961).

6. G. Hofstede, "Motivation, Leadership, and Organization: Do American Theories Apply Abroad?" *Organizational Dynamics,* Summer 1980, pp. 42–63.

7. E. Hall, *Beyond Culture* (Garden City, New York: Doubleday, 1976).

8. Paul A. Argenti, *Corporate Communication,* 3rd edition (Boston: Irwin/McGraw-Hill, 2003).

9. Paul A. Argenti and Janis Forman, *The Power of Corporate Communication* (New York: McGraw-Hill, Forthcoming.)

CHAPTER 3

1. Peter D. Bennett, ed., *Dictionary of Marketing Terms* (American Marketing Association, 1995).

2. J. Paul Peter and James Donnelly, *A Preface to Marketing Management,* 6th edition (Burr Ridge, IL: Irwin, 1994), pp. 56–73.

3. Abraham Maslow, *Motivation and Personality,* 2nd edition (New York: Harper & Row, 1970).

4. Philip Kotler, *Marketing Management: Analysis, Planning, Implementation, and Control* (Upper Saddle River, NJ: Prentice-Hall, 2000).

5. Kevin Keller, *Strategic Brand Management* (Upper Saddle River, NJ: Prentice-Hall, 1998), p. 4.

6. David Aaker, *Building Strong Brands* (New York: The Free Press, 1996) pp. 7–8.

7. Kevin Keller, *Strategic Brand Management* (Upper Saddle River, NJ, Prentice-Hall, 1998), p. 69.

CHAPTER 4

1. James G. March and Herbert A. Simon, *Organizations* (Cambridge, MA: Blackwell, 1993).

2. Robert R. Blake and Jane S. Mouton, *The Managerial Grid III: A New Look at the Classic That Has Boosted Productivity and Profits for Thousands of Corporations Worldwide* (Houston, TX: Gulf Publishing Company, Book Division).

3. Fred E. Fiedler and Martin M. Chemers, *Leadership and Effective Management* (Glenview, IL: Scott, Foresman, 1974).

4. Kenneth H. Blanchard, *Management of Organizational Behavior: Utilizing Human Resources* (Englewood Cliffs, NJ: Prentice-Hall, 1988).

5. J. French and B. Raven, "The Basis of Social Power," in *Studies in Social Power,* D. Cartwright, ed. (Ann Arbor: University of Michigan Press, 1959).

6. Richard Hackman et al., *Perspectives on Behavior in Organizations* (New York: McGraw-Hill, 1983).

7. Roger Fisher (*International Conflict for Beginners* (New York: Harper & Row, 1969).

CHAPTER 8

1. "Embracing Innovation: Entrepreneurship and American Economic Growth," National Commission on Entrepreneurship (NCOE) White Paper, 1999; and National Commission on Entrepreneurship web site, *www.ncoe.org.*

2. William Bygrave, *The Portable MBA in Entrepreneurships* (New York, John Wiley & Sons, 1994), p. 1.

3. Ibid, p. 2.

4. Alexander Russo, "Five Myths About Entrepreneurs: Understanding How Businesses Start and Grow," National Commission on Entrepreneurship, March 2001, p. 14.

CHAPTER 9

1. Fred L. Steingraber, "How to Succeed in the Global Marketplace," *USA Today* magazine, Vol. 126, 11/01/1997.

2. Bartlett and Ghoshal, *Managing Across Borders: The Transnational Solution* (Cambridge, MA: Harvard Business School Press), p. 56.

3. Michael Porter, *The Competitive Advantage of Nations* (New York: The Free Press, 1990), p. 6.

4. Michael Porter. "Raising National Competitiveness," April 1997, Taipei, Taiwan.

5. Keith H. Hammonds, "Good News—It's a Small World," *Fast Company,* 5/1/2000, p. 90.

Aaker, David, 70
Accenture, **47**
Accounting, 133–174
   balance sheet, 140–145
   cash flow statements, 149–155
   financial (external), 139–140,
      295
   income statement, 145–149
   managerial (internal),
      134–139, 311
   overview, 133–134, 170
   ratio analysis, 155–170
   resources, 170–174
Accounts receivable, liquidity of,
   144
Accrual-based accounting, and
   GAAP, 147
Activity-based costing (ABC), 137,
   259
Activity cost drivers, 259
Advertising:
   comparison, 275
   corporate image, 45, 279
   defined, 259
   online, 75
   point-of-purchase, 321–322
   of products, 75–76
Advertising frequency, 260
Advil, 70
Advocacy programs, corporate,
   45
Aggregate demand, 260
Aggregate supply, 260
Alliances, business. See Joint
   ventures
Allianz Holding, 166–168
Allocation function, 260
Allocative efficiency, 260–261
Amazon.com, 76
American Marketing Association,
   53, 70
Analysis:
   audience, 26
   BCG matrix, 7–8
   competitor, 9–12, 275–276
   constituency, 277
   cost-benefit, 280–281
   discounted cash flow (DCF),
      192–195
   economic, 120–121
   financial statement (ratio),
      155–170
   job, 306
   marginal, 125–128
   perceptual maps, 63, 67–70
   sensitivity, 330
   statistical, 54, 68
Anchoring theory, 87, 261
Angel investors, 214, 261
Annual report to shareholders,
   140
Antidilution of ownership, 261
Apple (computers), 71, 206

Arbitrage pricing theory, 261
Arbitration, 261
Area of dominant influence (ADI),
   261
Asch, Solomon, 96, 262
Asian versus Western corporate
   cultures, 38
Asking price, 262
Asset acquisition, 262
Assets, 142–143
   and capital budgeting, 180–182
   liquidity of, 144
Asset turnover ratio, 157–158,
   169
AT&T, 76, 200
Attribution, 262–263
Audience analysis, 26, 263
Augmented product, 263
Autos, perceptual mapping exam-
   ple, 68–69
Available market, 263

Backward integration, 263
Balance of payments, 263
Balance of trade, 264
Balance sheet, 140–145,
   180–182, 264
Bank for International Settle-
   ments (BIS), 264
Bank of England, 271
Bank of Japan, 271
Banks:
   commercial, 118–119
   development, 213–214, 285
   investment, 306
   regional, 327
   resume, 328
Banner ads, 75
Bargaining, positional, 322
Bartlett, Christopher, 221
Bayer, 166–168
Bear market, 264
Behavior:
   group, 96–103
   individual, 82–95
   organizational, 81–82,
      103–112
Ben & Jerry's, 159, 182
Benchmarking, 264
Benefits packages, 265, 297
Bernays, Edward, 40
Best efforts offering, 265
Beta measure, 265, 268
Bid price, 265
Blackberry (PDAs), 65
Blake, Robert R., 93, 311
Blanchard, Kenneth H., 93, 330
Blockbuster Video, 234
Blue sky laws, 265
Bondholders versus shareholders,
   185
Bond indenture, 265

Book value, 142, 167–168
Boston Consulting Group (BCG),
   7–8
Bottom line, on income state-
   ment, 145
Bounded rationality theory, 88
Brainstorming, 266
Brand:
   defined, 266
   equity, 70, 222
   as intangible asset, 143
   related terminology, 266
Branding, 67–71
Break-even point, 266
Bridge financing, 266
Budget, operating, 316
Budget deficit, 266–267
Budweiser frog ads, 75
Building Strong Brands (Aaker),
   70
Bull market, 267
Bureaucracy, 267
Bureau of Economic Analysis,
   116–117, 277
Bureau of Labor Statistics,
   115–116, 289
Burn rate, 267
Burson, Harold, 40
Burson Marsteller (PR firm), 40
Business cycle, 115, 267, 287
Business plan, 210–212, 267
Buying process, 55–57

Calculative theory of motivation,
   91–92
Call option, 268
Calvin Klein, 73
Cannibalization, 69, 268
Capital. See also Venture capital
   (VC)
   budgeting, 180–184, 269
   expenditures, 269
   flight, 269
   gain, 269
   markets, 175, 186–187
   sources of, 212–215
   stock, 269
   structure, 269–270
   working, 339
Capital asset pricing model
   (CAPM), 268–269
Capitalism, globalization and, 229
Capitalization rate, 270, 285–286
CareerBuilder Inc., 254
Career plan, 235–237. See also
   Job search
Carnegie, Dale, 36
Carried interest, 270
Carrying value, 142
Cartel, 270
Case interview, 268
Cash budget, 270

Cash cow, 8
Cash flow analysis. *See* Discounted cash flow (DCF) analysis
Cash flow statement, 270. *See also* Statement of cash flows
Causality and correlation, 270–271
Central bank, 118, 271
Centralization, 271
Certainty equivalent (CE) risk analysis, 193
Challenge interview, 271
Change management, 107
Charles Schwab (investment brokerage), 176
Charts, as communication tool, 35
Cheer (detergent), 56
Chevy, 68
China:
    corporate culture in, 38
    WTO entry, 219
Chronological resume:
    defined, 271
    example of, 243–244
Clairol (hair products), 76
Coaching, team, 98
Coca-Cola:
    cannibalization example, 69
    comparative ratio analysis, 166–168
    competitor analysis example, 9–10
    EVA and, 200
    top of mind status example, 64
Cognitive dissonance, 84, 271–272
Cohesiveness, 272
Cold call, 272
Collateral, 272
Collectivism, 272
Command process, 272–273
Commercial banks, 118–119
Commodity, 273
Common Market, 291
Common stock, 273
Communication:
    business, 23–52
    channels, 273
    crisis, 283
    cross-cultural, 36–38, 219
    defined, 267, 279
    distribution channels for, 28–30
    employee, 288–289
    external, 38–48, 296
    internal, 24–38, 288–289
    listening skills, 309
    management, 311
    managerial writing/presenting, 30–36
    nonverbal, 316
    organizational, 318
    overview, 23–24, 48–49
    public relations, 38–48
    resources, 49–52
    strategy, 273–274
    style, 274

Community relations, 274. *See also* Public relations (PR)
Compaq (computers), 66
Compensation, performance-based, 321
Competition:
    global (*see* International business)
    perfect, 320
Competitive advantage, 270
Competitive Advantage of Nations, The (Porter), 221
Competitive Strategy (Porter), 3–4, 275
Competitor Response Profile, 9–11
Competitors, analysis of, 9–12
Conditioning, 276
Confidentiality agreement, 276–277
Conflict management, 101
Conformity. *See* Group behavior
Constituencies (corporate), 23, 39, 43–44
Constituency analysis, 277
Consumer, 54. *See also* Customers
Consumer price index (CPI), 117, 277
Consumption function, 277
Contingency model, 93, 277–278, 293
Contractual joint ventures, 224
Contribution margin, 278
Conversion ratio, 278
Convertible security, 278
Coproduction, 278
Copyright, 278
Core competency, 278–279
Core product, 279
Corporate communication, 279. *See also* Communication
Corporate culture, 36–38, 105, 279, 318
Corporate structure, 103–105
Corporate vision, 280
Corporation, 216, 280
Correlation and causality, 270–271
Cost-benefit analysis, 280–281
Cost center, 281
Cost drivers, 318
Cost of capital, 198–199, 281
Cost of debt, 281
Cost of equity, 281
Cost of goods sold, 148–149
Cost of money. *See* Macroeconomics
Cost-plus pricing, 282
Costs:
    activity-based, 137
    calculating, 123–124
    fixed versus variable, 148–149, 338
    full, 298
    incremental, 303
    minimizing, 127
    standard, 331
Cost structure, 282

Counterpurchases, 319
Countertrade, 282
Covariance, 282
Covenants, 179, 282
Cover letter, 282
Credibility, corporate:
    and communication strategy, 25–27, 321
    and reputation, 327
    and shareholder value, 188–189
Creditors, 183
Credit policies, 158–159, 284, 336
Crisis management, 48, 283
Crocker Bank, 327
Cross-cultural communication, 36–38, 283
Cross-price elasticity, 283
Culture differences. *See* Cross-cultural communication
Currency, 290–291, 301
Current account, 284
Current ratio, 156, 169
Customer relationship management (CRM) defined, 61
Customers:
    buying process of, 55–57
    defined, 284
    marketing to, 54–55
    retention of, 58–61
    understanding, 6–7

Dale Carnegie courses, 36
Dartmouth, 24, 137, 251
Database marketing, 62, 76
Debenture, 284
Debt, long-term, 310
Debt capacity, 161
Debt/equity swaps, 284
Debt ratio, 160–161, 169
Debt service, 153
Debt versus equity, 144–145, 180–184
Decentralization, 284
Decision making:
    behavioral factors in, 84–88
    top-down versus participatory, 105–106
Deferred taxes expense, 148
Deficit spending, 266–267
Degree of operating leverage, 284
Dell (computers), 66
Demand function, 284–285. *See also* Supply and demand
Demming, W. Edwards, 335
Depreciation expense, 143, 147–148, 149–150, 169
Depreciation tax shield, 285
Determinants of National Advantage model (Porter), 222–223
Devil's advocate, 285
Dialectic inquiry, 285
Direct marketing, 285
Discounted cash flow (DCF) analysis, 192–195, 286, 322
Discounted earnings method. *See* Present value

Discount rate, 195, 285–286
Discover card, 62
Diseconomies of scale, 286
Disposable income, 286
Distributive bargaining, 286
Dividends:
  defined, 286–287
  as harbinger of performance, 189
  payout policy decisions, 191
Dividend yield ratio, 167
Divisional structure, 287
Document design, 287
Dodge (autos), 68
Dog (business term), 8
Double jeopardy, 287
Dow Jones Average, and beta risk, 265, 268
Drafting, role in managerial writing, 31
Due diligence, 287
Dumping, 287
Du Pont, 163
DVDs, as product life cycle example, 66
Dynamic pricing strategy, 74–75

Earnings dilution, 189–190
Earnings per share (EPS), 189–192
Ebay, 142–143
Economic indicators, 114–117, 308
Economic theory, 113–132
  macroeconomics, 113–121, 287–288, 292–293
  microeconomics, 113, 122–128
  overview, 113, 128
  resources, 129–132
Economic value added (EVA), 198–200, 288
Economies of scale:
  defined, 65, 288
  effect on pricing, 72
  in global industries, 221–222, 228
Economies of scope, 288
Edge Act, 288
Editing, in managerial writing, 31–32
Eisner, Michael, 177
Elasticity:
  cross-price, 283
  demand, 72–73, 124–125, 288
  income, 302
  price, 323
Electronic resume, 242
E-mail, 28–30, 277
Employees:
  intercompany communications, 47, 288–289
  and managerial accounting function, 134–136, 138–139
  stock ownership plans (ESOP), 289

Employment. See also Job search
  defined, 289
  as economic indicator, 115–116, 337
Employment Situation, The (Bureau of Labor Statistics), 116
Empowerment, 213, 289–290
Enterprise resource planning (ERP), 138–139
Entrepreneurs, 205–218
  business plan writing, 210–212
  characteristics of, 206–207
  opportunities for, 207–210, 228
  overview, 205, 216
  resources, 217–218
  sources of capital, 212–215
  types of businesses, 215–216
Equity joint ventures, 224
Equity shares, 175–176, 181
Equity theory, 91, 290
Era (detergent), 56
Escalating commitment theory, 84
ESOP, 289
Eurobond, 290
Eurocurrency, 290, 310
Eurodollars, 119, 290–291
European Community (EC), 291
Exchange rate, 291
Eximbank, 292, 297
Exit strategy, 291
Expansion financing, 291
Expectancy theory of motivation, 91–92
Experience law (of marketing), 292
Export-Import Bank, 292, 297
ExxonMobil, 45, 166–168

Factoring, 292
Fair market value, 166
Federal funds rate, 293
Federal Open Market Committee (FOMC), 118, 293
Federal Reserve, 118–121, 271, 292–293
  and economic indicators, 116, 117, 304, 308
  and monetary policy, 113–114
Feedback, effective, 102, 293
Festinger, Leon, 271
Fiedler, Fred E., 93
Fiedler contingency model, 293
Finance, corporate, 175–203
  goals of, 177–178
  management of, 178–187
  measuring value, 192–200
  overview, 175–176, 200
  resources, 201–203
  shareholder value maximization, 187–192
Financial accounting, 295. See also Accounting
Financial Accounting Standards Board (FASB), 140
Financial communications, 46, 138–139, 296

Financial leverage ratio, 160, 296
Financial statements. See also Accounting
  analysis, 155–170
  examples, 140–155
  pro forma, 326
Finn, David, 40
Firm commitment offering, 293
First Book (philanthropic organization), 280
First Chicago Bank, 327
First-in, first-out (FIFO), 293
First-round/first-stage financing, 293, 294
Fiscal policy, 294
Fisher, Roger, 101
Five Cs of obtaining credit, 294
Five forces model (Porter), 294–295
Five Ps marketing model, 62–76
Fixed costs, 124, 295. See also Costs
Flak era of public relations, 39
Flat organization, 296
Focus group interview, 297
Follow-up, interview, 297
Ford (autos), 68
Forecasting, role of financial managers, 186
Foreign Credit Insurance Association (FCIA), 297
Foreign exchange rate, 297
Foreign markets. See International business
Forward integration, 297
Framing theory, 87–88
France, work-related values, 37
Franchising, 297–298
Free cash flow, 298
French, J., 94
Full costs, 298
Functional resume:
  defined, 298
  example of, 241–242
Functional silo, 298
Fundamental attribution error, 262
Futures contract, 298
Future value, 298–299

Gain (detergent), 56
Gap model (of customer satisfaction), 58–61, 299
Gateway (computers), 66, 70
General Agreement of Tariffs and Trade (GATT), 299
General Electric, 166–168, 196–198
Generally accepted accounting principles (GAAP), 140, 142–143, 147, 296
General Mills, 191–192
General Motors (GM), 16
Germany:
  comparative ratio analysis, 166–168
  corporate culture in, 38

Gersick, Connic, 323–324
Ghoshal, Sumantra, 221
Ghost shopper, 299
Globalization, 299–300. *See also* International business
Goal-setting theory, 89, 300, 311
Golden handcuffs, 300
Golf magazine, 61
Goodwill, as balance sheet item, 143
Google.com, 208
"Got Milk" ads, 75
Government, U.S. *See also* United States
  deficit spending, 266–267
  relations (lobbying), 48, 300
  as source of venture capital, 213
Grants, as source of capital, 213
Graphics, as communication tools, 35
Greenhalgh, Len, 251
Gross domestic product (GDP), 114–115, 120–121, 260, 300, 308
Gross national product (GNP), 260
Group behavior, 96–103, 315–316
Groupthink:
  defined, 96, 300
  risks of, 99
Grove, Andy, 233
Growth potential:
  and BCG matrix, 7
  as intangible asset, 150
Growth rate, sustainable, 165
Guide to Managerial Communication (Munter), 24–25

Hacker, 301
Hackman, Richard, 98, 306
Hall, E., 37–38
Halo effect, 88, 301
Hamel, Gary, 15
Handspring (PDAs), 65
Harrigan, Kathryn Rudie, 224–225
Harvard Business Review, 15, 25
Harvard Business School, 24
Headhunters, 291–292
Health and Fitness magazine, 62
Hersey, Paul (p. 330 shows *Hershey*), 93
Heuristics, 84–85, 301
Hewlett-Packard, 75, 206
Hierarchy of needs (Maslow), 55–56, 89, 301
High-context cultures, 37–38
High-potential venture, 302
Hill and Knowlton (PR firm), 40
Historical value, 142
Hofstede, G., 37
Honda (autos), 16, 279, 280
Hostile takeover, 178
Housing industry, 117, 120
Housing starts, 302
Human resources, 106–107, 138

Hybrid joint ventures, 224
Hygiene factor, 302
Hypertext markup language (HTML), 302
Hypertext transfer protocol (HTTP), 302

IBM, 66, 189–190, 200, 279
Identity, corporate, 279. *See also* Public relations (PR)
Image, corporate. *See* Public relations (PR)
Impression management, 95
Incentives. *See* Rewards
Income
  elasticity of, 302
  net, 145–146, 315
  personal, 116–117, 286
  residual, 328
Income statement, 145–149, 303
Incremental cost, 303
India, global competitiveness of, 221
Indicators, economic. *See* Economic indicators
Industrial goods, 303
Industrial market, 303
Industrial policy, 303
Industrial production:
  defined, 304
  as economic indicator, 117
Inflation, 114, 168, 304
Information sharing, 102–103, 188–189
Initial public offering (IPO), 293, 304, 336
Innovation:
  defined, 304
  entrepreneurship and, 205, 207–208
  and globalization, 228, 229
"Institutionalized deviants," 97, 100
Intel, 233
Interest coverage ratio, 161
Interest rates:
  defined, 304–305
  and monetary policy, 114, 116, 118–121
Internal communications. *See* Employees
Internal rate of return, 305
International business, 219–232
  advantages of, 220–223
  backlash against, 228–229
  entrepreneurial opportunities, 208–209
  foreign exchange, 290–291, 292, 297
  joint ventures, 223–228
  overview, 219–220, 229
  resources, 230–232
Internet. *See also* Internet resources; Technology
  impact on constituency analysis, 277

job shopping, 237, 240, 245–246
marketing, 74–76
Internet resources:
  Accountingweb, 170
  Ad Age Global, 77
  AILEENA World Media Index, 230
  American Demographics (marketing tools), 77
  American Marketing Association, 77
  America's Job Bank, 255
  ASTD (performance-oriented strategies), 108
  Bloomberg, 230
  BradyNet Financial Information, 201
  Brassring.com (job searching), 255
  Business Week, 230
  CNNfn (financial network), 201
  Dismal Scientist (economic analysis), 129
  Dow Jones Interactive, 49
  E-Business Forum, 18
  Economy.com, 129
  Entreworld.org (entrepreneur-oriented), 217
  Expansion Management, 230
  Facilitation Factory, 49
  Finweb.com (finance, economics), 201
  Forbes Global News, 129
  Foreign Affairs Magazine, 129
  High Technology Career Magazine, 255
  Idea Cafe (entrepreneur-oriented), 217
  Ideas@Work on the Air, 18
  IMA (accounting issues), 170
  International Herald Tribune, 230
  Investor Words (acronyms, terms), 201
  Joboptions.com, 255
  Jobweb.com, 255
  Journal of Computer-Mediated Communication, 108
  Kiersey Temperament Sorter, 255
  Management Accounting Quarterly, 170
  MarketingProfs.com, 77
  Marketing Resource Center, 77
  McKinsey Quarterly, 18
  MediaNet Presentation Skills, 49
  Monster.com (career site), 61, 255
  Nationjob Network, 255
  New York Times, 129
  PR Week, 49
  Quick MBA, 18, 217
  Recruiter on-line, 255
  Rutgers Accounting Web, 170
  Salary.com, 255

Social Science of Research Network, 18
Society for Industrial and Organizational Psychology, 108
Society for Organizational Learning, 108
Startup Journal, 217
thevault.com (employee grievances), 27
2000–01 Occupational Outlook Handbook, 255
Vault.com (job-related), 256
Venture Wire, 217
Wetfeet.com (job-related), 256
Workforce Magazine, 108
Yahoo (financial), 201
Interviewing, job, 247–254, 319, 321, 330
Intranets, corporate, 47
Inventory turnover ratio, 159, 306
Investment and savings curve (IS). See IS/LM analysis
Investments:
    mutually exclusive, 315
    risks versus rewards, 176
    role of financial managers, 186
Investment tax credit, 306
Investor relations (IR), 46, 296
Investors. See Shareholders
IS/LM analysis, 120–121
Israel, work-related values, 37

Japan:
    comparative ratio analysis, 166–168
    corporate culture in, 38
Job-related terminology, 306–307
Job search, 233–258
    career plan, 235–237
    interviewing, 247–253
    networking, 246–247
    online help, 237, 245–246
    overview, 233–235, 254
    rejections, 253–254
    resources, 255–258
    resumes, 237–246
Johnson, Lyndon B., 85
Johnson & Johnson, 43
Joint ventures, 223–228
Just-in-time inventory management, 307

Keiretsu, 308
Keller, Kevin, 70–71
Kennedy, John F., 15
Keynesian economics, 120
Kia (Korean car company), 41–42
Kluckhohn, F., 36–37
Kmart, 197

Labor, division of, 287
Land, accounting treatment of, 143
Leadership, 92–93, 308, 330–331, 336

Leading economic indicators. See Economic indicators
Lease, 308–309
Lee Hecht Harrison (pollsters), 237
Letter of credit (LOC), 309
Leverage:
    defined, 160
    financial, 296
    operating, 284, 317
    and ROE, 164
Leveraged buyout (LBO), 310
Liabilities, 144–145, 181
Lien, 309
Lifetime value of a customer (LVC), 58
Limited partnership, 216
Liquidity, 144, 155–156, 169, 309
Listing (stock), 309
LM curve. See IS/LM analysis
Loans, as source of capital, 213–214
Lobbying, as corporate strategy, 48
Locke, Edwin, 300
Locus of control, 309
Logos, and corporate identity, 43, 279
London Interbank Offered Rate (LIBOR), 310
Low-context cultures, 37–38
Low-income areas, venture capital for, 213

Machiavellianism, 83, 95
Macroeconomics, 113–121
    defined, 113–114, 310
    Federal Reserve monetary policy, 118–121, 271, 292–293
    fiscal policy, 294
    leading economic indicators, 114–117
Macrowriting, 32–33, 310
Management:
    defined, 310
    financial, 179–180, 184–192
    participative, 319
    related terminology, 311
    strategic concepts for, 4, 16–17
Managerial accounting, 133–139
Managerial grid, 311
Managerial writing, 30–36, 311–312
Managing Across Borders (Bartlett and Ghoshal), 221
Managing for Joint Venture Success (Harrigan), 224
March, James G., 84
Marginal analysis, 125–128, 313
Marginal cost, 72, 126, 313
Marginal revenue, 72, 126, 313
Marketing, 53–79
    advertising, 75–76
    branding, 67–71
    buying process, 55–57

customer issues, 54–55, 58–62
global, 299–300
overview, 53–54, 76–77
packaging, 76
plan for, 211
pricing, 72–75
product life cycle, 62–76
related terminology, 312–313
relationship, 327
resources, 77–79
Market-related terminology, 312–313
Market segmentation, 61–62, 313
Market share, 7, 313
Market-to-book (M/B) ratio, 167–168
Market value, 142, 166, 196–198
Maslow, A. H., 55, 89, 301
Mass market, 54, 314
Matrix structure, 314
MBO, 311
McClelland, David, 89, 335
McDonald's (fast-food restaurants), 208
McGregor, Douglas, 335
McKinsey Wheel (business model), 12–14, 17, 314
Mean, 314
Mechanistic organizational structure, 104
Media relations, corporate. See Public relations (PR)
Mellon bank, 327
Mergers and acquisitions, 314
Merrill Lynch (investment brokerage), 176
Microeconomics, 122–128
    defined, 113
    elasticity of demand, 124–125
    optimization theory, 125–128
    revenue, cost, profit equations, 123–124
    supply and demand curves, 122–123
Microsoft, 193, 194, 234, 279
Microwriting, 32–33
Middle Eastern value systems, 37
Milgram experiments, 96
Minorities, venture capital for, 213
Minto, Barbara, 27
Monetary policy, 314–315. See also Federal Reserve; Macroeconomics
Money markets, 175
Mortgages. See Housing industry
Motivation:
    defined, 315
    human resource management, 106–107
    theories of, 88–92
Motivation and Personality (Maslow), 55
Mouton, Jane S., 93, 311
MSN online service, 234
Multidomestic versus global industries, 221–222

Munter, Mary, 24–25, 28–29, 32, 273
Mutually exclusive investment, 315

NASA, 15
National Association of Purchasing Management (NAPM) Diffusion index, 117
Needs theory, 89, 335
Net income:
  accounting treatment of, 145–146
  defined, 315
Net present value (NPV):
  defined, 315
  and IRR, 305
  and MVA, 197–199
Net transfer payments, 117
Networking, 246–247, 315
Net working capital, 150–151, 182
New Markets Venture Capital (NMVC) program, 213
Nike, 70, 266
Nippon Denko Co., 167
Nippon Telegraph & Telephone, 166–168
Nominal group technique, 315–316
Noncash expenses, 147
Noncollateralized loan, 213
Nonverbal communication, 28, 35–36, 316
Norms, 96–97
North American Free Trade Agreement (NAFTA), 316
Norwest Bank, 327
Not-for-profit entity, 216

Offshore financial center, 316
Ohio State University leadership studies, 93, 316
Online job search, 237, 245–246
Operating budget, 316
Operating profit, 198
Operational control processes, 138
Opportunity cost, 188, 190, 193–194, 198, 317
Optimization theory, 125–128, 317
Oracle software (CRM-related), 61
Oral presentation, 317
Organic organizational structure, 104
Organizational behavior, 81–112
  managing individuals, 82–95
  managing organizations, 103–107
  managing teams, 96–103
  overview, 81–82, 108
  resources, 108–112
Organization for Economic Development, 317–318

Organization of Petroleum Exporting Countries (OPEC), 270, 318
Out of cash, 318
Outsourcing, 319
Over the counter, 319

Packaging techniques, 76
Palm Pilots (PDAs), 65, 76
Panel interview, 319
Parallel trade, 319
Parity, 319
Partnership, 216, 319
Patents, 143, 320
Pavlovian conditioning, 276
Payback period, 320
Payout ratio, 165
PC industry:
  as product life cycle example, 66
  as profit margin example, 162
PDAs, as product life cycle example, 65
Peer pressure. See Group behavior
Penalty systems. See Rewards
Penetration pricing strategy, 73, 320
Pepsi, 9, 64
Perceived value, 72, 73, 320
Perceptual maps, 63, 67–70
Performance:
  appraisal, 321
  bonuses, 195–196
  evaluating via EVA analysis, 198–200
  as a function of motivation, 88–89, 106–107
  and managerial accounting, 134–136, 321
Period costs versus product costs, 148–149
Personal income, 116–117, 286
Personal Income and Consumption, The (Bureau of Economic Analysis), 116–117
Personality, and corporate behavior, 82–84
Persuasion, 321
Peru, work-related values, 37
Philanthropy, corporate, 280. See also Public relations (PR)
Philip Morris, 42–43, 45
Phone interview, 321
Point-of-purchase advertising, 321–322
Politics, organizational, 95
Porter, Michael:
  on analyzing competitors, 8–11
  competitive advantage model, 221, 222–223, 228
  competitive forces model, 3–4, 56–57, 275, 294–295
  and strategic intent, 15, 17
  on understanding customers, 6
Portfolio, 322
Power, 93–95, 322

Power distance, 37
PowerPoint, 35
Prahalad, C. K., 15
Presentations. See Speaking
Present value, 322–323
Press. See Public relations (PR)
Prevention magazine, 62
Price discrimination, 323
Price elasticity, 323
Price-to-earnings (P/E) ratio, 166–167, 323
Pricing strategies, 72–75, 124–125, 282, 320
Prime lending rate, 118–119
Privacy issues, and database marketing, 62
Private placement, 323
Probability misunderstanding theory, 86–87
Procter & Gamble, 54
Producer market, 303
Producer price index (PPI), 117, 325
Product:
  advertising, 75–76
  branding, 67–71
  costs, 148–149
  defined, 326
  five Ps marketing model, 62–63
  generic, 299
  life cycle, 63–67, 324–325
  margin, 326
  packaging, 76
  pricing, 72–75
Product bundling, 76
Productivity:
  defined, 325
  and global competitiveness, 221, 229
  group contributions to, 103
Product-line costing, 259
Profit:
  center, 325
  economic, 288
  equations, 123–124
  margin, 326
  maximizing, 127–128, 189–192
  measuring, 161–162
Profit and loss statement. See Income statement
Profit margin ratios, 161–162
Pro forma financial statements, 326
Promotion. See Advertising
Prospectus, 326
Proxy fight, 178
Psychology of management. See Organizational behavior
Public affairs. See Government, U.S.
Public relations (PR), 38–48
Pull strategy, 323
Punctuated equilibrium model, 101, 323–324
Punishment, as motivator, 89–91. See also Rewards

Purchasing decisions. *See* Buying process
Push strategy, 324
Put option, 324

Q ratio, 167–168
Question mark (business term), 8
Quick ratio, 156–157

Ralph Lauren (clothing), 70
R&D. *See* Research
Ratio analysis, 155–170
Rational optimizing model, 84
Raven, B., 94
Real-time pricing. *See* Dynamic pricing strategy
Receivables turnover ratio, 158–159
Recession:
    defined, 326
    GDP as indicator of, 115
    and monetary policy, 114, 292
Recognition. *See* Rewards
Recruiters, executive, 291–292
Redd, Baxter, 3
Redd, Bill, 2–17
Redd, Joan, 2–17
Redd's Fun Park, case study, 2–17
Red herring, 326
Reengineering, 327
Regression analysis, 54, 327
Reinforcement theory of motivation, 89–91
Relationship marketing, 327
Repeat purchase rate, 327
Reputation, corporate, 143, 327.
    See also Public relations (PR)
Research:
    as intangible asset, 143
    opportunity costs of, 188
    and venture capital, 213
Reserve requirements, 118
Residual income, 328
Resource allocation:
    supply and demand curves, 122–123
    team-related, 98–99
Response rate, 328
Resumes:
    online, 245–246, 328
    types of, 240–244, 298
    writing, 237–240, 282
Retail clothing industry, as example of skimming pricing strategy, 74
Retention ratio, 165
Retrenchment, 328
Return on assets (ROA), calculating, 163–164
Return on equity (ROE), calculating, 164–165
Return on Investment (ROI), 74, 328

Revenue:
    defined, 328
    equations, 123–124
    on income statement, 145
    maximizing, 126–127
Rewards. *See also* Risks
    benefits as, 265, 297
    incentive-based compensation, 195–196, 200
    as motivator, 89–91, 106–107
    performance-linked, 98, 107
    as power source, 94
    role in career planning, 235–237
    shareholder-value-related, 178–180
    sign-on bonuses, 252
Risk-adjusted discount rate (RADR), 193
Risks. *See also* Rewards
    interest rate–related, 305
    joint ventures and, 224–225
    management of, 88, 188–192, 329
    opportunity costs, 193–195
    premium for excess, 329
    systemic, 265, 333
    venture capital, 214
Robinson, Linda, 40
Rolling Stone magazine, 206
Russia, global competitiveness of, 221

Sales, 328, 329. *See also* Marketing
Saudi Arabian versus U.S. value systems, 37
Savings, 329
SBUs, 7–8
Schmidt, W., 25, 274
Schumpeter, Joseph, 206
S corporation, 216, 332
Sears, as example of database marketing, 62
Second-round financing, 329
Securities analysts, and investor relations, 46
Securities and Exchange Commission (SEC), 140, 329
Seed financing, 329
Segment margin, 330
Selective perception theory, 86
Self-managed teams, 330
Self-monitoring, 330
Self-serving bias, 263
Sensitivity analysis, 330
Sequential interview, 330
7S model. *See* McKinsey Wheel (business model)
7 Up, 67
Shandwick (PR firm), 40
Shank, John, 137, 332
Shareholders:
    defined, 183
    financial communications to, 139–140, 296
    liability of, 181

maximizing wealth of, 177–178, 187–192, 196–198
    ownership rights of, 145, 176
    as source of capital, 214
Shares, ownership. *See* Shareholders; Stock
Shelf life, 159
Sherman Antitrust Act, 270
Shortage, 330
Siemens, 166–168
Sign-on bonuses, negotiating for, 252
Simon, Herbert A., 84
Singapore, global competitiveness of, 221
Situational leadership theory, 330–331
Skimming pricing strategy, 73–74, 331
Skinner, B. F., 276
Small Business Administration (SBA), 212, 213
SMART, 89
Social information processing model, 331
Social security income, 117
Sociology, and group behavior, 96–97
Sole proprietorship, 215–216, 331
Solvency ratio, 155–156
Soviet Union, 219
Span of control, 331
Speaking:
    as communication medium, 28
    oral presentation, 33–36, 317
Speeches. *See* Speaking
Sprite, 64, 67
Standard & Poor's (S&P) Index, 265, 268
Standard business units (SBUs) defined, 7–8
Standard cost, 331
Star (business term), 7, 8
Start-up financing, 332
Statement of cash flows, 149–155, 332
Statement of financial condition. *See* Balance sheet
Statement of operations. *See* Income statement
Statistical analysis, in marketing research, 54, 68
Stereotyping, 85–86, 332
Stewart, Martha, 206
Stock:
    common, 273
    as compensation, 195–196
    convertible, 278
    defined, 175–176
    listing, 309
    preferred, 320
Stockholders' equity:
    accounting treatment of, 145
    (*See also* Shareholders)
    and capital budgeting, 181
Strategic alliances. *See* Joint ventures

Strategic cost management, 332
Strategic inflection point, 233, 332
Strategy, business, 1–21
  BCG matrix, 7–8
  competitors and, 9–12, 275–276
  customers and, 6–7
  defined, 268, 280
  implementing, 12–14
  intent of, 14–17
  overview, 1–2, 17–18
  Redd's Fun Park case study, 2–6
  resources, 18–21
Strodtbeck, F., 36–37
Subchapter S corporation, 216, 332
Sunk cost, 333
Supply and demand:
  elasticity of, 124–125
  for goods and services, 122
  for money, 119–121
Surplus, 333
Sustainable growth rate, calculating, 165
Sweden, work-related values, 37, 334
Switzerland:
  corporate culture in, 38
  global competitiveness of, 221
Syndicate, 333
Synergy, 333
Systemic risk, 265, 333

Tangible product, 333
Tannenbaum, R., 25, 274
Target audience, 75, 209, 333
Target return pricing, 74–75, 334
Task theory of motivation, 89, 334
Tax avoidance, 334
Technology:
  entrepreneurship and, 205, 207–208
  globalization and, 219, 220, 225–226, 229
  impact on accounting, 133
  impact on communication, 28–30
  impact on pricing, 74–75
  impact on product life cycle, 64–66
  strategic inflection points, 233–234
Texas Instruments, 66
Theories X and Y (McGregor), 335
3Com, 47

Tide (detergent), 54, 55
Timberland Company:
  balance sheets, 141–142
  cash flow statements, 150–155
  income statement, 145–146
  ratio analysis, 155–165
Time:
  impact on costs, 148–149
  and shareholder value issues, 188, 190–195
Time value of money, 192, 335
Tivo, 65
Tobacco companies, 48
Tokyo Electric Power, 166–168
Top of mind status, 64
Total Quality Management (TQM), 335–336
Toyota Motor, 166–168
Toys, as product life cycle example, 67
Trade balances terminology, 336
Trademarks, 143, 336
Transactional leader, 336
Transfer price, 336
Transformational leader, 336
Treasuries, U.S., 195, 305
Tuck School of Business (Dartmouth), 24, 137, 251
Tufte, Edward, 35
Turnover ratios, 157–159, 169
Tylenol crisis, 43

Ultimate TV, 65
Underwriting, 336–337
Unemployment:
  during the 1990s, 115
  as economic indicator, 117, 337
United States:
  balance of payments, 263
  comparative ratio analysis, 166–168
  current account, 284
  employment measures, 289
  entrepreneurship in, 205, 208–209, 216
  industrial production index, 304
  producer price index, 325
Unity of command, 337
University of Michigan leadership studies, 93
Utility companies, and government relations, 48

Valuation models, 337
Value additivity, 337–338
Value chain, 338

Value measurement, corporate, 192–200
Value systems, impact on corporate culture, 36–38, 337
Variable costs, 124, 338. *See also* Costs
Variance, 337
Venezuela, work-related values, 37
Venture capital (VC):
  entrepreneurship and, 210
  providers, 338
  sources of, 212–215
Vietnam, 38, 85
Visual aids, 35, 338–339
Volkswagen (autos), 71
Volvo, 99, 334
Vroom, Victor, 93, 308
Vroom-Yetton leader-participation model, 93

Wall Street, impact of interest rates on, 117
Wall Street Journal, 248
Walt Disney Company, 177
Warrant, 339
Web:
  addresses (*see* Internet resources)
  job shopping on, 237, 240, 245–246
Weber, Max, 267
Wenner, Jann, 206
Western versus Eastern corporate culture. *See* Cross-cultural communication
White knight, 339
Windows 2000, 194
Win-win solutions, in group negotiations, 102
Women, venture capital for, 213
Woolite (detergent), 54
Working capital, 339
World markets. *See* International business
World Trade Organization (WTO), 219, 228
World War I reparations, 264
World Wide Web. *See* Internet; Internet resources; Technology
Wozniak, Steve, 206
Writing, managerial, 30–36

X and Y theories (McGregor), 335
Xenocurrencies, 290
Xerox, 99

Yetton, Phillip, 93, 308